The Concord Quartet

Also by Samuel A. Schreiner Jr.

Nonfiction

The Passionate Beechers
Henry Clay Frick
Code of Conduct (with Everett Alvarez Jr.)
Cycles
Mayday! Mayday!
The Trials of Mrs. Lincoln
A Place Called Princeton
The Condensed World of the Reader's Digest

Fiction

The Van Alens
The Possessors and the Possessed
Angelica
Pleasant Places
Thine Is the Glory

The Concord Quartet

Alcott, Emerson, Hawthorne, Thoreau, and the Friendship That Freed the American Mind

Samuel A. Schreiner Jr.

John Wiley & Sons, Inc.

Published by John Wiley & Sons, Inc., Hoboken, New Jersey
Published simultaneously in Canada

Photo credits: Pages 8, 9 (both), 59, 107, 108 (both), 132, 133, 145 (both), 146, 208, and 209 courtesy of the Concord Free Public Library; pages 81 and 82 courtesy of the Peabody Essex Museum.

Library of Congress Cataloging-in-Publication Data:

Schreiner, Samuel Agnew.
    The Concord quartet : Alcott, Emerson, Hawthorne, Thoreau, and the friendship that freed the American mind / Samuel A. Schreiner, Jr.
        p. cm.
    Includes bibliographical references (p.) and index.
    ISBN-13 978-0-471-64663-1 (cloth : alk. paper)
    ISBN-10 0-471-64663-6 (cloth : alk. paper)
    1. Authors, American—19th century—Biography. 2. Authors, American—
19th century—Homes and haunts—Massachusetts—Concord. 3. Transcendentalists
(New England)—Biography. 4. Literary landmarks—Massachusetts—Concord.
5. Concord (Mass.)—Intellectual life—19th century. 6. Alcott, Amos Bronson,
1799–1888—Friends and associates. 7. Emerson, Ralph Waldo, 1803–1882—
Friends and associates. 8. Hawthorne, Nathaniel, 1804–1864—Friends and
associates. 9. Thoreau, Henry David, 1817–1862—Friends and associates. I. Title.
    PS128.S37 2006
    810.9′003—dc22

                                                                              2005031915

Printed in the United States of America
10 9 8 7 6 5 4 3 2 1

For the supportive women in my life:
Dorrie, my love and my wife, and my daughters,
Beverly Schreiner Carroll and Carolyn Schreiner Calder

Contents

Acknowledgments

One good thing can often lead to another. In this author's case, my last book, *The Passionate Beechers*, led to this one about another group of Americans living and working through the middle years of the nineteenth century and also making a difference to our lives today. On this voyage to the past, I had the same fine people in the crew: my agent, Phyllis Westberg of Harold Ober Associates; my editor, Hana Umlauf Lane of John Wiley & Sons; and Blanche Parker and her colleagues at the reference desk of the Darien Library. I am also indebted to Constance Manoli-Skocay of the special collections staff at Concord, Massachusetts, Free Library for aid in finding illustrations.

Prologue

In his book covering more than five centuries of the American people's experiences, the historian Samuel Eliot Morison equated an early event in this book's narrative to the start of the Revolutionary War with respect to its effect on the nation's development. "The year 1836, when Emerson published his *Essay on Nature*, may be taken as opening a period in American literary culture, corresponding to 1775 in American politics," Morison wrote. The author of that document, which Morison credits with starting a renaissance in American intellectual life, was a then little-known young ex-minister named Ralph Waldo Emerson, who, by reason of heritage, happened to live in Concord, Massachusetts, the town where that earlier political revolution erupted in war.

Emerson's essay was a seed that flowered into a movement called transcendentalism, which Morison defined as "an intellectual overtone to democracy, a belief in the divinity of human nature . . . a belief in the soul's inherent power to grasp the truth. Historically speaking, transcendentalism was an attempt to make Americans worthy of their independence, and elevate them to a new stature among the mortals."

At the time it came into being, transcendentalism flew in the face of the traditional beliefs of most Americans. The nation's few institutions of higher learning—the supposed seats of intellectual life—were generally founded and staffed by Protestant Christian clergy of largely Calvinist persuasion. They held that the Bible was divinely inspired and literally true and that, because of Adam's fall,

all human beings were born sinners and headed for damnation unless they underwent a conversion process to accept Christ as their only savior. Americans seeking enlightenment from other sources or enrichment from virtually any of the fine arts looked to Europe as the source and, when possible, went abroad for the experience. Schooling in general in the still new United States of America was a haphazard affair of mixed private and public facilities where harsh discipline and rote learning of the three R's—reading, 'riting, and 'rithmetic—took place in the few weeks of the year when children were not needed to labor on the farm or in the factory. The American writers and artists of any note got their grounding abroad and avoided realism about contemporary or local affairs in their work.

Beginning in the 1830s, coincidences that seem almost miraculous in retrospect brought together in Concord as friends and neighbors four men of very different temperaments and talents who shared the same conviction that the soul had "inherent power to grasp the truth" and that the truth would make men free of old constraints on thought and behavior. In addition to Emerson, a philosopher, there was Amos Bronson Alcott, an educator; Henry David Thoreau, a naturalist and rebel; and Nathaniel Hawthorne, a novelist. This book is the story of that unique and influential friendship in action, of the lives the friends led, and their work that resulted in an enduring change in their nation's direction.

1

A Homecoming

ON A CRISP OCTOBER DAY in 1834, Waldo Emerson and his mother boarded a stagecoach in Boston that would take them to Concord some seventeen miles to the north and west. During the four hours that the coach rattled and rocked its way along, there was lively talk among its passengers about the beauties of a country-side ablaze with fall colors and the sorry state of public affairs. It was not surprising that one of them, a resident of Concord, a place of natural features bearing Indian names such as the Muske-taquid River and still yielding arrowheads and other Indian arti-facts from a precolonial settlement with every spring plowing, should harangue his captive audience about the cruel action by President Jackson—"King Andrew the First," he called him—in uprooting the Seminoles from their native Florida. Ordinarily, Emerson might have participated in the conversation, and he cer-tainly would have been looking forward to the rest and recreation that visits to the family homestead had provided over the years. But not on this trip. He squeezed himself into a corner of the coach and kept glumly silent while contemplating the circum-stances in which he found himself. It was not sentiment or plea-sure that prompted this return to Concord. It was need. He could no longer afford to rent suitable quarters for himself and his mother in Boston and might never again be able to do so. Through tragedy and an exercise of his own stubborn will, his once golden personal and professional lives had turned to dross.

Having heard, when they boarded, the names of the young man and the woman who looked to be his mother, the driver needed no prompting to pull his team to a halt before the stone gateposts of the property in Concord known to have housed Emersons for as long as anybody could remember, instead of carrying them on to his usual stopping place at a tavern in town. For Waldo this courtesy was a bright glimmer in a dark day. It made him realize that few of his new neighbors could know the details of what he had been through in the six years since he had last been in Concord, and he would be accorded respect, however undeserved. While the driver offloaded their luggage, the Emersons stood together between moss-furred posts that had not held a gate for years and stared down the long tree-lined pathway to the door they would soon enter. The momentary lift to Waldo's spirits subsided. Signs of neglect and decay were everywhere to be seen. Magnificent compared to surrounding dwellings when his grandfather built it as an appropriate manse for the First Parish Church, the weathered gray house and unkempt grounds now reflected the physical decline and dated theology of the grumpy old man who would be their host.

Perhaps fortunately, Waldo's mother did not share his gloom. "Oh, isn't it good to be home!" she said. The best Waldo could manage in response was, "Yes, I suppose it is." With no other evident choice, he would try to make the best of it. In the journal he had kept since college days, he would note the homecoming by writing a kind of prayer: "Hail to the quiet fields of my fathers! Not wholly unattended by supernatural friendship and favor, let me come hither. Bless my purposes as they are simple and virtuous."

Waldo's description of the Concord area as "the fields of my fathers" was no idle boast. The first white party to replace the Indians on the banks of the Musketaquid two years earlier had been led by one of his direct ancestors, the Reverend Peter Bulkeley. In 1775, standing in the study of the house he had recently built, Waldo's grandfather, William Emerson, had been witness to the

first battle of the Revolution; two slain British soldiers had been
buried in unmarked graves on the grounds of the manse. Filled
with patriotic fervor, thirty-three-year-old William Emerson had
then signed on as chaplain to the American troops and had died
of dysentery at the siege of Ticonderoga. He left a young widow,
Phebe; a seven-year-old son, William; and a two-year-old daughter, Mary Moody. To make ends meet, Phebe took in boarders,
one of whom was the Reverend Ezra Ripley, who replaced her
husband in the pulpit, and within a year in her bed. Ezra Ripley
buried Phebe in 1825 but, now eighty-three, still clung to the job
and house he had inherited. His invitation for his stepdaughter-
in-law, Ruth, and her son to share the house was not entirely a
charitable gesture; confined to his bedroom by illness, he was as
much in need of their help as they were of his space.

In building his manse, Grandfather Emerson had evidently intended to beget a large family as well as live up to his status in the
community. Massachusetts had long been a theocracy in which
the state supported the churches of an approved Protestant persuasion, and the clergy were thus accorded an unofficial influence
and power in civic affairs. It had in fact only been in the last year
that the state's constitution had been amended to establish a sep-
aration of church and state as the founders, led by Jefferson, had
done in forming the federal government. Waldo had no doubt that
Dr. Ripley would view this development with a dismay similar to
that of Lyman Beecher down in Connecticut when that state dis-
established his Congregational church back in 1818. Whatever
his host might think of the demotion, Waldo welcomed it even
though it might become a bone of contention between them unless he could avoid discussion of matters theological or political
with the old man. He was hoping that the original creation of
many rooms, however small, for children would allow for a comfortable privacy and for his younger brother, Charles, and his aunt
Mary Moody, who had been born in the manse, to join them.

Whether from weariness or unanticipated graciousness, Dr.
Ripley greeted Waldo with a precious gift. A place for concen-
trated labor on writing sermons had been a professional necessity

for William Emerson, and he had kept that in mind while planning the manse. In a corner of the second floor, above and apart from the bustle of housekeeping and entertaining, he had outfitted a room as a study. Dr. Ripley had been told that Waldo had given up one of the most prestigious and financially rewarding pastorates in Boston because he would not participate in a Christian rite that even Unitarians performed. Utter foolishness in old Ezra's way of thinking, and he understood that Mary Moody and one of Waldo's smart younger brothers agreed with him. Apparently, Waldo was trying to earn something by giving lectures to people who would pay to hear him, filling pulpits wherever and whenever asked, and writing a book. None of these ventures sounded promising, but Ezra knew from long experience that they would require the facilities for thought. So almost as soon as he heard their voices when they entered the manse, he summoned them up to his bedside and told Waldo that he could have exclusive use of the study for as long as he needed it.

Much as he had wanted and hoped for such a gift, Waldo felt obliged to offer a feeble protest: "But you'll soon be getting back to the pulpit, and . . ."

"Don't give a thought to that, my boy. I don't need it. I've written thousands of sermons, most of them packed away up in the attic. I've been dusting them off and reusing them for years, as you will one day. Now I know you've got a lot to do to settle in."

The next morning after breakfast, Waldo mounted to the study and began moving to the attic more of the theological material dating back well beyond Ripley's tenure to make room for the books and papers that he had brought. It was honest and necessary labor, and he began feeling much better about his prospects. From time to time he would pause to look through the small cracked panes of the double window in the west wall. Much of the bare-limbed orchard between the willow shading the house and the river had been planted by Dr. Ripley since he and his mother and younger brothers, Edward and Charles, had spent most of 1827 and 1828 here. At the breakfast table that morning, Ruth

Emerson had clucked with delight over all the fresh fruit she had found in the larder. Out of the single window on the north side, Waldo could see that historic spot where the rebels and redcoats had first exchanged shots on the North Bridge. There would be anniversary ceremonies there in the next spring for which he had been asked to prepare suitable remarks before anyone knew that he might then be living in Concord. Perhaps this was another indication that his fall from grace was not known here.

While moving things around, Waldo ran into some papers of his grandfather's, and hanging on the wall of a little hideaway apartment in the attic was a crude likeness by a country painter of a solemn, bewigged man just about his own age but looking a great deal older in his antique attire. These objects reminded him of the weight of tradition that he had carried on his shoulders throughout most of his years of awareness. Although only seven when his father, William, died of stomach cancer, Waldo was conscious of the honor conferred upon him and the whole family by his father's position as pastor of Boston's First Church. In addition, there were all those other ministers who were talked about within the family circle—seven generations of them, some said—and the christening of his brother Robert Bulkeley Emerson carried the line back to that famous founder of Concord. Honor was just about all that the second William Emerson left behind him except for the five of eight children—all sons—who had survived infancy. As had her mother-in-law before her, Ruth Emerson took in boarders. To help her run the establishment in Boston, she had put the boys to work so consistently that Waldo would always refer to his youth as "hard." An even tougher taskmistress for the boys than Ruth was her sister-in-law, Mary Moody, who moved in with her to help out. A tart-tongued maiden lady of strict religious views, Mary Moody wanted to groom all of her five nephews for the ministry. It was the fate for which Emersons were destined. Waldo's one memorable respite from the rigorous Boston regime had come at age nine when he was sent to Concord for a lengthy stay with the Ripleys to escape the uncertainties of the war in 1812.

An artist's look at the town of Concord, Massachusetts, in the 1830s when Ralph Waldo Emerson returned to his ancestral home seeking solace after the death of his bride and a crisis in his once promising career as a Unitarian minister.

Referred to in disgust as "Mr. Madison's War," the conflict was causing little but misery in Boston, where it disrupted the commerce on which the port thrived. The fear in households like the Emersons' was that there would be riots and pillaging. But for an imaginative boy like Waldo, the safety of Concord was no comfort; it was banishment from the excitement of running down to the waterfront with other boys to watch the warships under sail and dream of glory.

To make ministers of the brood under their care, Ruth and Mary Moody knew that it meant somehow getting them through college. In Boston that meant going to Harvard, an institution over in Cambridge that, according to a statement by its founders in 1636 and carved on its gates, was intended to "advance learning and perpetuate it to Posterity; dreading to leave an illiterate Ministry to the Churches, when our present ministers shall lie in the Dust." The Emerson women could not know how much more than literacy was being taught in Harvard when, following in his brother William's footsteps, Waldo enrolled in 1817. For more than half a century beginning in 1673, there had been ongoing

All who knew him were warmed by Emerson's gentle smile, which reflected the kindliness and optimism of his nature regardless of many personal trials and tribulations and a deepening dismay over the course of a dividing nation.

The Old Manse in Concord, built just before the Revolutionary War by Emerson's grandfather, then pastor of the First Parish Church, was Emerson's first refuge in the town and would later become the honeymoon nest of Nathaniel and Sophia Hawthorne.

disagreements among the clergymen who made up the institution's Board of Overseers between those who clung to the Calvinist conservatism of the founders and those who were open to newer theological thinking. By the mid-eighteenth century, the conservatives were so outnumbered that they withdrew and went across the border into Connecticut to join Yale, "a school of the prophets." In 1792, the first layman took a seat on Harvard's Board of Overseers, and in 1805 a Unitarian was made a professor of theology. Wide-ranging reading and discussion or friendly argument over what they learned from it was the favorite recreation of the Emerson brothers, and they entered college eager to grasp any new knowledge or experience that would excite their minds.

College authorities recognized not only the financial need, but also the scholastic promise of the Emerson boys. Waldo was given the coveted position of a bed in the then president John T. Kirkland's house in return for his services as an orderly—a kind of all-around servant. When he moved to a dormitory in sophomore year, he went on waiting table and taking summer teaching jobs to cover expenses. By junior year, in a gesture indicative of how college was changing him, the young man dropped his given first name, Ralph, for the more unusual middle name he favored, and he would thereafter be Waldo to friends and family who did not insist on sticking to the formality of "Mr. Emerson." His curriculum was largely classical, and he became familiar with the histories and philosophies of Greece and Rome and, of course, mother England. He did not turn out to be a star student; he graduated thirtieth in a class of fifty-nine. But he did win prizes for essays on ethics and Socrates, and he enjoyed oratory enough to agree to deliver the class poem after half a dozen others turned the honor down. As a public speaker he had an asset for which he could claim no credit—a resonating baritone voice.

Degree in hand, Waldo had little choice as to what he should do. William had started a girls' school to help out with family finances, and he recruited Waldo for the enterprise. Money was needed for the care of brother Bulkeley, who had only a child's mind, and for the education of Edward and Charles, both brilliant and Harvard-bound. It was the beginning of a depressing period in Waldo's life. He had no taste for teaching and a bad case of low self-esteem. He told his journal that "the dreams of my childhood are all fading away and giving place to some very sober and very disgusting views of a quiet mediocrity of talents and condition— nor does it appear to me that any application of which I am capable, any efforts, any sacrifices, could at this moment restore any reasonableness to the familiar expectations of my earlier youth." His harsh analysis of his own personality was that he suffered from "a sore uneasiness in the company of most men and women, a frigid fear of offending and jealousy of disrespect." Whatever Waldo thought of himself, it apparently did not show, since the girls in his care would recall him as a good and amiable teacher. Slight and straight, he just missed being strikingly handsome by reason of a long nose and long neck. His "fear of offending" caused him to adopt an attitude and expression best described by a kitchen maid who was asked when she emerged from one of his lectures, "Do you understand Mr. Emerson?" She laughed. "Not a word, but I like to see him stand up there and look as if he thought everyone was as good as he was."

Waldo's hope that teaching might be a brief interlude in getting started on a more appealing career soon went glimmering. Members of the Harvard faculty who had enjoyed time abroad came back with enthusiasm for the German writers and philosophers whose work was becoming the rage among intellectuals in Britain and on the Continent. Persuaded by them that study in Germany was essential to anyone wishing to become a minister, William left Waldo in charge of the school and, in effect, of earning the family bread while he took off for Europe. During his brother's absence, Waldo had a debate with himself, much of which he confided to his journal, as to his own future. That rather harsh view of his character caused him to rule out the law as a possible profession because it "demands a good deal of personal address, an impregnable confidence in one's own powers." Medicine, too, was out of the question, because "it also makes large demands on the practitioner for a seducing mannerism." With a kind of resignation, he settled on the ministry, noting that "in Divinity I hope to thrive. I inherit from my sire a formality of manner and speech, but I derive from him, or his patriotic parent, a passionate love for the strains of eloquence. What we ardently love we learn to imitate. My understanding venerates and my heart loves that cause which is dear to God and man—the laws of morals, the Revelations which sanction and the blood of martyrs and triumphant suffering of the Saints which seal them. In my better hours, I am the believer (if not the dupe) of brilliant promises, and can respect myself as the possessor of those powers which command the reason and passions of the multitude."

No sooner thought than done. While carrying on with the school, Waldo began ministerial studies. Edward was helping with the school on vacations from Harvard, where he was outperforming Waldo scholastically and developing the kind of personality that made his plans to study law after graduation quite realistic in his older brother's view. But it was something of a shock when William returned from Germany also intending to study law. Instead of enriching the faith that William had planned to preach, his encounter with German thinking had shaken it. Nevertheless, he urged Waldo to go to Germany himself, or at least read up on it. Already four years out of college, Waldo was too impatient to get on with his chosen profession to waste time in Europe, and he enrolled in Harvard Divinity School instead. But he was interested in what William told him and intended to keep an open mind. Possibly to counter the feeling of following too meekly in the path of family tradition, he had written a youthful declaration of independence for himself: "Who is he that shall control me? Why may I not speak and write and think with entire freedom? What am I to the universe, or, the universe, what is it to me? Who hath forged the chains of wrong and right, of Opinion and Custom? And must I wear them? I say to the universe, Mighty One! thou art not my mother. Return to chaos if thou wilt. I shall still exist. I live. If I owe my being, it is to a destiny greater than thine. Star by star, world by world, system by system shall be crushed,— but I shall live."

There would be no escape from German influence in divinity school. One of Waldo's best friends there was Frederic Henry Hedge, son of a professor, who had been to Germany before entering Harvard College. His experience there did not deflect him from the ministry as in William's case, but it did alter his thinking as to how the faith should be presented, and he would share his views with an appreciative Waldo. One Germanic theme that the young Bostonians found very appealing was *Bildung*. First sounded by the great Goethe, it was translated as "self-culture" in America by Henry Wadsworth Longfellow, who would describe it in Harvard lectures as Goethe's "great study from youth to age" that made him "like the athlete of ancient story, drawing all his strength from earth. His model was the perfect man, as man; living, moving, laboring upon earth in the sweat of his brow." Longfellow added that through *Bildung* Goethe "beheld beauty in everything and God in everything. This was his religion." William Ellery Channing, Boston's most illustrious Unitarian minister and a mentor to young Emerson, suggested thinking of culture in this context as cultivating or tilling. "To cultivate anything, be it a plant, an animal, a mind, is to make it grow. Growth, expression, is the end," he said. *Bildung* was a natural fit with Emerson's personal declaration of independence.

Of more importance to Waldo's development was what Hedge prevailed upon him to absorb from the works of the German philosopher Immanuel Kant. The philosopher, who died a year after Emerson's birth, left behind him a massive body of work that challenged conventional views on just about everything from the structure of the mind itself to the mind's use in the realms of religion and politics. Kant called his conclusions about the working of the mind "transcendental philosophy" since they postulate an inherent element of the mind that transcends the experience of the senses. This was a seed that would take strenuous tillage by

Emerson and his like-minded friends before it would flower into an influential American school of philosophy. But, like *Bildung*, the seed of transcendentalism had landed in the fertile soil of an open mind.

There was a strain of physical weakness, threatening the lungs and nervous system, in all of the Emerson boys. Edward was hit first and hardest and had to give up his law studies temporarily in 1825 and sail for Europe in hope of recovering. With William in New York reading law in Wall Street, the trip was made possible by Waldo's own troubles: the reading connected with his theological studies overtaxed his eyes to the point where he gave up and opened a school in Cambridge to provide family income.

Within a year, however, Edward felt strong enough to come back and accept an invitation to learn his law in the offices of Senator Daniel Webster, and Waldo went back to an exhausting round of study with "mended" eyes and preaching in hope of a "call" to a paying position in some church. It was too much. Although he was "approbated to preach" by the Middlesex Association of Ministers in the fall of 1826, he considered a tightness in the chest as a warning that he too shared his brother's affliction. When a well-to-do uncle, Samuel Ripley, offered to finance a trip to Florida, he set sail for St. Augustine.

The time Waldo spent in the South did as much for his mind as his lungs. He found himself living in the same boardinghouse as Achille Murat, a nephew of Napoleon and former crown prince of Naples. Achille's father, married to Napoleon's youngest sister, Caroline, and crowned king of Naples by Napoleon, had been executed after Waterloo and the son had been exiled from Europe. It was no hardship for the young man, who had hated his uncle, and only three years into residence he had become such an enthusiast for American democracy that he was writing a book about it. The fellow boarders had youth—Waldo at twenty-four and Achille at twenty-six—in common and a lively interest in matters of the mind. Murat had purchased a plantation near Tallahassee and staffed it with slaves, with one of whom he had fathered a child.

In his book in progress, he argued that slavery was valuable economically to the whole nation and personally to the plantation owner, who was freed by slave labor to "cultivate his mind." Murat was also an atheist. Yet Waldo found somewhat to his surprise that they could be friends, particularly after they spent days together in the cabin of a small sailing ship weathering a storm during its passage from St. Augustine to Charleston, South Carolina. They could discuss their differences without agreeing or losing respect for each other. On his trip homeward in early 1827, Waldo summarized for his journal how the southern experience had hardened his feelings against slavery and softened his feelings about people who did not share his faith.

> *St. Augustine, February 27*: A fortnight since I attended a meeting of the Bible Society. The Treasurer of this institution is Marshal of the district, and by a somewhat unfortunate arrangement had appointed a special meeting of the Society, and a slave-auction, at the same time and place, one being in the Government house, and the other in the adjoining yard. One ear therefore heard the glad tidings of great joy, whilst the other was regaled with "Going, gentlemen, going!" And almost without changing our position we might aid in sending the Scriptures to Africa, or bid for "four children without a mother" who had been kidnapped therefrom.

> *Charleston, April 6*: A new event is added to the quiet history of my life. I have connected myself in friendship to a man who with as ardent love of truth as that which animates me, with a mind surpassing mine in the variety of research, and sharpened and strengthened to an energy for action to which I have no pretension, by advantages of birth and practical connexion with mankind almost all men in the world,—is, yet, that which I had ever supposed only a creature of the imagination—a consistent Atheist—and a disbeliever in the existence and, of course, the

immortality of the soul. My faith in these points is strong and I trust, as I live, indestructible. Meantime I love and honour this intrepid doubter. His soul is noble, and his virtue, as the virtue of a Saducee must always be, is sublime.

In the summer of 1827, Ruth Emerson was living in the manse in Concord, where she could provide a place of rest and recreation for her busy and sometimes overstressed sons. On summer vacation from Harvard, Charles was with her most of the time, except for a speaking appearance at a college exhibition in July. Often complaining of not feeling well, Edward came down weekends to rest up from his work in Webster's Boston office and get into shape for accompanying the senator and his family to Washington in the fall. At Harvard commencement exercises in August, where he received an honorary master's degree, Edward gave an oration that Waldo criticized in a letter to William as falling rather flat. Suspecting that his disappointing delivery might have been caused by health problems, Waldo warned William in a postscript, "You will say to Edward if you say anything that you have heard from Waldo of his success for, I have heard today that 'it was the perfection of speaking' & he looks sad under the suspicion that it was not." As for Waldo himself, he was earning ten dollars on Sundays preaching in different churches and spending weekdays with Charles roaming the familiar fields around Concord. He found the combination of hot weather and walking a wonder-working tonic.

At the very end of that year, one of Waldo's preaching dates took him to Concord, New Hampshire. There on Christmas Day, he was entertained in the home of one of the town's most prominent citizens, Colonel William A. Kent, and introduced to his sixteen-year-old stepdaughter, Ellen Tucker. She was vivacious and pretty and possessed of a handsome legacy from her late father, Bezaleel Tucker, who had owned and operated a Boston rope factory. She was almost as interested in words as in animals, as witnessed by her giving the name Byron to her pet spaniel, one member of her menagerie that included a lamb, a canary, and some white mice. The developing eloquence of the young visiting preacher impressed her. Not only was the voice golden, but there was a new shine to the words it carried. Although this Mr. Emerson started his sermon dully enough with a text from the Bible, he went on to illustrate his points with examples from nature that she loved and with quotations from other great thinkers going back to the Greeks. His message was that each of them sitting there in front of him had the need and capacity to think deeply about spiritual matters and his or her own path to becoming a better person.

Waldo was appreciative of the warm reception that he got at the Kent household—and particularly from this bright young girl who was obviously well read for her age and well versed, too, as he could tell from a bit of poetry that she shyly showed him. He hoped that the rest of the congregation shared her reaction. Even if a congregation called itself Unitarian, Waldo could never be sure that he would not shock his audience, many of whom still cherished the lingering rites and pieties of the Calvinism in their background. In the matter of denying the Trinity—Father, Son, and Holy Ghost—as worshiped in orthodox Christianity, he argued in a letter to a friend, "All I said was this—that a priori, we know no reason why God may not exist in a threefold unity; but that since the manner of such an existence is inconceivable to our minds, he would never have revealed to us such an existence which we can neither describe nor comprehend. Infinite wisdom established the foundations of knowledge in the human mind so that twice two could never make anything else than four. So soon as this can be otherwise, our faith is loosened and science abolished. Three may be one, and one three." He had doubts about a great many other aspects of orthodoxy and openly wondered whether he would have been "approbated to preach" if the examiners could have looked into his mind. But he had no doubts at all about the moral truths to which Jesus of Nazareth witnessed in his life and with his death, and these he was preaching with conviction when Ellen Tucker first heard him.

Throughout the next year, Ellen and Waldo corresponded. He could not help but be moved and flattered by her openness. "I am entirely yours now and ever shall be," she wrote in one letter, and in another, "Dear Waldo I love you says Ellen T. I dream about you again night and day." Although it was distressing to Waldo, he found the sad fact that she suffered from tuberculosis, which had killed her brother, all too familiar; it was his own family's affliction. She treated it lightly, proposing that a "drop of blood vermeil" be made into the family crest. Her letters revealed a saving wit, as for instance, "I want to tell you that I love you very much and I would like to have you love me always if consistent with your future plans." Ellen was definitely in Waldo's future plans, and the thought of their being together helped to sustain him when Edward went through a fit of madness so severe that he had to be briefly institutionalized. Waldo attributed his brother's derangement to an overdose of energy. In typical self-deprecating fashion, he noted that he was saved from such a fate by a "mixture of silliness" in his makeup. By year's end, Waldo and Ellen became engaged, while Edward gave up his taxing apprenticeship to Senator Webster and set sail for Puerto Rico.

The engagement virtually forced Waldo early in 1829 to settle down and take one of the permanent jobs with salary attached that he was being offered. He chose to sign on as assistant pastor at the historic Second Church, the religious home of the famous Increase and Cotton Mather. Apparently as wealthy as it was famous, the church paid Waldo twelve hundred dollars a year, an impressively large sum. When Waldo was only a few months into the job, the senior minister, Henry Ware, convinced that the congregation liked his junior, resigned to take a teaching position at Harvard. Waldo's compensation was raised to an amazing eighteen hundred dollars in July, and by September he felt wealthy enough to marry Ellen and bring her to Boston. It was the beginning of a romantic idyll for Waldo. The love that they shared for each other was oddly strengthened by her occasional sick spells when she coughed up blood. Waldo enthusiastically cooperated in any treatment the doctors suggested, such as taking her on a two-hundred-mile bumpy buggy ride to shake the sickness out of her system, and buying dumbbells to join her in home exercises. The consciousness of what her illness might lead to caused them to communicate their feelings constantly in notes and poetry if not in person. In the midst of reading or writing at home, Waldo was sometimes heard to look up and call out, "O Ellen, I do dearly love you." But in a sermon on death just months after their marriage, he told the congregation that "our own pleasant dwelling has been the house of pain. The lamp of our life is burning already in the socket."

Low as it might have been, the flame was bright. With the money that Ellen brought with her and with Waldo's salary, they were able to live well—each of them to have a buggy, for instance, and Ellen to have her mother and sisters with her. Waldo had enough money left over to keep his mother and brothers in comfort, too. Ellen soon discovered that she had married a personage rather than a parson. Like his father before him, Waldo was named chaplain to the Massachusetts legislature and elected to the Boston School Committee. Although he enjoyed crafting sermons, Waldo was less enthralled with other aspects of his job. He was soon in conflict with his congregation over administering the sacraments, and he literally dreaded making pastoral calls. In that process, he was known to mix up addresses and visit perfect—and astonished—strangers who had no connection to his church. When he did get to the right person, he could be nearly tongue-tied by shyness. One story widely circulated about him had to do with his effort to ease the passing of a dying veteran of the Revolutionary War. Waldo could think of nothing hopeful to say until his eyes lighted on the sick man's medicine bottles and he began discussing glassmaking. "Young man, if you don't know your business, you had better go home," the old soldier grumbled.

While he had Ellen to go home to, Waldo could put up with anything in order to keep her happy and comfortable. But in early 1831 there came a time when it was obvious that he could no longer help her. It was an event that he had anticipated. At the height of their happiness he had written to his aunt Mary, "You know—none can know better—on what straightened lines we have all walked to manhood. In poverty and many troubles the seeds of our prosperity were sown. Now all these troubles appeared a fair counterbalance to the flatteries of fortune." After pointing out how well his brothers were doing at the time, he went on:

> Waldo is comparatively well and comparatively success-ful,—far more so than his friends, out of his family, antic-ipated. Now I add to all this felicity a particular felicity which makes my own glass very much larger and fuller, and I straight away say, Can this hold? Will God make me a brilliant exception to the common order of his dealings, which equalizes destinies? There's an apprehension of re-verse always arising from success. But is it my fault that I am happy, and cannot I trust the Goodness that has up-lifted to uphold me? I cannot find in the world without or within, any antidote, any bulwark against this fear, like this: the frank acknowledgment of unbounded dependence. Let into the heart that is filled with prosperity the idea of God, and it smooths the giddy precipices of human pride to a substantial level; it harmonizes the condition of the individual with the economy of the universe.

The fear proved valid when Waldo was compelled to make this terse entry in his journal: "Boston, February 8, 1831—Ellen Tucker Emerson died, 8th February, Tuesday morning, 9 o'clock."

Waldo was devastated. That "bulwark against this fear" was not there. For a year he walked every morning to her father's vault in Roxbury where Ellen lay to deliver thoughts he had of her, poems he wrote to her. When not thinking of Ellen, he was dwelling on an increasing conviction that the conventional min-istry was not for him. It involved mouthing words and conducting rituals unchanged for more than a thousand years that, in his view, distorted and obscured what should be a living faith. He could no longer honestly administer the sacrament of communion, or the Lord's supper, in which the wine is held to be the blood, and the bread the flesh, of Jesus. If, as claimed, its purpose was "in remembrance" of Jesus, Waldo agreed with his Quaker friends that the physical acts of drinking and eating profaned what should be a spiritual experience. He was at a loss as to how to handle his feelings in this matter until a fateful day in early 1832. On his regular daily visit to the cemetery, he performed an act that he recorded in his journal without elaboration: "I visited Ellen's tomb and opened the coffin."

However grisly the act might appear to others, it was life-changing for Ralph Waldo Emerson. He had a new birth of freedom. Ellen was truly gone beyond recall, and he no longer had to cling to a job that he would have needed to support her and any family that they might have had. In fact, he had been made aware that her considerable legacy would come to him when the estate was finally settled, and become the source of a livable income. No eccentric act he now performed could bring shame upon his love, and he was emboldened to take up the communion issue with leaders of his congregation. After many meetings in which there was no agreement, Waldo retreated to the mountains to meditate. He came back with a sermon on the subject that would cause his resignation.

At a September service, Waldo told his people that he did not believe from his understanding of the Bible that Jesus meant his last supper with his disciples to be perpetual and that the effect of doing so was "to clothe Jesus with an authority which he never claimed." He went on to say that

> the importance ascribed to this particular ordinance is not consistent with the spirit of Christianity. The general object and effect of this ordinance is unexceptionable. It has been, and is, I doubt not the occasion of indefinite good; but an importance is given by Christians to it which never can belong in any form. My friends, the apostle well assures us that "the kingdom of God is not meat and drink, but

righteousness and peace and joy, in the Holy Ghost." I am not so foolish as to declaim against forms. Forms are as essential as bodies; but to exalt particular forms, to adhere to one form a moment after it is out-grown is unreasonable, and it is alien to the spirit of Christ. If I understand the distinction of Christianity, the reason why it is to be preferred over all other systems and is divine is this, that it is a moral system; that it presents men with truths which are their own justification; that if miracles may be said to have been its evidence to the first Christians, they are not its evidence to us, but the doctrines themselves; that every practice is Christian that praises itself; and every practice unchristian which condemns itself. I am not engaged to Christianity by decent forms, or saving ordinances; it is not usage, if not what I do not understand, that binds me to it—let these be the sandy foundations of falsehoods. What I revere and obey in it is its reality, its boundless charity, its deep interior life, the rest it gives to my mind, the echo it returns to my thoughts, the perfect accord it makes with my reason through all its representations of God and His Providence; and the persuasion and courage that come out thence to lead me upward and onward. Freedom is the essence of this faith. It has for its object simply to make men good and wise. Its institutions, then, should be as flexible as the wants of men. That form out of which the life and suitableness have departed, should be as worthless in its eyes as the dead leaves that are falling around us.

Although some younger hearers thought that their minister made sense, the general reaction was expressed by a lady who cornered him after the service and said, "You have taken my Lord away and I know not where you have laid him." His stand did not go down too well even in his own family. His usually adoring brother Charles expressed concern that he had gone too far in "the expression of individual opinion." Aunt Mary Moody felt that he was repudiating the work and reputation of his father and all that she had hoped for him even though he said, "I have sometimes thought that to be a good minister it was necessary to leave the ministry." Fellow ministers thought that he had gone "Quakerish," and there were even rumors that he had gone mad. Oddly enough, his strongest supporter was a fire-breathing Methodist minister, Father Edward Taylor, who had been aided by Waldo in founding a Seamen's Mission. When fellow Methodists complained of the association and insisted that Waldo "must go to hell," Taylor thundered, "It does look so, but I am sure of one thing: if Emerson goes to hell, he will change the climate there, and emigration will set that way."

Instead, Waldo went to Europe. The strain that the Emersons had been under since Ellen's death played havoc with their weak constitutions. Charles developed alarming symptoms of tuberculosis and departed for Puerto Rico to be with Edward. Before leaving, he informed Aunt Mary Moody that he had never seen Waldo so "disheartened." In addition to general malaise, Waldo was dealing with persistent diarrhea. He did not know what to do about it until he heard of a ship sailing for southern Europe on Christmas Day, and he found himself almost unwittingly aboard when it cleared Boston harbor. The voyage restored his health, and he enjoyed seeing places he knew only by reading, such as Rome, Paris, and London. He overcame his shyness enough to call on his favorite authors—Coleridge and Wordsworth in England and Carlyle in Scotland. He had been fascinated by Thomas Carlyle's essays on the new thinking coming out of Germany, but he hadn't been prepared for the effect of meeting him. Although very different personalities, their mutual attraction was such that Waldo offered to get the Scotsman's book published in America and noted in his journal, "Carlyle is so amiable that I love him."

Sailing homeward, Waldo had a great deal of time for thinking about what he would do and where he would do it. The loss of a pulpit had been his own choice, and he was determined to justify it by carrying on his ministry in any available way. To do so, he felt obliged to come up with a response to that woman in his lost congregation who wanted to know where he had laid her Lord. He used the idle time aboard ship to frame an answer that might satisfy her and all like-minded souls:

> Before I parted from you I anxiously desired an opportunity of speaking to you upon the subject of that change which seems to be taking place under our eyes in the opinions of men on religious questions; of that teaching which all men are waiting for; of that Teacher who has been predicted, and hath not yet come. Who is that Teacher? Let Jesus answer. Even the Spirit of truth. He would say that there is constant effort of the Divine Providence for the instruction of man. Time, the great teacher, is always uttering his lessons; every day is exposing some of the falsehoods that have deceived us; every day the Almighty Father accumulates knowledge in the mind of the race, from endless sources. The Teacher is one, but he speaks by a thousand lips. To drop all personification, the progress of society, the simple occurrences of every day, are always instructing men, undeceiving them; and every event, big with what crimes and misfortunes soever, carries with it this beneficial effect. So with the highest truth, the relations, namely, of man to God, and the character of God. The perspective of time, as it sets everything in the right view, does the same by Christianity. We learn to look at it now as a part of the history of the world; to see how it rests on the broad basis of man's moral nature, but is not itself that basis. I cannot but think that Jesus Christ will be better loved by not being adored. He has had an unnatural, an artificial place for ages in human opinions, a place too high for love. There is a recoil of affections from all authority and force. In the barbarous state of society it was thought to add to the dignity of Christ to make him King, to make him God.

But will it not come to be thought the chief value of his teaching that it was a brave stand made for man's spiritual nature, against the sensualism, the forms, and the crimes of the age? The value of his particular lessons is something less to us than it was to his contemporaries, because, like every wise and efficient man, he spoke to his times, in all their singular peculiarities. He speaks as he thinks, but he is thinking for them. And it is the great mark of the extraordinary force of his mind that, notwithstanding this occasional character, his sayings have a fullness of meaning, a fitness to human nature, and an universality of application which has commended them to the whole world. Christianity is the most emphatic affirmation of spiritual nature. But it is not the only nor the last affirmation. There shall be a thousand more. Very inconsistent would it be with a soul so possessed with the love of the real and unseen as Christ's to set bounds to that illimitable ocean. He never said, "All truth have I revealed." He plainly affirms the direct contrary: "I will send you another Teacher, another Comforter, even the Spirit of truth; he will guide you into all truth." His word is a mustard seed; it is a little leaven; but, with a prophet's eye, he sees it quicken the minds of good men, and run, like something endued with life, from soul to soul, from land to land— searching, agitating, educating society; touching with sympathy all heroic minds, and preparing hearts to conceive and tongues to utter yet more lofty and significant revelations. "Greater things than these shall he do." We see with our eyes the verification of his promise. In the place of unsupported virtues of solitary individuals that sparkle in the darkness of antiquity, of the little, stingy, rapacious intercourse of those days, the nations of the globe are brought together by pacific and equitable commerce; liberal, humane, Christian associations are correcting the manners and relieving the sufferings of vast masses of men:

are they not all the fruit of the life and teachings of the lowly Nazarene?

There is a revolution of religious opinion taking effect around us, as it seems to me the greatest of all revolutions which have ever occurred; that, namely, which has separated the individual from the whole world, and made him demand a faith satisfactory to his own proper nature, whose full extent he now for the first time contemplates. A little while ago men were supposed to be saved or lost as one race. Adam was the federal head, and his sin a federal sin, which cut off the hopes of his posterity. The atoning blood of Christ again was sacrifice for all, by which the divine vengeance was averted from you and me. But now man begins to hear a voice that fills the heavens and earth, saying that God is within him; that there is the celestial host. I find this amazing revelation of my immediate relation to God a solution to all the doubts that oppressed me. I recognize the distinction of the outer and inner self; the double consciousness that, within this erring, passionate, mortal self, sits a supreme, calm, immortal mind, whose powers I do not know, but it is stronger than I; it is wiser than I; it never approved me in any wrong; I seek counsel of it in my doubts; I repair to it in my dangers; I pray to it in my undertakings. It seems to me the face which the Creator uncovers to his child. It is the perception of this depth in human nature, this infinitude belonging to every man that has been born, which has given a new value to the habits of reflection and solitude. In this doctrine, as deeply felt by him, is the key by which the words that fell from Christ upon the character of God can alone be well and truly explained. "The Father is in me: I am in the Father, yet the Father is greater than I."

As he sat in the quiet of his study in the Concord manse reading over his journal, Waldo was aware that it would take him many years and require many forms of expression to spread this message that, in another entry at sea, he had condensed into a sentence: "The highest revelation is that God is in every man." He would need allies in the process, one of whom would certainly be brother Edward, whose only quarrel with the new thinking was a too frequent use of the word *reason* instead of the word *soul*. On his first walk to the post office, Waldo found a letter from Puerto Rico. Since Charles had long ago returned home, more to court a Concord girl than to try to practice law, in Waldo's estimation, the letter should be from Edward. But Waldo did not recognize the handwriting on the envelope. Fearful of what that could mean, he tore it open right there in the post office and read the worst possible news. A friend was informing the Emerson family that twenty-nine-year-old Edward had died almost on the day that they had moved to Concord. That night Waldo told his journal that "I see I am bereaved of part of myself."

For Waldo, Edward's death was the last sad straw on the load of calamity befalling him since Ellen had left him. He could have given in to despair, but doing so would have meant denying his belief that the Comforter was within him. What he did do was to plunge into work. He was in the act of putting together his thoughts on nature to make a book. Done rightly, it would be a fitting memorial to Ellen, who had so loved nature. What Ellen saw in nature, and what he saw better through her eyes, was uplifting beauty. As he thought about that, he wrote, "Beauty in its largest and profoundest sense is one expression for the universe; God in the all-fair. Truth and goodness and beauty are but different faces of the same All." He began feeling better with every scratch of the pen. Coming to Concord, where beauty could be seen from every window, gave promise of a move in the right direction instead of a retreat from defeat.

2

A Meeting of Minds

SHE WAS NO BEAUTY, and yet there was something about her that attracted attention. Tall and slender, she moved with a grace left over from dancing lessons in her youth. Her height was accentuated by a twist of dark brown hair held in place by a high tortoiseshell comb. The effect of her bearing and a faraway look in her gray eyes was to lift her above her surroundings in the view of beholders. Although she was classed as an old maid at thirty-three by the pilgrim society of Plymouth, Massachusetts, Lydia Jackson's bearing and pursuits made it clear to all that she was not to be pitied.

By that time in her life, however, Lydia had experienced enough in the way of tragedy and disappointment to leave a shadow of sadness in those dreamy eyes. Her father, a prosperous merchant and shipowner, and her mother, a tubercular invalid, had died in the same year when she was sixteen. Left to fend for themselves, Lydia and her sister, Lucy, and brother, Charles, had at least been blessed with adequate incomes from the estate, numerous nearby relatives, and a showplace colonial mansion known as the Winslow House. Lucy eventually married a local merchant of good reputation named Brown and bore him two children before he absconded, having borrowed and lost much of the family inheritance. Lydia took Lucy and the children into Winslow House with her and felt obliged to share what income she had left with

Lucy and Charles, who was just starting a practice as a physician in Boston.

In view of these misfortunes, Lydia treasured all the more an inheritance worth more than money—a fine mind. She read everything that came to hand, including books in the several languages that she had mastered. In addition to these normal uses of the mind, Lydia was surprised and intrigued by unwanted and accurate incidences of clairvoyance. On what had been an ordinary January day in 1835, she started up the stairway in Winslow House and was startled to see herself in bridal dress coming down the stairs hand in hand with a man whom she instantly identified as Mr. Emerson. Although she hardly knew him, she was sure of who it was for a rather peculiar reason. Back in the 1820s, she had gone to church on a visit to Boston and taken a seat near the pulpit. She was at first disappointed to learn that the sermon would be delivered by a young visiting preacher. But when he arose and climbed into the pulpit, she was fascinated—first by the fact that he had the longest neck she had ever seen, and then by the words that came out of him in mellifluous tones. She never expected to encounter that preacher again, but in 1834 George Bradford, her German teacher, arranged for a Plymouth appearance by a man named Emerson who was gaining fame for the lectures on great personalities that he was delivering around the Boston area. Not one to miss a cultural event, Lydia attended the lecture and was introduced to the speaker. This time she was not aware of his neck but of the pleasant circumstance that, at six feet, he looked slightly down on her through gem blue eyes and gave her a soft, sweet smile. In their flurry of conversation, it was evident that they might have a meeting of minds on important subjects such as the shortcomings of the Unitarian Church and the value of learning. But she had since entertained no thought of him that would fit the bridegroom image. When the vision faded, she found herself blushing from embarrassment and claiming aloud, "I don't deserve this."

Lydia was just as unprepared when later that month—January 26, precisely—Mr. Emerson's smiling face appeared briefly before her and again faded away. This was more than embarrassing. It was frightening. On the very next afternoon, a letter addressed in an unknown hand was delivered to her while she was resting on the parlor sofa. It was just as well that she was so safely supported. She might have dropped in a faint when she absorbed the message:

Concord 24 January 1835

To Miss Lydia Jackson:

I obey my highest impulses in declaring to you the feeling of deep and tender respect with which you have inspired me. I am rejoiced in my Reason as well as in my Understanding by finding an earnest and noble mind whose presence quickens in mine all that is good and shames and repels from me my own weakness. Can I resist the impulse to beseech you to love me? The strict limits of the intercourse I have enjoyed have certainly not permitted the manifestation of that tenderness which is the first sentiment in the common kindness between man and woman. But I am not less in love, after a new and higher way. I have immense desire that you should love me, and that I might live with you always. My own assurance of the truth and fitness of the alliance—the union I desire, is so perfect, that it will not admit the thought of hesitation— never of refusal on your part. I could scratch out the word. I am persuaded that I address one so in love with what I love, so conscious with me of the everlasting principles, and seeking the presence of the common Father through means so like, that no remoteness of condition could separate us, and that an affection founded on such a basis cannot alter.

I will not embarrass this expression of my heart and mind with any second considerations. I am not therefore blind to them. They touch the past and the future—our friends as well as ourselves, even the Departed. But I see clearly how your consent shall resolve them all.

And I think it not strange, as you will not, that I write rather than speak. In the gravest acts of my life I more willingly trust my pen than my tongue. It is as true. And yet had I been master of my time at this moment, I should bring my letter in my own hand. But I had no leave to wait a day after my mind was made up. Say to me therefore anything but no. Demand any time for conversation, for consideration, and I will come to Plymouth with a joyful heart. And so God bless you, dear and blessed Maiden, and incline you to love your true friends.

Ralph Waldo Emerson

Lydia did demand a conversation, and Waldo came to Plymouth posthaste. Having thought hard about the amazing letter and composed an answer in her mind, Lydia proceeded to deliver it with her eyes shut in order not to see his reaction. It was a litany of reasons why she would not make a good wife, as, for instance, that she might not be up to the demands of housekeeping, at which she was inexperienced and probably inept. She was not willing to trade a way of life that she liked for another that might not suit her unless she was convinced that his need and love for her was great enough to overcome her doubts. She went on so long in this vein that she was afraid he might be bored. "Do you find all this uninteresting?" she asked, opening her eyes and meeting his. "Uninteresting? It is heaven! You are not saying no," he said.

Waldo assured her of both his need and his love. From his study of the lives of great men, he was learning that a "perfect sympathy between like minds," such as he believed theirs to be, was very rare. Indeed, he felt that she was a "commissioned spirit." Far from being a rash, spur-of-the-moment act, his letter had been brewing in his mind since first he saw her. His was a form of love at first sight. As proof he recited an entry in his journal dating back to that time: "It happened once that a youth and a maiden beheld each other in a public ceremony for the first time. The youth gazed with great delight upon the beautiful face until he caught the maiden's eye. There are some occult facts in human nature that are natural magic. The chief of these is the glance. The mysterious communication that is established across a house between two entire strangers, by this means moves all the springs of wonder."

The conversation that began so negatively ended so well that they publicly announced their engagement the very next day. Waldo could not linger in Plymouth to share what he called "a very sober joy" with his betrothed. There was much to do in both Concord and Boston to make a wedding possible. In addition to already scheduled lectures and a book in progress, he had felt obliged to agree to preach every Sunday at a Lexington, Massachusetts, church to earn steady income, much as he had done to provide for Ellen. In this instance, however, he would not be taking on the sacramental and pastoral duties that had driven him from his Boston church. Despite the ease with which Lydia and Waldo reached an agreement, there remained a number of issues in their relationship to be settled, mostly by letter. One was Waldo's desire to change her name to Lidian, since he felt that it would sound better with Emerson than Lydia, which New Englanders tended to pronounce as "Lydiar." Although Lydia had no trouble going along with that wish, she had a hard time coming to terms with Waldo's insistence that they live in Concord rather than in her ancestral Plymouth.

There was no way that Waldo would leave Concord. He had fallen in love with the place almost as surely as with his betrothed. At about the time that he and Lydia were discussing the matter, Waldo had noted in his journal:

Sunday evening. I went at sundown to the top of Dr. Ripley's hill, and renewed my vows to the genius of that place. Somewhat of awe, somewhat grand and solemn, mingles with the beauty that shines afar around. In the west, where the sun was sinking behind clouds, one pit of splendor lay as in a desert of space,—a deposit of still light, not radiant. Then I beheld the river like God's love journeying out of the gray past into the green future.

To Lidian he wrote that he could not live in Plymouth because "Plymouth is streets; I live in the wide champaign. I must win you to love it." Somewhat mysteriously, he added that leaving Concord would deprive him of "some important resources." When Lidian reluctantly gave in, Waldo knew what his next step toward the altar had to be. "I hope to hire a house and set up a fireside next September," he wrote to brother William. "Perhaps Charles also; and, a year hence, shall we not build a house on grandfather's hill, facing Wachusett, Monadnoc, and the setting sun?"

The Concord for which Waldo wanted to win his bride's love was a working town. Although most of its two thousand citizens gained a livelihood from farming, there was a cotton mill, a pipe factory, a steel smithy, two sawmills, two gristmills, and home shops in which artisans were turning out everything from carriages and furniture to pencils crafted by a family named Thoreau. There were three large taverns that did too thriving a business, in the view of some sober citizens. But there was a Society for the Supression of Intemperance to compete with the publicans, and people could congregate in a library, a lyceum, a schoolhouse, or a church. Waldo was no snob. He enjoyed absorbing native wisdom from his encounters with fellow Concordians in the "lukewarm dog-days of common village life." The only thing Waldo missed in Concord was the stimulus of intellectual discussion, and he made up for that by socializing with old friends on his business trips to Boston. While the search for a suitable fireside was going on, this made possible face-to-face meetings of the lovers, since Lidian could invite herself to visits with her Boston friends. Often informal social gatherings took place after some cultural meeting, and at one of these on a July evening in 1835 Waldo Emerson made contact with a person who would play a leading role nearly as important as Lidian's in the drama of his life.

Whether Lidian herself was at this particular meeting has not been recorded, but there were many of the women with whom she would likely be associated, including her frequent Boston hostess, Mrs. Bliss. Brightest stars of the gathering were two of the Peabody sisters from Salem, Elizabeth and Mary; the shyest would have been Elizabeth Hoar, the young Concord woman engaged to Waldo's brother Charles; the most eccentric was undoubtedly Waldo's acerbic aunt, Mary Moody. Hosting them in the rooms his family occupied at 3 Somerset Court was a man a few years older than Waldo who could easily qualify as the celebrity of the moment in Boston's intellectual circles. His name was Amos Bronson Alcott, and he was owner, operator, and chief instructor at a new and intriguing school for children of the city's elite.

Unlike the men in the circles he now frequented, this master to whom they were entrusting their children had not gone to Harvard. He had, in fact, enjoyed only a few months of formal education in all of his thirty-five years. He had, however, endured more hard learning experiences and quite probably had read more books than any distinguished member of the faculty in Cambridge. Alcott was born and reared in northern Connecticut on a hilly, rocky farm that barely provided food for the family. Physical labor almost from the first step he took had given him a muscled, stocky body that exuded strength. He had large features with shaggy brows overhanging kindly eyes, a forehead sloping up to a head clearly capable of housing an ample brain. Despite rather formidable looks, his expression and demeanor were gentle and open, inviting quick and easy acquaintance. His was the classic story of the child impoverished in every way but his mental inheritance. His father was illiterate, but an understanding mother helped and encouraged him to learn his letters by writing them with charcoal on the kitchen floorboards by firelight. Other than his mother, few around him understood his ambition and hunger for knowledge, but he always cherished a childhood in which he learned love in the context of a hardworking, caring family and developed a rich and rewarding inner existence.

"I knew a boy once who lived in a small farmhouse under the brow of a hill covered with trees and beautiful retired coves and solitudes," he liked to recall, "and he used to rise early in the morning and go out and choose one of these beautiful places, when the dew was on the ground and the trees and birds were singing and the sun was glittering, and there he would say his prayers; and he found it easy to be good and kind all day when he practised this. I knew this boy intimately." His prayers were a form of meditation on all that he knew or was discovering about life. Lacking companions with understanding and sympathetic ears, he took to jotting his thoughts down in a journal and thus acquired a lifelong habit that would stand him in good stead.

Disappointed by his brief experience with formal schooling and anxious to alleviate the family poverty, if possible, Alcott turned himself into another classical American figure at age seventeen by becoming a "Yankee peddler." Loaded down with mostly household wares made in Connecticut, he tramped through Virginia and the Carolinas selling his goods to homeowners. He slept and ate wherever and whenever he could. His amiable personality and lively interest in new people and new experiences opened most doors, including those of the manor houses on large plantations. He was impressed and inspired by the erudition and gracious manners of the planters as well as the fine furnishings and artifacts with which they surrounded themselves. He returned home determined to improve his own circumstances and behavior. He also returned home four hundred dollars in debt and thus acquired another and less rewarding lifelong habit. In an effort to clear the debt assumed by his father, Alcott stuck to peddling for six years while his mind absorbed book learning like a dry sponge soaking up water. In still deeper monetary debt but richly funded with self-acquired knowledge, Alcott turned to teaching in his early twenties.

By most people's standards, Alcott was as unsuccessful at teaching as at peddling. He bounced around from school to school, town to town. Although pupils liked him, parents and the communities at large were upset by his beliefs and methods. As to beliefs, he was an admiring worshiper of Jesus of Nazareth but not an adherent of any orthodox form of Christianity. As to method, it was best described by one of his daughters, Louisa May: "My father taught in the wise way which unfolds what lies in the child's nature, as a flower blooms, rather than crammed it, like a Strasbourg goose, with more than it could digest." Alcott was admittedly indebted to the Swiss educator Johann Heinrich Pestalozzi for some of his ideas, as well as to the Greeks, especially Plato and Socrates. But he invented most of his instructional techniques right in the classroom as he went along, and this proved to be anathema to conservative traditionalists who are generally the people with the wealth and power to establish schools and who tend to favor orthodoxy and established authority in all matters. Nevertheless, by 1830, Alcott managed to secure sponsorship for an experimental school in suburban Philadelphia that promised to last long enough to permit his marriage to Abigail—known as Abba—May, a brilliant, well-educated, fiery member of an established Boston family.

As usual, Alcott lost his job within a few years, but the marriage brought him food for new thought and opportunities beyond expectation. From the moment that daughters Anna and then Louisa May were born during the Philadelphia years, Alcott used his discipline of journal keeping to record everything that he observed about their lives and the interaction between them and with their parents. By the time he arrived in Boston he had a massive manuscript that he called *Psyche, Or the Breath of Childhood* in hand. When failure in Philadelphia was reported to the avant-garde in Boston through the May connections, two of its leaders—the venerable Reverend William Ellery Channing and the young, ambitious Elizabeth Peabody—set about collecting funds and pupils for another new Alcott school that opened its doors in the fall of 1834 at the fashionable Masonic Temple on Tremont Street. Alcott's capacity to shrug off reverses and take on a new challenge with verve and optimism comes through in his journal entries on that occasion:

Sept. 22, 1834. I opened today with thirty children (between three and twelve) and am assisted in their instruction by Miss Elizabeth Peabody whose reputation both as regards original and acquired ability is high,—she unites intellectual and practical qualities of no common order. Her proposition to aid me comes from the deep interest she feels in human culture, and her friendly desire to establish me in this city. I have obtained very fine rooms in the temple and have made arrangements to fit up the interior in style corresponding to the exterior and what is of more importance, in adaptation to those who are to assemble there for the formation of tastes and habits.

I have spared no expense to surround the senses with appropriate emblems of intellectual and spiritual life. Painting, busts, books, and not inelegant furniture have been deemed important. I wish to fill every form that addresses the senses with significance and life, so whatever is seen, said or done shall picture ideal beauty and perfection, thus placing the child in a scene of tranquil repose and spiritual loveliness. I would bring external circumstances into harmony with that serenity of spirit and vivacity of portraiture which are the native attributes of unspoiled childhood,— planting, as it were, a prop around which tendrils may fasten, and thus lift its aspiring energies to the skies.

My pupils seem favored by nature with good capacities. I am glad to find them so free from the usual entailment of school habits. They seem to have been well taught, having few vicious tendencies either of spirit or body. About half are girls,—a circumstance most favorable to the exertion of a pure and final moral influence on the formation of character, and preserving the social relations unbroken during the impressionable period of life.

By present arrangement, I shall never be occupied with practical instruction more than five hours daily, and ultimately, perhaps, not more than three. I shall be able also to do better justice to my family than I have done. Thirty pupils (there will doubtless be more) will bring me an income of $1800,—sufficient to support us comfortably and soon free me from debt. The sensation of thrift is to me a delightful one and the more so from the continuous suffering with untoward circumstances to which I have been subjected. This income may at least take from the toil of life some anxieties and impediments to progress in the celestial life and may serve to open out powers which have struggled amid severer conditions.

At that July gathering in Alcott's rooms, Elizabeth Peabody filled Emerson's ears with praise about what was happening at the school. She was so impressed that she had taken copious notes of the proceedings and was going to publish a book about it. Alcott firmly believed in the preexistence of the soul and that, as his favorite poet Wordsworth put it, "trailing glory do we come / From God, who is our home." He would tell his pupils that "all truth is within. My business is to lead you to find it in your own Souls." Amazingly, he was doing just that with his Socratic method. Knowing that this was very like what Emerson preached, Miss Peabody suggested that he come to the school and hear it himself.

It was an invitation that Waldo with his own teaching experience could not resist, and he visited the Temple School on several occasions. He was particularly fascinated by what came out of the mouth of a six-year-old boy named Josiah Quincy. In one exchange with Alcott, the boy said, "If you call Jesus God and God God, then I think there would be two Gods, and that is the same as worshipping statues." No Unitarian divine could say it better, but few divines would have dared to give Josiah's answer to a question as to were there any idolaters in Boston: "Yes; a great many of them. They worship money." Josiah thought that there was a Supernatural element in life that he called Spirit, and a Natural one that he called Clay. Waldo was astonished when he heard Josiah say, "Mr. Alcott, we think too much about Clay. We should think of Spirit, not Clay. I should think a mother now would love her baby's Spirit; and suppose it should die, that is only the Spirit bursting away out of the Body. It is alive; it is perfectly happy, I really do not know why people mourn when their friends die. I should think it would be a matter of rejoicing. For instance: now, if we should go out into the street and find a box— an old dusty box—and put into it some very fine pearls, and by and by the box should grow old and break, why, we should not even think about the box; but if the pearls are safe, we should think of them and nothing else. So it is with the Soul and Body. I cannot see why people mourn for bodies."

In addition to inspiring this kind of thought in children, Alcott enriched their days with drawing, taught by a leading artist, Washington Allston, and with music led by his wife, Abba. Alcott did not believe in using the rod on a disobedient child; instead, he would make the culprit strike him. This proved to be a very effective form of discipline since the child was not only reluctant and embarrassed to carry it out but was also made aware by doing so that his or her wrongdoing hurt others. Although an impressed Waldo was determined to get to know this unusual schoolmaster better, in that July there was another development that demanded his attention and time. As in the case of other rather momentous events, this was treated tersely by a single line in his journal: "I bought my house and two acres six rods of land of John T. Coolidge for 3,500 dollars." But in another letter to brother William he reported a bit more fully:

> *July 27, 1835.* Has Charles told you that I have dodged the doom of building and have bought the Coolidge house in Concord, with the expectation of entering it next September? It is in a mean place, and cannot be fine until trees and flowers give it a character of its own. But we

shall crowd so many books and papers, and, if possible, wise friends into it, that it shall have as much wit as it can carry. My house costs me thirty-five hundred dollars, and may next summer cost four or five hundred more to enlarge or finish. The seller alleges that it cost him seventy-eight hundred.

A square, wooden structure in colonial style, the house was relatively new, having been built in 1828. It was just on the outskirts of town on the Cambridge Turnpike, across from a schoolhouse. Set well back from the road, the house was large enough to accommodate Ruth Emerson and brother Charles in addition to the newlyweds and some live-in help. It was served by a barn for horses and equipage and surrounded on three sides by meadow through which a path in back led across a brook to open fields and Walden beyond. It satisfied a need of Waldo's that he had expressed when a friend objected to keeping cows because of the land they needed: "But a cow does not need so much land as my eyes require between me and my neighbor." Once they knew where they would live, the couple was able to set a wedding date. Since Waldo was scheduled to give an oration on the two hundredth anniversary of his ancestor's founding of Concord on Saturday, September 12, he suggested an evening wedding in the Winslow House on the following Monday.

In the interim, there were visits in Plymouth and Concord to let Lidian and the Emerson family get to know each other. One of these nearly derailed the romance. During a few days that she spent at Winslow House, Aunt Mary Moody behaved so strangely and rudely that Lidian was glad to see her go when Waldo came for her in a carriage. In the next letter she received from Waldo, Lidian found herself accused of being too fond of herself and too judgmental of others. Her hurt feelings weren't assuaged until Aunt Mary Moody delivered herself of a confession during Lidian's visit to the manse in Concord: "I spent the whole time we were riding to Concord in trying to make Waldo give you up, and ran you down in every way I could. I cannot bear to lose my nephews and I did the same when Charles was engaged to Eliza-beth." But before that confession Lidian understandably wore—in Waldo's words—"her air of lofty abstraction, like Dante." While Waldo liked this characteristic of his bride, one aspect of it did upset him: she insisted on calling him Mr. Emerson instead of Waldo. In an effort to persuade her otherwise during that visit he gave her a ring he had inherited from his great-uncle Waldo and told her, "The inscription inside is the name you should call me by." She held the ring up to the light for a close look and laughed. "I do! It says *Mr. Waldo Emerson!*" Waldo knew then for sure that he had met his match in quick wit.

By the wedding day, they were in such a blissful agreement that they talked too long in the parlor after Waldo arrived at Winslow House and had to rush upstairs to dress for the seven-thirty ceremony. Waldo was waiting at the foot of the stairs in good time, but there was no sign of Lidian. He started up the stairs to alert her and met her on the landing. As they went down together, hand in hand, Lidian was nearly overcome by the eerie replay of her January vision. She had no time to worry about what that could mean. Late in the afternoon of the next day, they arrived in the yard of a Concord house that she had never seen, since it was held to be improper for a lady to look at her future home before her marriage. Lidian had sent two cartloads of furni-ture a few weeks earlier, and a fraction of it had been unpacked by Charles and Ruth Emerson, who were on hand to meet them with Nancy Colesworthy, a cook, in tow. Preparations were under way for tea, even though there was nothing to serve it on but saucers, when sister Lucy Brown and a maid from Plymouth named Hitty, who had followed them by stagecoach, arrived. At that point, an evening that should have been joyful turned into a waking night-mare for a woman fearful of her adequacy as a housekeeper, and the cause of it all was an unanticipated flaw—or virtue—to be seen in the character of her very new husband, depending upon the viewer's angle of vision.

When Lidian led her sister up to one of the few rooms with a bed to change her travel-dusted clothes, Lucy broke down and started to sob; the move was just too much for her in many respects. Lidian started to comfort her, but there was a knock on the door and Waldo stuck his head in. He was smiling broadly as he told Lidian that old friends, the Rodmans, had stopped by on a carriage trip through New England. Thrilled to be at last master of his own ample establishment, Waldo had asked them to stay to tea and spend the night, and they had been delighted to accept. Lidian felt that letting her husband down this early in the marriage could be the beginning of the end of it. So, summoning Nancy and Hitty to her aid, she managed to lay a carpet, set up a bedstead, and move a washing stand, dressing table, and some chairs into an empty room. It was ten-thirty before she could show the Rodmans to their chamber. And then the proverbial straw fell upon her. Mrs. Rodman announced that she had left everything— nightclothes, hair brushes, the works—back at the inn where they had planned to stay. Digging through packing cases, Lidian managed to furnish these, too, and finally fell into bed, totally exhausted. Anything in the way of a honeymoon went on hold.

Lidian was much happier with her husband's social nature a month later when he brought her old German teacher, George Bradford, who had been their Cupid, and the much-discussed Boston schoolteacher Bronson Alcott to their home for a weekend. Alcott was a fascinating talker who had interesting ideas about everything, and he included her in the discussions. Without any prompting from Waldo, Lidian let a departing Mr. Alcott know that he would be welcome in their home at any time. Waldo went right to his journal and wrote, "Last night came hither Mr. Alcott and spent the Sabbath,—a wise man, simple, superior to display and drops the best things as quietly as the least. Every man, he says, is a revelation and ought to write his own record, but few with the pen. *His* book is his school in which he writes all his thoughts. He thinks Jesus is a pure deist and says all children are deists."

Like his new friend, Emerson, Alcott recorded his impressions of the visit as soon as he could get to his journal:

> On Saturday afternoon I came to Concord with Mr. Bradford. We reached the residence of Mr. Emerson after a ride of three hours. The evening was passed in very interesting conversation. On Sunday various interesting topics of an intellectual and spiritual character were resumed. On most subjects there was a striking conformity of taste and opinion. We have much talk on the character and life of Christ. On this there was some diversity of idea—more the effect, as I deem, of difference of association than of thought. Mr. E's fine literary taste is sometimes in the way of the clear and hearty acceptance of the spiritual. I have not found a man in whose whole mind I felt more sympathy than his. With Mrs. E I was also much pleased. These two persons have and represent a new idea of life.
>
> I have been quite interested in this visit. I have found a man who, with all his tastes for Grecian literature and philosophy, can apprehend something spiritual in Christianity. To him it is "not altogether foolishness," for he has the sense of the human, and the love and faith for the pure and perfect universal Man.
>
> With his brother, Mr. C. Emerson, I had some interesting conversation. He has much of his brother's spirit. They are both scholarlike in their views and tastes, and yet the man is not lost in the scholar. I shall like to renew my acquaintance with them on fit occasions. To have a few such friends is the joy and content of life. In communion with such the spirit finds itself, and for the brief time of their presence forgets its independent life, being lost in the common being of humanity.

On the very next day, Alcott told his journal, "On returning from Concord I visit the gaol with my wife and see Garrison."

The Garrison in question was William Lloyd Garrison, Boston's—and quite possibly the nation's—leading abolitionist, and he had been jailed by the police to protect him when a riot broke out in Washington Street after he had spoken to a meeting of his followers. Emerson would certainly have approved of Alcott's jailhouse visit; as pastor of the Second Church in 1831 he had been the first Boston intellectual to validate the abolitionist movement by turning his pulpit over to one of their speakers. For the most part, abolitionists were looked upon as extremists by Bostonians, and they were actively feared and disliked by a commercial community that relied on business with the cotton states. That same fall, Harriet Martineau, a visiting British author, was threatened by a mob when she spoke disparagingly about slavery as she had observed it in the South. She later reported that "at the time of the hubbub against me in Boston, Charles Emerson stood alone in a large company in defense of the right of free thought and speech, and declared that he had rather see Boston in ashes than that I or anybody else should be debarred in any way from perfectly free speech. His brother Waldo invited me to be his guest in the midst of my unpopularity." The anti-abolitionist feeling was national. Gangs in the South broke into post offices and seized and burned any anti-slavery literature they found. Basing it on a fear of "insurrection," outgoing president Jackson ordered the post office to stop sending abolitionist material addressed to anyone in the South.

During her visit to Concord, Martineau was so smitten by her host that she wrote of him in her book *Retrospect of Western Travel* that "he has modestly and silently withdrawn himself from the perturbations and conflicts of the crowd of men, without declining any of the business of life or repressing any of his human sympathies. He is a thinker without being solitary, abstracted, and unfitted for the time. He is ready at every call of action. He lectures to the factory people at Lowell when they ask. He preaches when the opportunity is presented. He is known at every house along the road he travels to and from home, by the words he has dropped and the deeds he has done. The little boy who carries wood for his household has been enlightened by him; and his most transient guests owe to him their experience of what the highest graces of domestic manners may be. Earnest as is the tone of his mind, and placidly strenuous as is his life, an exquisite spirit of humor pervades his intercourse. A quiet gaiety breathes out of his conversation; and his observation, as keen as it is just, furnishes him with perpetual material. If, out of such harmony, one leading quality is to be distinguished, it is, in him, modest independence, and independence equally of thought, of speech, of demeanor, of occupation, and of objects in life; yet without a trace of contempt in its temper or of encroachment in its action."

"Placidly strenuous" was a very good description of the life that Waldo was pursuing once he was settled into marriage and a home of his own. In addition to preaching and lecturing, he was working hard on his book about nature when the Emerson family was visited by tragedy once more on a May day in 1836. A bright spirit in the household, brother Charles would often lighten the atmosphere when conversation got too sad or serious by cracking jokes or getting up and dancing around the room. For months work had been going forward at the house that Waldo and Lidian had decided to call "the Bush" on adding rooms to accommodate Charles and fiancée Elizabeth Hoar after their planned marriage in September. But it was so apparent that the Emerson lung affliction was eating away at Charles that on a day when she was measuring the new rooms for her piano, Elizabeth broke into tears and said, "It's of no use. It never will be." A few weeks later, Charles went to visit his brother William, and Waldo reported the outcome in his journal entry for May 16: "Charles died at New York, Monday afternoon, 9 May. His prayer that he might not be sick was granted him. He was never confined to a bed. He rode out on Monday afternoon with Mother, promised himself to begin his journey with me on my arrival, the next day; on reaching home, he stepped out of the carriage alone, walked up the steps and into the house without assistance, sat down on the stairs, fainted and never recovered. Beautiful without any parallel in my experience of young men, was his life, happiest his death. Miserable is my own prospect from whom my friend is taken. Clean and sweet was his life, untempted almost, and his action on others all-healing, uplifting and fragrant. I read now his pages, I remember all his words and motions without any pang, so healthy and human a life it was, and not like Edward's, a tragedy of poverty and sickness, tearing genius.

"His senses were those of a Greek. I owe to them a thousand observations. To live with him was like living with a great painter. I used to say that I had no leave to see things until he pointed them out, and afterwards I never ceased to see them."

After a period of intense grief which he shared with Elizabeth, who would remain permanently close to the family as Charles's "widow," Waldo took up his pen again and drove through to the completion of his book. Published in the fall as an anonymous work, it was a critical, if not commercial, success, and the thinking found in it was so original that readers were either inspired or shocked. One of those who was inspired was a Harvard student from Concord named Henry David Thoreau, who found it on the college library shelves. There is no record that he then related "anonymous" to the Mr. Emerson living down the road whom he had yet to meet. The shocking aspect of the book was its anticipation of the work of Charles Darwin, who in that year had just arrived back in England on the *Beagle* after a voyage of discovery that would result in his theory of evolution. Self-styled as a poet rather than a theologian or scientist, Emerson compressed this thought into a short prelude:

> A subtle chain of countless rings
> The next unto the farthest brings;
> The eye reads omens where it goes,
> And speaks all languages the rose;
> And striving to be man the worm
> Mounts through all the spires of form.

The whole work might be called a prose poem in praise of the beauty and wonderful working of nature of which man is a part. Emerson suggests that creation did not stop with Genesis but is a continuing process in which man also shares through the spiritual aspect of his being. "Spirit, that is, the Supreme Being, does not build up Nature around us, but puts it forth through us, as the life of the tree puts forth new branches and leaves through the pores of the old." As in his lectures and sermons, Emerson made his arguments with impressive sentences. Among them: "Nothing in nature is exhausted in its first use. When a thing has served an end to the uttermost, it is wholly new for an ulterior service." . . . "Each creature is only a modification of the other." . . . "Nor has science sufficient humanity so long as the naturalist overlooks that wonderful congruity which subsists between man and the world, of which he is lord, not because he is the most subtile inhabitant, but because he is its head and heart, and finds something of himself in every great and small thing, in every mountain stratum, in every new law of colour, fact of astronomy, or atmospheric influence which observation or analysis lay open."

One appreciative reader of Emerson's *Nature* was Bronson Alcott. Much of it came very close to his own thinking as he had tried to spell it out in his journal only months before: "I set out from the wide ground of Spirit. This is; all else is its manifestation. Body is Spirit at its circumference. It denotes its confines to the external sense; it individualizes, defines Spirit, breaks the Unity into Multiplicity and places under the vision of man parts of the great Whole which, standing thus separate, can be taken in by the mind—too feeble to apprehend the whole at once and requiring all save an individual thing to be excluded at a single view—Infinitude is too wide for man to take in. He is therefore permitted to take in portions and spread his vision over the wide circumference by little and little; and in these portions doth the Infinite shadow forth itself; God in all and all in God."

Thanks largely to Henry Hedge, Waldo's friend from Harvard Divinity School days, he and Alcott would not be alone in sharing and spreading such heretical views. Hedge had a pastorate in Bangor, Maine, and he felt even more remote from intellectual companionship than Waldo had in Concord. At a celebration of Harvard's bicentennial, Hedge met with Emerson and two other unorthodox Unitarian ministers, George Ripley and George Putnam, and proposed forming a group that would hold periodical meetings for intellectual discussion that he would be able to attend. Within days, the first meeting was held at Ripley's Boston home with a wider circle, including Bronson Alcott, in attendance. Talk went so well that several more meetings were held in members' homes that fall to discuss such subjects as "American Genius— the causes which hinder its growth, and give us not first rate productions"; "Education of Humanity"; and "What is the essence of Religion as distinct from morality?" Called at first just "The Club," it was soon known as "The Transcendental Club" because of its members' common belief in much of Kant's philosophy.

Emerson, who would lecture and write essays on the law of compensation, experienced it in action in his own home on October 31, 1836. He noted it with the brevity he reserved for momentous occasions: "Last night, at 11 o'clock, a son was born to me. Blessed child! a lovely wonder to me, and which makes the universe look friendly to me." The boy, named Waldo, was new life replacing life lost. He was also another link to the man named Bronson. With a much more sympathetic eye, Emerson worked his way through Alcott's *Psyche* and his journals for the year 1835 when another Alcott daughter, Elizabeth, had been born—a thousand handwritten pages. The point Alcott was making in his book was that every child is the "Incarnate Word. The Supernatural is quickened into life and asketh for its own forms of significance" and becomes a soul growing in a body. Emerson liked Alcott's thinking but informed his new friend in a kindly way that he was overwriting and misusing devices like the "eth" endings on verbs. Alcott valued the criticism and promised a rewrite.

Meanwhile, Alcott was heading into serious trouble as a result of another book that he did have published toward the end of

1836. The collection of Elizabeth Peabody's that appeared in book form as *Record of a School: Exemplifying the General Principles of Spiritual Culture* had been so successful in bringing attention and pupils to the Temple School that the pair decided to put out another collection entitled *Conversations with Children on the Gospels*. While this was in preparation, Alcott and Peabody had an unfortunate falling-out. Having continued his chronic indebtedness by borrowing to furnish his school, Alcott was unable to pay Peabody for her services and instead took her into his household to provide room and board in the place of salary. Another young intellectual with literary aspirations and private income, Margaret Fuller, took her place in the school. Charging that Bronson or Abba Alcott had entered her room and read her personal correspondence, Elizabeth Peabody broke off relations with them, dropped work on the book, and asked that her name not be associated with much of it. Her younger sister, Sophia, who had come to "adore" Mr. Alcott, thought that Lizzie, as she called her, was wrong in her accusation, and Sophia stepped in to work along with Miss Fuller to finish the book.

As it turned out, Elizabeth may have been using a personal peeve to protect her professional reputation. There were questions and answers in the conversation that she perceived would go beyond the pale of propriety if published. Although Alcott's avowed purpose was to learn something new and unexpected from the children whom he credited with spiritual insight, he occasionally felt called upon to give them some guidance in the right direction. In dealing with the birth of Jesus, for instance, he was astonished to discover how totally innocent they were of the physiology of birth. One child, for instance, thought that bodies came out of the ground and laid around until God put spirit into them. Trying to be as delicate as he could, Alcott explained that "a mother suffers when she has a child. When she is going to have a child she gives up her body to God, and He works on it in a mysterious way and, with her aid, brings forth the child's Spirit in a little Body of its own; and when it has come she is blissful." Letting children know that much struck adult readers as bad enough, but raising the question of birth at all produced much worse in the way of truth from Josiah, the school's six-year-old seer, who said that birth resulted from "the naughtiness of other people." Even after the break, Lizzie Peabody tried to warn Alcott about such passages, to no avail.

When the book came out, Miss Peabody's hunch about public reaction proved to be right on the mark. Newspapers blasted it editorially as "indecent and obscene"; ministers denounced it from the pulpit as profane. Parents began withdrawing pupils until there were only ten left for the first quarter of 1837. With his uncanny knack for doing the right thing at the wrong time, Alcott augmented this small group by admitting a black girl, and the rest of the student body melted away. In a vain effort to wipe out his debts and keep bread on the table, he auctioned off all the fine furnishings he had acquired to educate the eye of his charges. He started holding "conversations" for adults in people's parlors for a modest fee, but when asked by his mother what he was doing, he wrote that he was "still at my old trade—hoping."

Alcott had goodly company in dealing with hard times that year. The nation was going through one of its earliest and worst depressions. There was a failure of the wheat crop, a drop in the price of cotton, and financial anarchy as a result of President Jackson's dissolving the central bank and then stipulating that all obligations to the United States be paid in specie. In May all the banks of Boston suspended payment, which worked a special hardship on Waldo Emerson. Although the last of Ellen's estate finally came through, bringing the total to twenty-three thousand dollars, which should yield an annual income of some twelve hundred dollars, much of it was in temporarily unyielding bank stock. At the same time, brother William called on Waldo for help in covering some sixty-five hundred dollars that he needed to hold on to his properties and investments. Even with an offer of 20 percent interest, William could not find a lender in New York. Somehow Waldo managed to bail William out, but their finances would be irritatingly intermingled for years. In his journal, Emerson said of the times that "the land stinks with suicide."

In matters other than financial, 1837 was a good year for Emerson. He had become Concord's leading citizen in only three years and, as such, was invited to deliver remarks at the dedication of a new monument to the opening battle of the Revolution. A hymn that he wrote for the occasion began with lines that became universally known:

> By the rude bridge that arched the flood
> Their flag to April's breeze unfurled,
> Here once the embattled farmers stood
> And fired the shot heard round the world.

Later in the year a less than stellar student named Ralph Waldo Emerson was called back to Harvard to give the annual Phi Beta Kappa speech on the topic "The American Scholar." When Emerson stepped up to the lectern and began to read in what a listener described as "that thrilling voice of his, so charged with subtle meaning and subtle music," his audience was not prepared for the surprise he sprung in the first paragraph: "Our day of dependence, our long apprenticeship to the learning of other lands, draws to a close. The millions, that around us are rushing into life, cannot always be fed on the sere remains of foreign harvests. Events, actions arise, that must be sung, that will sing themselves." Before finishing, he gave his audience a charge: "The scholar is that man who must take up into himself all the ability of the time, all the contributions of the past, all the hopes of the future. He must be an university of knowledges. If there be one lesson more than another, which should pierce his ear, it is, The world is nothing, the man is all; in yourself is the law of all nature, and you know not yet how a globule of sap ascends; in yourself slumbers the whole of Reason; it is for you to know all, it is for you to dare all. Mr. President and Gentlemen, this confidence in the unsearched might of man belongs, by all motives, by all prophecy, by all preparation, to the American Scholar. We have listened too long to the courtly muses of Europe."

The mostly young intellectuals listening to Emerson were thrilled. Dr. Oliver Wendell Holmes, not yet thirty, called the speech "our intellectual Declaration of Independence." James Russell Lowell, poet and editor-to-be, said, "We were socially and intellectually moored to English thought till Emerson cut the cable and gave us a chance at the dangers and glories of blue water." Recalling the event in later life, James R. Osgood wrote, "And who that saw the audience will ever forget it, where every one still capable of fire, or longing to renew in them the half forgotten sense of it, was gathered? Those faces, young and old, agleam with pale intellectual light, eager with pleased attention, flash upon me once more. I hear again the rustle of sensation, as they turned to exchange glances over some pithier thought, some keener flash of that humor that always played about the horizon of his mind like heat lightning. Emerson awakened us, saved us from the body of this death. It is the sound of the trumpet that the young soul longs for, careless what breath may fill it."

Perhaps anticipating the reaction he would get, Emerson had arranged for a meeting of the Transcendental Club at the Bush in Concord the next day. Rather slyly, he had Lidian invite Margaret Fuller, Elizabeth Hoar, and another bright woman named Sarah Ripley, all of whom she liked, to dinner with the club members before the meeting. It would be the worst of manners if the ladies were not invited to join in the discussion and thus integrate the all-male club. Emerson would not risk making his intention known; he would leave it up to Miss Fuller, whose wit and knowledge he had come to admire during an earlier three-week summer visit she made to the Emersons. The way he put it to her in his invitation was that "you shall gentilize their dinner with Mrs. Ripley if I can get her, and what can you not mould them into in an hour!" The ruse worked, and women were often present in future club affairs. Emerson had demonstrated that like minds can inspirit very different bodies.

3

A New Voice

LIFE WAS ANYTHING BUT DULL at the Parkman house in the center of Concord where John Thoreau manufactured pencils and his wife took in boarders, among them Lucy Brown. The surroundings were not as elegant as those in the Winslow House back in Plymouth, but Lucy found the company much more stimulating. She was especially entranced by the Thoreau boys, John and Henry, who had minds as fine as any she had ever encountered, not excluding that of her brother-in-law Waldo Emerson. Henry in particular carried on so much like Waldo that she thought she was hearing an echo. In a way she was, since young Thoreau was fond of quoting from Waldo's book on nature. She thought it a surprise and a shame that they didn't know each other. Even though they were fourteen years apart in age, they seemed to share a lot of the same knowledge, perhaps because they shared the Harvard experience. In fact, Lucy knew that Waldo had written to Harvard's president when old Dr. Ripley asked him to help get Henry a grant to cover his expenses, and enough money had come through to let the boy graduate. Now that Henry was going to be staying here in Concord and teaching school, Lucy was determined to see that they did meet.

Every time she was at the Emersons', which was often, Lucy would talk about Henry. Nothing she said really worked, until Henry did what she thought was the sweetest thing. At thirty and still married, though deserted, she thought that she must seem like an ancient aunt in the eyes of a twenty-year-old, until one day Henry tossed a gift through her open window. It was a bunch of violets wrapped in the manuscript of a poem that he had written. It was titled "Sic Vita," and she thought it quite good enough to show Waldo. If Henry had her uprooted life in mind as he wrote, it showed unusual sensitivity and understanding for one his age. She watched Waldo's face as he read:

> I am a parcel of vain strivings tied
>   By chance bond together,
> Dangling this way and that, their links
>   Were made so loose and wide,
>   Methinks
>   For milder weather.
>
> A bunch of violets without their roots,
>   And sorrel intermixed,
> Encircled by a wisp of straw
>   Once coiled about their shoots,
>   The law
>   By which I'm fixed.
>
> A nosegay which Time clutched from out
>   Those fair Elysian fields,
> With weeds and broken stems, in haste,
>   Doth make the rabble rout
>   That waste
>   The day he yields.
>
> And here I bloom for a short hour unseen,
>   Drinking my juices up,
> With no root in the land
>   To keep my branches green,
>   But stand
>   In a bare cup.

Some tender buds were left upon my stem
    In mimicry of life,
But ah! the children will not know,
    Till time has weathered them,
            The woe
    With which they're rife.

But now I see I was not plucked for nought,
    And after in life's vase
Of glass set while I might survive,
    But by a kind hand brought
            Alive
    To a strange place.

That stock thus thinned will soon redeem its hours,
    And by another year
Such as God knows, with freer air,
    More fruits and fairer flowers
            Will bear,
    While I droop here.

The poem was something of a surprise for Waldo, who was rather reluctant to get involved with young Thoreau in view of the reputation he had been creating for himself since his return from Harvard. The news of Henry's outrageous behavior as a teacher in the public school system could not have escaped Waldo's ears. Fresh from graduation, Henry had stepped into one of the best-paying jobs in Concord as one of two male teachers at the large Center Grammar School. His salary at age twenty was five hundred dollars a year when old Dr. Ripley, nearing ninety, was only making six hundred dollars a year, albeit with a house and a hundred and fifty dollars' worth of firewood thrown in. But the School Committee considered the salary in keeping with Henry's responsibility for a hundred students. After Henry had been at work for a couple of weeks, a member of the committee stopped by to check on him and discovered to his horror that

Henry refused to use physical punishment. "How can they learn without being birched? What kind of teacher are you?" he asked. Henry's response was to make a random selection of half a dozen boys and girls, whip them, and then walk out of the school forever. Most people viewed him as a strange and prickly character with a physical appearance and demeanor to match. Of medium height, thin and wiry, long-nosed, slope-shouldered, and bright-eyed, he moved quickly, as if fired by pent-up energy. He walked with head lowered, not from shyness but to study the ground over which he was passing for anything of interest in plant or animal life. Most often dressed in rough workman's clothing, he would never be taken for the scholar who had surpassed the elegant Mr. Emerson in academic standing at Cambridge.

Having watched Waldo's sometimes stern features soften as he read the poem over several times, Lucy was not surprised when he said, "Very good, indeed. Bring the young man over. I'd like to know him."

The success of Lucy's matchmaking can be judged by Emerson's journal entry for February 17, 1838:

> My good Henry Thoreau made this else solitary afternoon sunny with his simplicity and clear perception. How comic is simplicity in this double-dealing, quacking world. Everything the boy says makes merry with society, though nothing could be graver than his meaning. I told him he should write out the history of his college life, as Carlyle has his tutoring. We agreed that seeing the stars through a telescope would be worth all the astronomical lectures. Then he described Mr. Quimby's electrical lecture here, and the experiment of the shock, and added that "college corporations are very blind to the fact that that twinge in the elbow is worth all the lecturing."

Once met, well met, with walks following frequently and being noted, as on April 26: "Yesterday afternoon I went to the Cliff with

Although he grew up in Concord and was a near neighbor of Ralph Waldo Emerson, Henry David Thoreau did not meet the man who was to be his lifelong friend and mentor until his graduation from college. It was said that an admiring Thoreau soon learned to speak like Emerson and even looked like him, as this crayon portrait would suggest. Their admiration was mutual and supportive in their different endeavors.

Henry Thoreau. Warm, pleasant, misty weather, which the great mountain amphitheatre seemed to drink in with gladness. A crow's voice filled all the miles of air with sound. A bird's voice, even a piping frog, enlivens a solitude and makes the world enough for us. At night I went out into the dark and saw a glimmering star and heard a frog, and Nature seemed to say, Well do not these suffice? Here is a new scene, a new experience. Ponder it, Emerson, and not like the foolish world, hanker after thunders and multitudes and vast landscapes, the sea or Niagra."

Through association with Henry, Waldo was discovering that Concord could be a universe in itself. It certainly was to his young companion, who first viewed Walden Pond at the age of five and later wrote, "That woodland vision for a long time made the drapery of my dreams." From then on, Concord was his home, where he enjoyed an unusually happy childhood. Looking back on it, he reported that

> no experience which I have today comes up to, or is comparable with, the experiences of my boyhood. And not only is this true, but as far back as I can remember, I have unconsciously referred to the experiences of a previous state of existence. My life was ecstacy. In youth, before I lost any of my senses, I can remember that I was all alive, and inhabited my body with inexpressible satisfaction; both its weariness and refreshment were sweet to me. The earth was the most glorious musical instrument, and I was audience to its strains. I remember how glad I was when I was kept from school half a day to pick huckleberries on a neighboring hill all by myself to make a pudding for the family dinner. Ah, they got nothing but the pudding, but I got invaluable experience beside! A half day of liberty like that was like the promise of life eternal. It was emancipation in New England.

When he was not sent to pick berries, Thoreau was enlisted in the family enterprise, where he acquired a wide variety of skills.

"In his own home he was one of those characters who may be called household treasures; always on the spot with a skilful eye and hand to raise the best melons in the garden, plant the orchard with the choicest trees, act as extempore mechanic; fond of pets, the sister's flowers, or sacred Tabby, Kittens being his favorites—he would play with them by the half hour," a neighbor wrote of him. By the age of ten, he could handle well both gun and fishing rod in the interests of adding to the family food supply. His demeanor was so serious that one of the town's leading citizens, Squire Hoar, nicknamed the small boy "Judge." In speech he was so forthright and honest that his word was considered good, and he was noted for minding his own business. An anecdote related by that same neighbor who admired his home life is illustrative: "Being complained of for taking a knife belonging to another boy, Henry said, 'I did not take it.'—and was believed. In a few days the culprit was found, and Henry then said, 'I knew all the time who it was, and the day it was taken I went to Newton with father.' 'Well, then,' of course was the next question, 'why did you not say so at the time?' 'I did not take it,' was his reply."

During his college years—his only extended time away from the place—Thoreau showed every sign of wishing to be back in Concord. He found himself visually set apart from classmates by having to wear a green homespun coat instead of the customary black to chapel because he could not afford new clothes. He did not seem to care, according to a classmate, who recalled that "he was cold and unimpressible. The touch of his hand was moist and indifferent. How the prominent gray-blue eyes seemed to rove down the path, just in advance of his feet, as his grave Indian stride carried him down to University Hall! This down-looking habit was Chaucer's also, who walked as if a great deal of surmising went on between the earth and him. He did not care for people; his classmates seemed very remote. He had no animal spirits for our sport or mischief." Thoreau made it obvious that he was in college to learn, majoring in classics but minoring in mathematics and science, and doing it well. He stood near the top of his class but sought no honors. It would come as a surprise to nobody who knew him why Henry was so moved by reading passages like this in Emerson's *Nature*: "Build, therefore, your own world. As fast as you conform your life to the pure idea in your mind, that will unfold its grand proportions. A correspondent revolution in things will attend the influx of the spirit."

Thoreau's passage through Harvard was interrupted by bouts of ill health that seemed related to a family history of lung disease and by a chronic lack of funds. During sophomore year, he took six months off to take a teaching job in Canton, Massachusetts, in order to pay his tuition. This particular detour would prove as important to his future thought as any of his college courses. The man in Canton supervising the selection of a teacher was the Reverend Orestes A. Brownson, and he found Henry so fascinating that they stayed up till midnight talking on the day of their first meeting, and Brownson invited the young man to board in his own home. At thirty-two, Brownson had been a Presbyterian, a Universalist, and was then a Unitarian, and he was writing a book he called *New Views of Christianity, Society and the Church*. He was still searching for a form of faith to fit his convictions as something of a socialist and supporter of the Workingman's Party. Above all, he despised conformity and opposed any kind of orthodoxy or establishment that opposed social and political reform. He believed that religion should help men's lives on earth, that heaven could wait. Brownson and Henry explored each other's thinking extensively, and Brownson would later sit in on Transcendental Club meetings, as would Henry. About the time that he met Emerson, Henry wrote to Brownson, "I have never ceased to look back with interest, not to say satisfaction, upon the short six weeks which I passed with you. They were an era in my life— the morning of a new Lebenstag. They are to me as a dream that is dreamt, but which returns from time to time in all its original freshness. Such a one as I would dream a second and third time, and then tell before breakfast."

While taking delight in a new friendship with Thoreau, Emerson was doing his best that year to elevate the flagging spirits of his old friend Bronson Alcott. On his fairly frequent trips to Boston, Waldo would make a point of visiting Bronson, who was suffering physically and psychologically from the collapse of his school. The kind of help that Emerson gave Alcott is apparent in an entry in Alcott's journal: "Emerson's faith in me is most grateful. The faith of the faithful is noblest testimony to the simple soul. His confidence in my purpose serves to confirm me in it the more. It is the testimony of one instinct as active in two souls, and establishes its verity. 'I know of no man,' said he to me, as we threaded the street that led to his lodging, 'of diviner faith in the soul, or who, amidst every hindrance, stands as firmly by it as yourself. Abide by yourself and the world shall come round to you at last.'" Alcott knew what he meant because on another occasion Emerson had written him that "in the few moments broken conversation I had with you a fortnight ago, it seems to me that you did not acquiesce at all in what is always my golden view for you, as for all men to whom God has given 'the vision and the faculty divine'; namely, that one day you would leave the impractible world to wag on its own way, and sit apart and write your oracles for its behoof."

As sustaining to Alcott's spirits as Emerson's support was that of his family. While she was nursing Bronson through an undiagnosed depression after the collapse of his school, Abba wrote to her brother,

> You see how roughly they have handled my husband. He has been a quiet sufferer but none the less a sufferer because quiet. He stands to it, through it all, that this is not an ungrateful, cruel world. I rail. He reasons and consoles me as if I were the injured one. I do not know a more exemplary hero under trials than this same "visionary."
>
> I try not to believe it but the cruel sacrifices we are called upon to make daily compel me to despair of better

things yet awhile. Can Mr. Alcott have time to work out his problem, we may yet hide our faces and strike our breasts for shame at our incredulity. I say *ours* for I have been among the sceptics and he still thinks me impotent in faith. But his patient endurance staggers me. And the undaunted manner in which he assumes his burdens and cares, giving up with cheerful submission those things which I know are dear to his heart and lovely to his eye for the rigors of toil and privation, fill me with admiration. There is no sighing or complaining, but silent bowing to the dispensations of injustice and ignorance where he had reasonably expected intelligent cooperation or loving patience.

Let us, dear brother, sustain him. This is my resolution. Depend upon it, a reality is in him which does not show itself all on the surface. There is a depth from which pure and living waters well up to refresh thirsty souls—supplied from the very source of life.

However much they admired his purposes and disposition, Bronson could be a true trial to his family, and nobody knew this better than he. The self-diagnosis he recorded in his journal attests to this: "I have so long lived an inward, reflective life that the relations of external things to my temporal prosperity have been almost lost sight of. I am not perhaps sufficiently inclined to yield to the dictates of earthly prudence. I cling too closely to the ideal to take necessary advantage of the practical, and my wife and children suffer from this neglect. I may not sympathize with a true spirit in the deprivations to which this course subjects them. Disinclined from making much of outward success, I may seem un-kind, indifferent, improvident." Bronson did rise up from his bed and continue teaching small classes in his home and conducting "conversations" for pay with adults, but the family remained on very short rations, and he seemed incapable of mending his impractical ways.

Much as they loved him, Alcott's family frequently wished that his head was not so far up in the clouds and his feet so far from earth, and yet they were often left in awe at the way things turned out for him. In one memorable instance when the family finances were at their lowest ebb, a stranger knocked at the door while Bronson was home alone. The man told a plausible hard-luck story and asked for a five-dollar loan. It happened that a twenty-dollar gold piece had come into Bronson's possession that very day. Abba and the girls were out on a walk, looking into shops and making plans for how to spend this windfall. After hearing the stranger out, Bronson dug into his pocket, brought out the gold piece, and said, "I don't have the change you want, but here, take this twenty." The man grabbed the coin and left, and the usually understanding Abba indulged herself in a window-rattling blowup when she heard the story. As she anticipated, the newspapers the next day gave a description of the man and his method and reported that he had swindled a number of other people in the same neighborhood. Abba felt justified in her ire until an envelope arrived in which they found the gold coin and a hastily scribbled note: "I can't rob a man so simple hearted as to give me four times what I ask." The culprit was never caught, and none of the other victims recovered a penny. The Alcott household had been given more food for thought.

If following his heart sometimes turned out right, Bronson's well-intentioned efforts to go against his personal conviction to please others often turned out wrong. He was, for instance, a strict vegetarian. In view of the fact that vegetables—homegrown, if possible—were generally all that the family could afford to put on the table, it was easy to practice what he preached. But his wife and daughters did not share his views in this matter, and he did not think it fair to deny them meat when there was enough money in hand. Thus, this incident that he recorded in his journal: "The butcher again took advantage of my simplicity this morning at market. I asked for what I did not want, not speaking the dialect, nor having the air of the market. He, well knowing what I wanted, took me literally, saying, 'You see what it is; this must be the piece you want, and here I will cut it for you.' So he cut me my flesh. Instinctively, I felt he was cheating me. But who can chaffer with Blood? He knew what I wanted well enough; but any revision of the carnal code of practice was above his morality. The piece was sent home, and forthwith I was sent for, from the schoolroom, to survey the strange flitch as it lay on the kitchen table. I knew this marketing to be a fool's errand for me, and could only plead guilty of not knowing one piece of flesh from another. And so by that I might not be used in this service more."

When Alcott's spirits were at their lowest ebb, Emerson was emotionally equipped to give them a boost, and he was blissfully unaware of being on the way to needing understanding support himself. A letter to his British friend Carlyle speaks for itself:

> I occupy, or improve, as we Yankees say, two acres only of God's earth; on which is my house, my kitchen-garden, my orchard of thirty young trees, my empty barn. Besides my house, I have, I believe, $22,000, whose income in ordinary years is six per cent. I have no other tithe or glebe except the income of my winter lectures, which was last winter $800. Well, with this income, here at home, I am a rich man. I stay at home and go abroad at my own instance. I have food, warmth, leisure, books, friends. Go away from home, I am rich no longer. I never have a dollar to spend on a fancy. As no wise man, I suppose, ever was rich in the sense of freedom to spend, because of the inundation of claims, so neither am I, who am not wise. But at home, I am rich,—rich enough for ten brothers. My wife Lidian is an incarnation of Christianity,—I call her Asia,—and keeps my philosophy from Antinomianism; my mother, whitest, mildest, most conservative of ladies, whose only exception to her universal preference for old things is her son; my boy, a piece of love and sunshine, well worth my watching from morning to night;—these, and three domestic women, who cook, and sew and run for us, make

all my household. Here I sit and read and write, with very little system, and, as far as regards composition, with the most fragmentary result: paragraphs incompressible, each sentence an infinitely repellent particle.

Watching Wallie, as they called the boy, was a shared joy and an important bond in the Emerson marriage. Writing the letter, Waldo must have had in mind an occasion he noted in his journal: "Lidian came into the study this afternoon and found the towerlet that Wallie had built, half an hour before, of two spools, a card, an awl-case and a flower-box top, each perpendicularly balanced on the other, and could scarce believe that the boy had built the pyramid, and then fell into such a fit of affection that she lay down by the structure and kissed it down and declared she could possibly stay no longer with papa, but must go off to the nursery to see with eyes the lovely creature; and so departed." It was well that they had such a bond, because a few years of living together had exposed differences in their natures. Perhaps because he had seen and suffered so much of it in his family, Waldo abhorred illness and closed his eyes to it in himself or others, while Lidian very nearly rejoiced in ill health. She treated what ailed her with bed rest and/or cold—cold baths every morning, a cold house with doors and windows open even in winter—while Waldo was so fond of heat that he kept a fire burning in his study even in summer. Although she did not argue theology with her husband, Lidian was, as he informed Carlyle, more of a conventional Christian than he.

By 1838, Emerson had given up all pretense of any orthodoxy. He quit preaching at Lexington and could hardly endure sitting through the sermons of others. After one experience in Cambridge he noted that he was "nettled again & nervous (as much as sometime by flatulency or piddling things) by the wretched Sunday's preaching of Mr. H." What upset Waldo was that preachers stuck to biblical examples and quotations as if there had been no new revelation in nearly two thousand years, as if they were "permanent embryos which receive their nourishment through the umbilical cord & never arrived at a conscious and independent existence." Critiquing a sermon by the Reverend Barzillai Frost, Dr. Ripley's assistant, Waldo complained that he "had no one word intimating that ever he had laughed or wept, was married or enamoured, had been cheated, or voted for, or chagrined." In a journal entry that spring, he gave a clear indication of where he would worship: "In the wood, God was manifest, as he was not in the sermon."

In light of what was going on in Emerson's head, it is ironic that he was asked to deliver a midsummer address at Harvard Divinity School. He decided that the time had come to go public with his developing thoughts on religion. The invitation was not official; it came from a small group of students with whom he had met previously. They wanted him to speak on the evening of their graduation. The audience would be small—a few faculty members and invited friends—and, as Emerson thought, receptive to what he had to say. He felt confident in this, because he had gone to his informal meeting with the students "rather heavy hearted for I always find that my views chill or shock people at the first opening. But the conversation went well & I came away cheered." He was being uncharacteristically naïve in view of the composition of the larger audience. They were either teachers and preachers devoting their lives to spreading the Unitarian word or students who had been absorbing it well enough to be granted a degree. Although Unitarians by definition did not insist on the truth of the Trinity, they tended to go along with the New Testament's claims of miracles and Christ's divinity. They were not prepared for the words that would flow out on the mellow voice of a fellow divine.

Among the startling passages in his long address, the most arresting and challenging were these:

> Jesus Christ belonged to the true race of prophets. He saw
> with open eye the mystery of the soul. Drawn by its severe
> harmony, ravished with its beauty, he lived in it, and had

his being there. Alone in all history, he estimated the greatness in man. One man was true to what is in you and me.
He saw that God incarnates himself in man, and evermore
goes forth anew to take possession of his world. He said, in
this jubilee of sublime emotion, "I am divine. Through me,
God acts; through me, he speaks. Would you see God, see
me; or, see thee, when thou also thinks as I now think."
But what a distortion did doctrine and memory suffer in
the same, in the next, and the following ages! There is no
doctrine of the Reason which will bear to be taught by the
Understanding. The understanding caught this high chant
from the poet's lips, and said, in the next age, "This was
Jehovah come down out of heaven. I will kill you, if you
say he was a man." The idioms of his language, and the
figures of rhetoric, have usurped the place of his truth; and
the churches are not built on his principles, but on his
tropes. Christianity became a Mythus, as the poetic teaching of Greece and Egypt, before. He spoke of miracles; for
he felt that man's life was a miracle, and all that man doth,
and he knew that this daily miracle shines, as the character ascends. But the word Miracle, as pronounced by the
Christian churches, gives a false impression; it is Monster.
It is not one with the blowing clover and the falling rain.

And:

The stationariness of religion; the assumption that the age
of inspiration is past, that the Bible is closed; the fear of
degrading the character of Jesus by representing him as a
man; indicated with sufficient cleanness the falsehood of
our theology. It is the office of a true teacher to show us
God is, not was; that He speaketh, not spake. The true
Chrisitanity,—a faith like Christ's in the infinitude of
man,—is lost. None believeth in the soul of man, but only
in some man or person old and departed.

And in conclusion:

Let me admonish you to go alone; to refuse the good models, even those which are sacred to the imagination of men, and dare to love God without mediator or veil. Yourself a newborn bard of the Holy Ghost, cast behind you all conformity, and acquaint men at first hand with Deity.

Some members of his small audience were so shocked and alarmed at what Emerson said that they went public with their indignation. The one who caused the greatest stir was the Reverend Andrews Norton, a professor of biblical literature who had retired to write a book entitled *The Evidences of the Genuineness of the Gospels.* He wrote that his fellow faculty members were disgusted by what he called "a general attack upon the Clergy" and "an insult to religion." As a passionate defender of the Bible, he argued that the only way to be a true Christian was through the Bible and the authoritative church, that "there can be no intuition, no direct perception of the truth of Christianity." Norton ignited a firestorm of public attacks in which Emerson was accused of impiety, infidelity, and "foulest atheism." Some of his friends who had also been in the audience, like Elizabeth Peabody and the Reverend Theodore Parker, leapt to his defense, but their voices were drowned out by those of the offended. Emerson was astonished and upset by the attention his speech was getting—some thirty-six notices as compared to only eleven for his Phi Beta Kappa address. He decided to stay out of the controversy and hold his tongue in the hope that the fire would burn down. It never quite did, although he was gratified to discover when the fall lecture season began that his audiences were as large and warm as ever.

In that season, Thoreau gave up on his efforts to find a well-paying public school job despite efforts by those who knew him best to help—a hundred-dollar loan from Emerson to fund a job-searching trip as far as Maine, letters of recommendation from the president of Harvard and Dr. Ripley. His solution was to prevail upon his older brother, John, to start a private school in Concord. When not working, the brothers built a small, shallow-draft boat that could be powered by oar or sail with a riparian adventure in mind. Ever more frequent walks with Emerson continued, during which the older man felt free to express his feelings about the reaction to the divinity school address in view of Thoreau's skeptical attitude about authority of any kind. Although he still attended church and found favor in the eyes of Dr. Ripley, who could not see into his mind, Thoreau agreed entirely with his mentor's view that God was easier to find in the woods.

One of Thoreau's college classmates, David Greene Haskins, who met up with him again at Emerson's house a little more than a year after graduation, could hardly believe the effect of this intergenerational friendship on Thoreau in such a short time. "I was quite startled at the transformation that had taken place in him," he wrote. "His short figure and general caste of countenance were, of course, unchanged, but, in his manners, in the tones and inflections of his voice, in his modes of expression; even in the hesitations and pauses of his speech, he had become the counterpart of Mr. Emerson. Mr. Thoreau's college voice bore no resemblance to Mr. Emerson's, and was so familiar to my ear that I could readily have identified him by it in the dark. I was so much struck with the change, and with the resemblance in the respects referred to between Mr. Emerson and Mr. Thoreau, that I remember to have taken the opportunity as we sat near together, talking, of listening to their conversation with closed eyes, and to have been unable to determine with certainty which was speaking. It was a notable instance of unconscious imitation."

In the spring of 1839, the Thoreau brothers finished their boat, which they called *Musketaquid*. It was, as noted in Henry's journal, "in form like a fisherman's dory, fifteen feet long by three and a half in breadth at the widest part, painted green below, with a border of blue, with reference to the two elements in which it was to spend its existence." With plans in mind for a navigation of the Concord and Merrimack rivers come summer, they supplied it with "wheels in order to be rolled around falls, as well as two sets of oars, and several slender poles for shoving in shallow places, and also two masts, one of which served as a tent-pole at night; for a buffalo-skin was to be our bed, and a tent of cotton cloth our roof. It was strongly built, but heavy, and hardly of better model than usual. If rightly made, a boat would be a sort of amphibious animal, a creature of two elements, related by one half its structure to some swift and shapely fish, and the other to some strong winged and graceful bird."

Before they could get around to making their voyage, the brothers would find another, more emotionally stirring use for their new boat. Boarding in the ever active Thoreau household was a Mrs. Joseph Ward and her daughter Prudence. Impressed with the brothers' school, Mrs. Ward arranged with her family in Scituate, south of Boston, to send her eleven-year-old grandson, Edmund Sewall, to Concord as a pupil. So glowing were Edmund's reports to home that it was decided to send his seventeen-year-old sister, Ellen, for a two-week vacation with the Thoreaus. She was lovely and lively, and both brothers fell instantly in love with her. She liked nothing better than accompanying them on their walks in the woods, and especially on their shakedown cruises in *Musketaquid*. Not surprisingly, Henry was inspired to write poetry and indite a single enigmatic but telltale line in his journal: "There is no remedy for love but to love more."

Ellen reportedly shed a few tears when she had to leave for home, and there were promises of letters and perhaps visits to Scituate from the brothers. Despite being in love with the same girl, the brothers had an amicable and interesting voyage, which Henry recorded in his journal in some detail for future use. A typical entry: "Soon the village of Nashua was out of sight, and the woods were gained again, and we rowed slowly on before the sunset, looking for a solitary place in which to spend the night. A few evening clouds began to be reflected in the water, and the surface was dimpled only here and there by a muskrat crossing the stream. We camped at length near Penichook Brook, on the confines of what is now Nashville, by a deep ravine, under the skirts of a pine wood, where the dead pine-leaves were our carpet, and their boughs stretched overhead. But fire and smoke soon tamed the scene; the rocks consented to be our walls, and the pines our roof. A woodsite was already the fittest locality for us." One purpose of the trip was to restore John's health after the strain of teaching. He was a frail 117 pounds, a victim of colic and nosebleeds so violent that they caused him to faint. Genial and well groomed, John was the pride of the family, and especially of his younger brother, who considered him a model beyond imitation. The rugged life on the river did inspirit John, and he took off for Scituate with the avowed purpose of wooing Ellen as soon as they tied up again in Concord. Left to ponder what to do with his own feelings, Henry plunged into an orgy of writing.

Although she had moved into a house of her own, Lucy Brown maintained an interest in the Thoreau boys, and she decided to play matchmaker again—between Henry and Bronson Alcott, this time. She invited Henry to her house on an evening when Alcott was to be there, and her instinct proved as sound as it had with Henry and Waldo. Within days, an impressed Henry arranged for Alcott to hold one of his "conversations" for adults at the Thoreau house. In the view of Emerson, this gathering was not a success. In a journal report, he called the participants in a discussion on "Futurity" stupid and complained that Alcott did not "meet them wisely." Nevertheless, Henry would see to it that Alcott found welcome whenever he desired in the Thoreau home.

Another Concord house that always remained open to Alcott was the Bush, where Lidian Emerson kept her promise despite an increase in her duties and concerns brought on by the arrival of a daughter, as recorded in Waldo's journal.

February 25, 1839—Yesterday morning, 24 February at 8 o'clock, a daughter was born to me, a soft, quiet, swarthy little creature apparently perfectly healthy. My sacred child! Blessings on thy head, my little winter bud! And comest thou to try thy luck in this world, and know if the things of God are things for thee? Well assured, and very soft and still, the little maiden expresses great contentment with all she finds, and her delicate but fixed determination to stay where she is, and grow. So be it, my fair child! Lidian, who magnanimously makes my gods her gods, calls the babe Ellen. I can hardly ask more for thee, my babe, than that name implies. Be that vision, and remain with us, and after us.

Whether Waldo knew it or not, Lidian's insistence on naming the child Ellen Tucker Emerson stemmed from a dream in which she and Waldo encountered his first wife in heaven, and she left them there together. Waldo's joy in Lidian's gesture would indicate that she read his heart very well.

She could also read his mind, which may account for why she was as welcoming to Margaret Fuller as to Alcott. With his passion for beauty, Emerson was put off on Fuller's first visit to Concord as Lidian's guest by the young woman's plain looks and nasal voice and physical tics like blinking her eyes. For five years, Margaret had been the only child of an eccentric politician who served in the Massachusetts Senate and the United States Congress. As soon as Margaret could talk, her father personally drilled her in reading, writing, mathematics, history, music—in her own words, "tasks given me, as many and various as the hours would allow, and on subjects beyond my age; with the additional disadvantage of reciting to him in the evening." Although the pressure let up as the family expanded to include eight children, she blamed that early regime for her eye trouble and frequent headaches. But she caught from the experience an unquenchable fever for learning that she pursued through some brief stints of formal instruction and then on her own. Nearing thirty when she became a frequenter of the Bush, she had covered so much intellectual ground and could talk about it with such wit and fervor that Waldo began enjoying their tête-à-têtes in his study or on rambles in the countryside. Knowing that Waldo's interest was only in Margaret's mind, Lidian showed no jealousy. Far from it, she was such an admirer of Margaret that she would arise in the dark, take a cold bath, and catch the early stage to Boston to attend one of the "conversations"—an idea borrowed from Alcott—that Margaret held for adult women in Elizabeth Peabody's bookstore.

Much as she liked some of the individuals, Lidian was less than happy about the fact that her husband drew so many odd and sometimes seedy transcendental pilgrims to the Bush. Their relentless talk of reforming others or themselves or both and their intellectual snobbery was sometimes more than she could bear. Once when enjoying one of her bed rests for some ailment, she passed the time by composing what she called a "Transcendental Bible" and later read it aloud within the family. As to personal guidance, she read:

> Never hint at a providence, Particular or Universal,
> Never speak of sin. It is of no consequence to "The Being" whether you are good or bad.
> Never confess a fault. You should not have committed it and who cares whether you are sorry?
> Never speak of Happiness as the consequence of Holiness.
> Never speak of the hope of immortality. What do you know about it?

As to dealing with others, Lidian's version of transcendental thought was:

> Loathe and shun the sick. They are in bad taste and may untune us for writing the poem floating through our mind.
> Scorn the infirm character and omit no opportunity of insulting and exposing them.
> Despise the unintellectual and make them feel that you do by not noticing their remark.
> Abhor those who commit certain crimes because they indicate stupidity.

> Justify those who commit certain other crimes. Their
> commission is consistent with the possession of intellect.

Waldo laughed harder than anyone else at this new indication
of his wife's wit and independence. Since the nicknames they
often used for each other were "Queen" and "King," he called it
the "Queen's Bible." But he and his fellow transcendentalists did
not let her satire deflect them in their course. On the contrary,
they decided to try for a wider outreach of their thinking by
launching a new magazine called the *Dial*, and prevailed upon
Margaret Fuller to edit it. Among the contents of the first edition
would be the first published poetry and an essay by Henry David
Thoreau. Emerson's role as a mentor to Thoreau was clear in a
letter to Fuller while the *Dial* was being put together: "Thoreau
was in my house this eve. & when I repeated to him some of your
criticism on his lines, he boggled at Nature 'relumes,' and prefers
his own honest 'doth have,' which I told him should be restored.
Othello's melodious verses 'that thy light relume,' make that word
sacred always in my ear. But our tough Yankee must have his
tough verse, so I beg you will replace it. You need not print it, if
you have anything better. He has left me with a piece of prose for
you, which I will send now or presently. I am to read it first."
Thoreau's debut was not an unqualified success. One of his fellow
contributors, Theodore Parker, noted in his own journal, "Emerson expressed to me his admiration of Thoreau, & his foolish article on 'Aulus Persius Flaccus' in the Dial. He said it was full of
life. But alas the life was Emersons, not Thoreau's, & so it had
been lived before. However he says T is but a boy. I hope that he
will write for newspapers more & less for the Dial. I would rec-
ommend him to the editor of the New World to keep the youth
out of mischief."

In that summer of 1840, Thoreau could not have cared less
about such criticism. His smothered love for Ellen Sewall had
again burst into flame. Pursuing what he thought to be a welcome
suit, brother John went to Scituate and proposed to Ellen while

they were walking the beach. For unexplained reasons, she turned him down flat. When a sad John returned to Concord, Henry had the grace not to let him know how he felt, but in his journal he wrote of the two days that his brother had been gone as "an aeon in which a Syrian empire might rise and fall—How many Persias have been lost and won in the interim—Night is spangled with fresh stars." After nursing the good news for a while, he noted that "a wave of happiness flows over us like sunshine over a field."

Ellen's father sent her to Watertown, New York, to be out of reach of the Thoreau brothers. But after a nervous wait until November, Henry worked up the nerve to propose to Ellen himself by letter. He did not have to wait long for an answer. Its nature is evident in a letter that Ellen wrote to her aunt Prudence, who was boarding with the Thoreaus: "Last week Tuesday, the day I sent my last letter to you I received one from Father. He wished me to write immediately in a 'short, explicit and cold' manner to Mr. T. He seemed very glad that I was of the same opinion as himself with regard to the matter. I wrote to H.T. that evening. I never felt so badly at sending a letter in my life. I could not bear to think that both those friends whom I have enjoyed so much with would now no longer be able to have a free pleasant intercourse with us as formerly. My letter was very short indeed. But I hope it was the thing. It will not be best for either you or me to allude to this subject in our letters to each other. Your next letter may as well be to Mother perhaps, or to Edmund. By that time the worst of this will be passed and we can write freely again. I do feel so sorry H. wrote to me. It was such a pity. Though I would rather have it so than to have him say the same things on the beach or anywhere else. If I had only been at home so that Father could have read the letter himself and seen my answer, I should have liked it better. But it is all over for now."

Her rejection must have recalled for Henry one of those things that Ellen "enjoyed so much"—a boat ride that he recorded in his journal with uncanny foresight: "The other day I rowed in my boat a free—even lovely young lady—and as I plied the oars, she sat in the stern—and there was nothing but she between me and the sky. So might all our lives be picturesque if they were free enough—but mean relations and prejudices intervene to shut out the sky, and we never see a man as simple and distinct as the man-weathercock on a steeple." It was clear that Ellen's father mistrusted the Thoreau brothers as fit providers for his daughter. An indication that Ellen would eventually agree with him were remarks that she made in one of the letters that she wrote after that flirtatious summer in Concord. She wanted to know what "real work" Henry did and whether "Dr. Thoreau" was still giving free advice.

The suspicions of the Sewalls were well grounded. At about the same time, Emerson confided to his journal in a kind of admiration, "My brave Henry here who is content to live now, and feels no shame in not studying any profession, for he does not postpone his life but lives already—pours contempt on these crybabies of routine and Boston. He has not one chance but a hundred chances." In losing Ellen, Henry was learning the high price for pouring "contempt on the crybabies of routine." But what the Sewalls and others like them who viewed Henry as an idler without ambition would never understand was a thought that Emerson shared with his walking companion and later recorded in his journal for future use: "What is the hardest thing in the world? To think."

4

A Man Who "Looks Answers"

MUCH AS HE APPRECIATED their interest and help—Elizabeth Peabody in publicizing and marketing his work and Margaret Fuller in doing the dog work on the *Dial*—Waldo Emerson sometimes found the literary ladies of Boston exasperating. In the matter of this writer named Nathaniel Hawthorne they just would not let go. Elizabeth was the most persistent. For some years now, ever since the fellow's little fictions began appearing in little magazines, she had drawn Waldo's attention to them. Once she came all the way to Concord and stood over him while he read something Hawthorne called "Footprints on the Seashore," and she would not give up when Waldo told her bluntly, "There is no inside to it. Alcott and he together would make a man." When Waldo made the mistake of telling Elizabeth that he had heard good things about Hawthorne's work in the Boston Custom House from a mutual friend, she prevailed upon him to look through a volume of Hawthorne stories entitled *Twice-Told Tales*. His reaction to that was, "It's no easy matter to write dialogue. Cooper, Sterling, Dickens and Hawthorne cannot." He thought that Elizabeth's judgment might be warped by the fact that the Peabody and Hawthorne families were Salem neighbors. But it was almost alarming when Margaret, on whose editorial objectivity he relied for the success of the *Dial*, began singing Hawthorne's praises. Venting his bewilderment in his journal, he noted, "Nathaniel Hawthorne's reputation as a writer is a very pleasing fact, because his writing is not good for anything, and this is a tribute to the man."

From all Waldo knew of him, Hawthorne the man was something of a mystery. His lineage in Salem was as long as or longer than Emerson's in Concord, going back to an ancestor who had participated in that town's infamous witch trials. After graduation from Bowdoin College in Maine, Hawthorne had turned himself into a virtual hermit for ten years. To labor over the writing that Waldo found wanting, he shut himself up in a room of the old Salem house he shared with his mother and sisters. Only recently had his inability to generate significant income from writing forced him to emerge into the everyday working world. Weighing coal and salt on Boston's Long Wharf was an odd choice of occupation for a literary man, but mutual friend George Bancroft told Waldo that Hawthorne was "the most efficient and best of the Customs House officers." Lacking a talent for it in himself, Waldo admired people who were good at anything practical. And there was another intriguing report about Hawthorne to weigh in the balance: he was said to be so handsome that, according to one story, a gypsy woman who ran into him on a path near his college campus asked him, "Are you a man or an angel?" An appreciator of beauty in all its forms, Waldo could understand the effect that such a man might have on women like Elizabeth and Margaret.

In the summer of 1840, Waldo found himself more interested than irritated when it appeared that an acquaintance with Hawthorne the man, rather than Hawthorne the author, would be thrust upon him. Elizabeth Hoar had come up with the idea of having the youngest Peabody sister, Sophia, make a bust of her lost love, brother Charles. Waldo had encouraged the project, because he had met Sophia on a visit to the Peabody home during a lecture trip to Salem, and he had been impressed with her artwork. The bust had turned out so well that the artist was invited for a visit to the Bush so that all of the Emersons could thank her. Since Waldo had been told of Sophia's supposedly secret engagement to Hawthorne, he invited the writer as well.

When Nathaniel Hawthorne was in college, a woman passing him on a campus path was so struck with his beauty that she asked, "Are you a man or an angel?" An older Hawthorne who brought his bride to the Old Manse in Concord on the eve of their marriage had retained his looks, as is evident in this portrait, but he had developed a nearly pathological shyness that would stay with him for life.

Hawthorne's bride was one of the accomplished Peabody sisters of Salem, Massachusetts, their mutual ancestral town. Bright and gay and nearly as gifted with words as her novelist husband, Sophia recorded their lives and the life of Concord in the letters she wrote to her parents and sisters. She worshiped Nathaniel and compensated for his shyness by recruiting friendships.

Hawthorne declined on the grounds that his work had turned him into a "business machine" unfit to mingle with the intelligentsia. Sophia did not let Hawthorne's attitude dampen her enthusiasm over the opportunity to get to know the Emersons better.

Sophia Peabody was one of Waldo's most adoring admirers. After getting acquainted with him in Salem, she had written to her sister Elizabeth, "I think Mr. Emerson is the greatest man that ever lived. *As a whole* he is satisfactory. Everything has its due in him. In all relations he is noble. He is a unit. His uncommon powers seem used for right purposes. It is often said, 'Oh, such a one must not be expected to do thus and thus,—so gifted!' Such nonsense Mr. Emerson proves it to be, does he not? Because he is gifted, therefore he cannot be excused from doing everything and being equal to everything. He is indeed a 'Supernal Vision.'" In accepting the Emerson invitation, Sophia apparently revealed some of these feelings, since Waldo warned her in reply, "In regard to certain expressions in your letter, I ought to say, you will presently be undeceived. Though I am fond of writing, and of public speaking, I am a very poor talker and for the most part very much prefer silence. Of Charles's beautiful talent in that art I have no share; but our common friend, Mr. Alcott, the prince of conversers, lives little more than a mile from our house, and we will call in his aid, as we often do."

Alcott had recently given up on making it in Boston and, at Waldo's urging, rented a small place with a large garden on the Hosmer farm in Concord for fifty dollars a year, christened it Dove Cottage, and moved his family to within walking distance of the Bush. Sophia was well acquainted with the Alcotts from her work with them in Boston, and their presence contributed to making her Concord visit so delightful that she almost persuaded Hawthorne to regret his not coming. Responding to her glowing reports of the experience, he wrote, "Would that we could build our cottage this very now amid scenes which thou describest. My heart thirsts and languishes to be there, away from the hot sun, and the coal-dust and the steaming docks, and the thick-pated, stubborn, contentious men, with whom I brawl from morning till night. It gladdens me that thou meetest with sympathy there and that thy friends have faith that thy husband is worthy of thee. I do not press thee to stay, but leave it all to thy wisdom. I must not forget to thank Mr. Emerson for his invitation to Concord, but really it will not be in my power to accept."

If Sophia had been reporting to her Nathaniel from Dove Cottage instead of the Bush, his reaction would have been different. Apart from the promise of eventually dining from vegetables growing in their garden, the move to Concord had not improved circumstances for the Alcotts. Still thousands of dollars in debt and with a fourth daughter due to arrive before frost, Bronson not only toiled on his own land but helped his neighbors cradle grain and lay in wood for whatever they were willing to pay him. He had little hope for any return from intellectual labor. His contribution of fifty "Orphic Sayings" to the first issue of the *Dial* brought only derision, with one critic calling it "a train of fifteen coaches going by, with only one passenger." But one of those sayings reflected his real enjoyment of the kind of work that he was doing: "Nature is not separate from me. She is mine, alike with my body; and in moments of true life I feel my identity with her; I breathe, pulsate, feel, think, will through her members, and know of no duality of being. It is such moods of soul that prophetic visions are beheld, and evangels published for the joy and hope of mankind."

Alcott did not let the labor weary him or turn him into a clod. He participated in teaching his three older daughters, helped his pregnant and then nursing wife with the housework, walked and talked with Emerson and Thoreau, held "conversations" when asked, kept up with his own reading and writing in his journal. Copying their father, the girls kept journals as well, and a glimpse of life in that first year at Dove Cottage can be seen in a few pages inscribed by Anna, the oldest:

Concord, Sept. 1, 1840. I helped mother iron and tend baby beside having my lessons with father. My sums were all right today. I read several pieces of poetry to father from the Commonplace Book of poetry. Father read us the Fairy Tale of Order and Disorder. I had a very interesting talk with Father about Jesus. He explained to me several things I wanted to know about what he did; about his feeding the five thousand people and about raising the dead to life, and stilling the tempest. I like conversations with father.

Thursday, Sept. 3, 1840. Father read from Pilgrim's Progress about the pictures at the Interpreter's house and made some pictures of our appetites and passions. We had baby in school, and she seemed to talk. She said, "coo, coo." She is not quite six weeks old. Elizabeth said and wrote almost all of her letters and Louisa wrote some with her pen. I was interested most in the conversation on God and the soul. I can see how a great many things can be without my seeing, tasting, hearing, smelling, touching or feeling them.

Sunday, Nov. 4, 1840. Louisa and I went to meeting and father too. We sat in Mr. Emerson's seat. When we were coming home it was raining and Mr. Thoreau asked us to go in and wait till it had done raining so we went in and took dinner there.

Far from being demeaning, Alcott's labor turned him into a kind of hero in the eyes of his transcendental friends. "I do rejoice that you are hiring yourself at daily labor," one of them wrote. "You are thus rendering a most essential service to the community and the age." The most ringing accolade was in the letter that old Dr. Channing, the mentor to them all, wrote to Elizabeth Peabody: "Mr. Alcott little suspects how my heart goes out to him. One of my dearest ideas and hopes is the union of Labor and Culture. I wish to see labor honored, and united with free development of the intellect and heart. Mr. Alcott, hiring himself out for day-labor and at the same time living in a region of high thought, is, perhaps, the most interesting object in our Commonwealth.

Orpheus at the plough is after my own heart; there he teaches a grand lesson,—more than most of us teach with the pen."

A true Concord soul mate for Alcott was Henry Thoreau, who was also earning what cash he needed as a sometime surveyor and jack-of-all-trades laborer. He became a frequent visitor at Dove Cottage and a surrogate older brother or young uncle to the girls. Like Channing, Emerson admired his friends for combining manual labor with mental labor, and he felt guilty for escaping the need to follow their example by reason of his invested inheritance and respectable lecture fees. He acknowledged this feeling in a letter to brother William: "I am quite intent on trying the experiment of manual labor in some considerable extent, and of abolishing or ameliorating the domestic service in my household. Then I am grown impatient of seeing the inequalities all around me; am a little of an agrarian heart, and wish sometimes that I had a smaller house, or else that it sheltered more persons. So I think that next April we shall make an attempt to find house-room for Mr. Alcott and his family under our roof; for the wants of the man are extreme and his merits extraordinary. But these last very few persons perceive; and it becomes more imperative that those few, of whom I am in some respects nearest, to relieve them. He is a man who should be maintained at the public cost in the Prytaneum; perhaps one of these days he will be. At all events, Lidian and I have given him an invitation to establish his household with us for one year, and have explained to him and Mrs. Alcott our views or dreams respecting labor and plain living; and they have our proposal under consideration."

While awaiting a decision by the Alcotts in early 1841, the Emersons tried an almost comic experiment in dignifying labor, which he also reported to William: "You know Lidian and I had dreamed that we would adopt the country practice of having but one table in the house. Well, Lidian went out the other evening and had an explanation on the subject with the two girls, Louisa accepted the plan with great kindness and readiness; but Lydia, the cook, firmly refused. A cook was never fit to come to table, etc. The next morning, Waldo was sent to announce to Louisa that breakfast was ready; but she had eaten already with Lydia, and refused to leave her alone. With our other project we are like to have the same fortune, as Mrs. Alcott is as much decided not to come as her husband is ready to come."

Fortunately for domestic bliss in both households, Abba Alcott's point of view prevailed. Her sound judgment was rewarded with one of the few strokes of good fortune that the Alcotts had ever enjoyed. Her father died that spring, leaving her thirty-one hundred dollars in his will. It represented only a future easement rather than a solution to their problems. If applied to their debts along with the proceeds of Alcott's only asset—five hundred unsold copies of *Conversations on the Gospels* that a trunk maker bought for five cents a pound—they would still owe thirty-four hundred dollars, according to Alcott's estimate. In view of this, Alcott remained intrigued by the concept of communal living as a way of providing life's necessities without becoming a "business machine" like Hawthorne, an idea that was finding favor among the transcendentalists. One of them, George Ripley, began recruiting followers and selling shares in an ambitious experiment just a long walk from Boston that he called Brook Farm. Participants would share the manual labor of the farm to provide food and some cash income and the living quarters, where they would share the stimulation of discussion and criticism of ideas on a daily basis instead of the infrequent meetings of the club. Ripley and the other organizers were surprised when what seemed to be prime candidates like Alcott and Thoreau decided not to join. They were even more surprised when the reclusive Hawthorne, seeking escape from coal dust and to find a possible living arrangement that would make marriage to Sophia affordable, quit his job, bought a share in Brook Farm, and walked out to join the group through an April snowstorm in 1841.

In that same month, Thoreau yielded to a persistent invitation from Emerson to move into the Bush, and Emerson virtually crowed about it to William: "He is to have his board, etc., for what labor he chooses to do, and he is thus far a great benefactor and physician to me, for he is an indefatigable and very skilful laborer, and I work with him, as I should not without him, and expect to be suddenly well and strong, though I have been a skeleton all the spring until I am ashamed. Thoreau is a scholar and a poet, and as full of buds of promise as a young apple tree." Thoreau was a better fit in the Emerson household than Alcott would have been since he did not carry a similar weight of family and debt. In fact, before moving he was able to settle his total indebtedness to his father for borrowing and board for $73.08. Thoreau did share the Emerson family table and occupied a favored room at the top of the stairs. The children welcomed him for the fun he provided in devising games and making toys. There were those in the family who thought that the help and instruction he provided in the orchard and garden was as useful for keeping the head of the house from harm as for beautifying the grounds. Watching his father hoe the potato patch before Thoreau arrived, four-year-old Waldo once cried out, "I wish you would not dig your leg!"

Emerson was in need of the kind of help Thoreau could provide that year. He was fully engaged in his primary occupation as a writer and lecturer. His first book of essays was turning out to be a popular and critical success. The essays all treated subjects with such broad appeal as "Friendship," "Self-Reliance," and "Intellect." They were not logical arguments for any point of view but compendiums of thoughts, observations, life experiences, and quotations from other thinkers that were drawn together to the theme like scattered iron filings to a magnet. For a reader as for a listener to his lectures, it would be almost impossible not to take away some memorable phrase or passage that was applicable to his or her life.

On friendship, for instance:

A friend is a person with whom I may be sincere. Before him I may think aloud. I am arrived at last in the presence of a man so real and equal that I may drop even those

undermost garments of dissimulation, courtesy, and second thought, which men never put off, and may deal with
the simplicity with which one chemical atom meets
another.

Or on self-reliance:

A foolish consistency is the hobgoblin of little minds,
adored by little statesmen and philosophers and divines.
With consistency a great soul has simply nothing to do.
He may as well concern himself with this shadow on the
wall. Speak what you think now in hard words again,
though it contradict every thing you said today—"Ah, so
you shall be misunderstood."—Is it so bad, then, to be misunderstood? Pythagoras was misunderstood, and Socrates,
and Jesus, and Luther, and Copernicus, and Galileo, and
Newton, and every pure and wise spirit that ever took flesh.
To be great is to be misunderstood.

Or on intellect:

God offers to every mind its choice between truth and
repose. Take which you please,—you can never have both.
Between these, as a pendulum, man oscillates. He in
whom love of repose predominates, will accept the first
creed, the first philosophy, the first political party he
meets,—most likely his father's. He gets rest, commodity,
and reputation; but he shuts the door of truth. He in
whom the love of truth predominates will keep himself
aloof from all moorings, and afloat. He will abstain from
dogmatism, and recognize all the opposite negations, between which, as walls, his being is swung. He submits to
the inconvenience of suspense an imperfect opinion, but
he is a candidate for truth, as the other is not, and respects
the higher law of his being.

Emerson did not hesitate to defend the core of transcendentalism, about which critics tended to be sarcastic, if not nasty. A powerful passage in an essay entitled "The Over-Soul" said it all:

If we consider what happens in conversation, in reveries, in remorse, in times of passion, in surprises, in the instructions of dreams, wherein often we see ourselves in masquerade— the droll disguises only magnifying and enhancing a real element, and forcing it on our distinct notice,—we shall catch many hints that will broaden and enlighten into knowledge of the secret of nature. All goes to show that the soul in man is not an organ, but animates and exercises all the organs; is not a function, like the power of memory, of calculation, of comparison, but uses these as hands and feet; is not a faculty, but a light; is not the intellect or the will, but the master of the intellect and will; is the background of our being, in which they lie,—an immensity not possessed and that cannot be possessed. From within or from behind, a light shines through us upon things, and makes us aware that we are nothing, but the light is all.

The essays established Emerson as a thinker to reckon with abroad as well as throughout America. In his often fault-finding account of his travels throughout the United States, *American Notes*, Charles Dickens said this of the essays:

There has sprung up in Boston a sect of philosophers known as Transcendentalists. On inquiring what this appellation might be supposed to signify, I was given to understand that whatever is unintelligible would be certainly Transcendental. Not deriving much comfort from this elucidation, I pursued the inquiry further, and found that the Transcendentalists are followers of my friend Mr. Carlyle, or, I should rather say, of a follower of his, Mr. Ralph Waldo Emerson. This gentleman has written a volume of Essays in which, among much that is dreamy and fanciful (if he will pardon me for saying so), there is much more that is true and manly, honest and bold. Transcendentalism has its occasional vagaries (what school has not?), but it has good healthful qualities in spite of them; not least among the number a hearty disgust of Cant, and an aptitude to detect her in all the million varieties of her everlasting wardrobe. And therefore, if I were a Bostonian, I think I would be a Transcendentalist.

If fame threatened to swell Emerson's head, all he had to do to deflate it was to walk down the road to the Thoreau house, where Henry's mother found him to be a little less impressive than her boys. A story that made the round of Concord was Mrs. Thoreau's comment after a visit from Emerson: "How much Mr. Emerson does talk like my Henry!" Failing that, he could read again his aunt Mary's disappointment with his essays, in which she found too much atheism. Both of these ladies clung to the gospel as dispensed by Ezra Ripley rather than Waldo Emerson. That being the case, it was a sad day in the Thoreau home when Henry penned a terse note early in 1841 to the clerk for the congregation stating that "I do not wish to be considered a member of the First Parish in this town" and, worse, refused to pay his church tax to the town. He would later try to explain this action by writing that "the State met me in behalf of the Church, and commanded me to pay a certain sum toward the support of a clergyman whose preaching my father attended, but never myself. 'Pay,' it said, 'or be locked up in jail.' I declined to pay. But, unfortunately, another man saw fit to pay it. I did not see why the schoolmaster should be taxed to support the priest, and not the priest the schoolmaster; for I was not the State's schoolmaster, but I supported myself by voluntary subscription. I did not see why the Lyceum should not present its tax-bill, and have the State to back its demand, as well as the Church. However, at the request of the selectmen, I condescended to make some such statement in writing:—'Know all men by these presents, that I, Henry Thoreau, do not wish to be regarded as a member of any incorporated society which I have not joined.' This I gave to the town clerk; and he has it. The State, having thus learned that I did not wish to be regarded as a member of that church, has never made a like demand on me since; though it said that it must adhere to its original presumption from that time. If I had known how to name them, I should then have signed off in detail from all the societies which I never signed on to; but I did not know where to find a complete list." It was partly because of this action that Emerson kept referring to Henry as "heroic."

Learning of this act by a member of what he regarded as a faithful church family, by a young man for whom he had written recommendations, must have been hard to take for the ninety-year-old pastor, as was the act of the whole congregation in turning his beloved church on its foundations and remodeling the interior in Greek revival style. As if he could not cope with these changes, Dr. Ripley died late that summer, and Waldo was chosen to deliver the eulogy. He could not resist remarking that Dr. Ripley "was identified with the ideas and forms of the New England Church, which expired about the same time with him." But he referred rather wistfully to the simplicity and discomforts of the church building as the departed had known it throughout his ministry, and he wrote to his grieving aunt Mary, "These Puritans, however in our last days they have declined into ritualists, solemnized the heyday of their strength by the planting and liberating of America. Great, grim, earnest men, I belong by natural affinity to other thoughts and schools than yours, but my affection hovers respectfully about your retiring footsteps, your unpainted churches, strict platforms, and sad offices; the iron-gray deacon, and the wearisome prayer, rich with the diction of ages."

What grieving took place in the Bush was mitigated by the promise of Lidian's condition that there would be a new life in the household within months. It was another proof of Emerson's law of compensation, a concept that he told Thoreau was fully understood only by the two of them and Alcott. Apart from that,

Emerson had to do something very practical about another loss. When he discovered that the City Bank would pay no dividend on his account, he had to plunge into an active season of lecturing to make ends meet. During Emerson's absences, Henry was quite literally the man of the house. In addition to the outdoor chores, he had to see to the entertainment and discipline of the children and provide a sympathetic companionship for Lidian, who was ill much of the time. And so it happened that Emerson returned from a lecture engagement late one November evening to find a new baby in Lidian's arms, an arrival that he recorded in his journal: "*Edith*. There came into the house a young maiden, but she seemed to be more than a thousand years old. She came into the house naked and helpless, but she had for her defence more than the strength of millions. She brought into the day the manners of the Night."

In view of her history of prophetic visions, it was very upsetting to Lidian when she was visited by a strange scene just days before Edith's birth. There was a little girl in a room with a beautiful statue, and they were having a deep discussion about the meaning of life. Suddenly the statue started to move and, as Lidian told it, "it gave the most forcible picture of decay and death and corruption, and then became all radiant again with sign of resurrection." In the first month of the new year—1842—the hand of death and corruption fell upon inhabitants of the Bush in the form of real-life events more gruesome than the disintegration of the dream statue. On New Year's Day, John Thoreau cut his finger while shaving. By the end of the week, the wound was infected; on January 9 he was racked with spasms of lockjaw; two days of agony later, he died in the arms of his brother Henry, who had come over from the Bush to nurse him. Worse was yet to come. Trying to play the stoic, Henry lapsed into a depressive calm until, back at the Bush on January 20, he developed alarming symptoms of lockjaw. Although these turned out to be psychological and lasted only a night, Waldo Jr. came down with scarlet fever and died on the evening of January 27.

Unlike Thoreau, Emerson tried to deal with his sorrow by venting it rather than smothering it. Frequent visitors to the Bush would have agreed with the grieving parents that Wallie was, as Emerson called him in a letter to his aunt Mary, the "world's wonderful child." Recording his feelings when awakened at three o'clock on the morning after Wallie's death because "every cock in the barnyard was shrilling," he wrote, "The sun went up in the morning sky with all his light, but the landscape was dishonored by this loss. For this boy in whose remembrance I had slept & awakened so oft, decorated for me the morning sun, & the evening sky." The child was precocious—only five and able to read and write and come up with poetic observations, such as one when a storm broke while he was playing his whistle: "My music makes the thunder dance." To Caroline Sturgis, a woman friend who admired Wallie, Emerson wrote that his son was "too precious & unique a creation to be huddled aside into the waste & prodigality of things." To prevent such a fate, Emerson spent much of the spring writing "Threnody," one of his finest poems. It is very long and includes interesting detail of the boy's life and character, but one passage reflects the father's feeling about his son's lost gifts:

> Not mine—I never called thee mine,
> But Nature's heir,—if I repine,
> And seeing rashly torn and moved
> Not what I made, but what I loved,
> Grow early old with grief that thou
> Must to the wastes of Nature go,—
> 'Tis because a general hope
> Was quenched, and all must doubt and grope.
> For flattering planets seem to say
> This child should ills of ages stay,
> By wondrous tongue, and guided pen,
> Bring the flown Muses back to men.
> Perchance not he, but Nature ailed,
> The word and not the infant failed.

It was not ripe yet to sustain
A genius of so fine a strain,
Who gazed upon the sun and moon
As if he came into his own,
And, pregnant with his grander thought,
Brought the old order into doubt,
His beauty once their beauty tried;
They could not feed him, and he died,
And wandered backward as in scorn,
To wait an aeon to be born.

Emerson did not let his memories of the dying get in the way of his ongoing concern for the living. Just weeks after burying Wallie, he sent a note to Bronson Alcott in which he suggested that Alcott spend the summer in England. Estimating that the trip would cost four or five hundred dollars, he wrote that "it will give me great pleasure to be responsible to you for that amount, and to more, if I shall be able, and more is necessary." However honored, Alcott's labor was not providing for his family; they had to rely on discreetly managed gifts from Abba's relatives and the Emersons. But there existed in England an institution ten miles from London called Alcott House. It was an experimental school founded by a businessman turned educator who admired and used Alcott's teaching methods after reading his books about the Temple School that Harriet Martineau brought back from her trip to America. Emerson thought that a much-needed lift to Alcott's sagging spirits from a visit to that school would be well worth the cost. The Alcotts agreed, and Bronson set sail for England in early May.

On the day before Alcott's departure, Sophia Peabody arrived in Concord with Nathaniel Hawthorne in tow. At the suggestion of Elizabeth Hoar, they had come to inspect a possible rental—the Old Manse, which had been standing idle since Ezra Ripley's death. The minister's son and heir, Samuel, had no desire to move to Concord and was willing to let the place go furnished for a hundred dollars a year. It was a visit begun with some anxiety for

Sophia. Finding an affordable place for them to live was her latest and most important move in a kind of romantic chess game that the couple had been playing for five years since they first laid eyes on each other in the parlor of the Peabodys' home in Salem. They had experienced an immediate, though improbable, mutual attraction when Sophia's sister Elizabeth, who was pushing publication of Hawthorne's work, introduced them. Their reaction was improbable because Sophia was subject to such frequent and blinding headaches that she was a virtual invalid; Nathaniel was so shy that he avoided all social contact except with a few college mates; she at twenty-eight and he at thirty-three were overage for romance in the custom of the times. But the attraction grew through correspondence and seeing each other under respectable circumstances until they agreed upon a secret engagement in 1839. The engagement had done wonders for Sophia's health but little for Nathaniel's reserve; she had been unable to persuade him to tell even his own family about the nature of their relationship until the spring of this trip to Concord.

As Sophia had hoped, Emerson joined Miss Hoar in showing them around the town and property, and the visit went well despite the reservations that both the men had expressed about each other's work and thinking. Reporting on the occasion, Sophia wrote that "Emerson received us with such welcoming, shining expression of face & figure that we were penetrated with joy. It was a fine afternoon & all things were new." Emerson noted that he would be "content" if they came to live in the manse and added, "I like him well." Hawthorne did not record his reaction, but he was in the mood for what looked like a quiet retreat after his disillusioning experience of communal living at Brook Farm. Not only had he tired of the endless high-minded talk among the residents; he had also found the labor on the farm—milking cows, chopping hay, shoveling manure, hoeing vegetables—nearly unbearable. After five months of it, he had fled back to a rooming house in Boston, losing his investment in the escape. In notes about the experience, he wrote: "It is my opinion that a man's soul may be buried and perish under a dung-heap or in a furrow of the field just as well as under a pile of money. Even my Custom-House experience was not such a thraldom and weariness; my mind and heart were free. Oh, labour is the curse of the world, and nobody can meddle with it without becoming proportionately brutified. Is it a praiseworthy matter that I have spent five golden months in providing food for cows and horses? Other persons have bought large estates and built splendid mansions with such little books as I mean to write; so that perhaps it is not unreasonable to hope that mine may enable me to build a little cottage, or at least to buy or hire one."

The manse was hardly a "little cottage," but Hawthorne liked the looks of the little study within it where Emerson told them he had written *Nature*, the book that had first brought him widespread attention. Having found the place, the lovers made arrangements with Samuel Ripley to occupy it after an early summer wedding. When they learned that their move would coincide with Margaret Fuller's planned visit to the Bush, Sophia wrote to her that "Mr. Hawthorne, last evening, in the midst of his emotions so deep and absorbing, after deciding, said that Margaret can now, when she visits Mr. Emerson, spend part of the time with us." A continuing admirer of Hawthorne, both as writer and man, Margaret responded that "if ever I saw a man who combined delicate tenderness to understand the heart of a woman, with quiet depth and manliness enough to satisfy her, it is Mr. Hawthorne."

The thought of having Hawthorne a short walk away was particularly pleasing to Margaret that summer, since she was having more than her usual trouble with getting Waldo Emerson to "understand the heart of a woman." Her notes of that visit are very revealing. On one occasion, she wrote that "we got talking, as we almost always do, on Man and Woman and Marriage,—W. took his usual ground. Love is only phenomenal, a contrivance of nature, in her circular motion. Man, in proportion as he is completely unfolded is man and woman by turns. The soul knows nothing of marriage, in the sense of a permanent union between

two personal existences. The soul is married to each new thought
as it enters into it. If this thought puts on the form of man or
woman, if it last you seventy years, what then? There is but one
love, that for the Soul of all Souls, let it put on what disguises it
will, still at last you find yourself lonely,—*the Soul*. Waldo said,
'Ask any woman whether her aim in this union is to further the
genius of her husband; and she will say, yes, but her conduct will
always be to claim a devotion day by day that will be injurious to
him, if he yields.'"

In the course of her seven-week stay, Margaret discovered that
Waldo was as good in action as his word. They spent hours together each day—taking walks, visiting back and forth in his
study or her guest room to read aloud a favorite passage or to test
a new idea. Suffering from a low fever and case of nerves that she
was treating with opium, Lidian was spending most of her time in
her room and missing out on the social life of the house. For the
first time she exhibited jealousy over the relationship between
Waldo and Margaret, in an incident that Margaret recorded in
fine detail:

> Yesterday she said to me, at dinner, I have not yet been
> out, will you be my guide for a little walk this afternoon. I
> said, 'I am engaged to walk with Mr. E. but'—(I was going
> to say, I will walk with you first) when L. burst into tears.
> The family were all present, they looked at their plates,
> Waldo looked on the ground, but soft & serene as ever. I
> said, 'My dear Lidian, certainly I will go with you.' 'No!'
> she said. 'I do not want you to make any sacrifice, but I do
> feel perfectly desolate, and forlorn, and I thought if I once
> got out, the fresh air would do me good, and that with
> you, I should have the courage, but go with Mr. E. I will
> not go.' I hardly knew what to say, but I insisted on going
> with her, & then she insisted on going so that I might re-
> turn in time for my other walk. Waldo said not a word; he
> retained his sweetness of look, but never offered to do the

least thing. I can never admire him enough at such times; he is so true to himself.

Margaret shrugged the incident off on the grounds that "L. knows perfectly well, that he has no regard for me or any one that would make him wish to be with me, a minute longer than I could fill up his time with thoughts. As to my being more his companion that cannot be helped, his life is in the intellect not the affections. He has affection for me, but it is because I quicken his intellect,—I dismissed it all, as a mere sick moment of L's." Margaret thought that Lidian would have more of these moments because "she has always a lurking hope that Waldo's character will alter, and that he will be capable of an intimate union." Although she was convinced that the Emersons' union would never be perfect, she was equally sure that both partners would remain faithful to it.

Perhaps to escape some of the tension at the Bush, Margaret walked down the road to the Old Manse one day to pay a surprise visit to the Hawthornes shortly after they had moved in. She found them in the parlor at midday locked in a fondling embrace. Breaking loose, Sophia stuttered an embarrassed apology for the disarray of her hair and the flush of her cheeks. Margaret laughingly assured them that it was wonderful to witness such affection. In her own mind she was reassured that her assessment of Hawthorne as a man who understood what women want was true; it was a virtue lacking in Emerson. But even with what she was witnessing, Margaret could hardly guess at the passionate nature of this new union. From the minute that the carriage bringing them from a brief and simple marriage ceremony in the Peabody apartments in Boston dropped them at the gates of the Old Manse, they felt that they were entering what they both described as Eden. They discovered that the freedom to fully explore at last each other's minds and bodies was well worth the wait. Sophia's letters to family and friends were rhapsodic, and Nathaniel's only a little less so.

Even the most idyllic marriages can run into rough patches as the partners try to adjust to each other's instinctive actions and reactions. The Hawthornes started keeping journals of their time in Eden, and Sophia's account of their first tiff is more revealing of the nature of their relationship than the embrace that Margaret witnessed. Out on a walk, Sophia started to go across a field of tall grass, and Nathaniel asked her to stay on the road with him. She kept going. "I was very naughty and would not obey, and therefore he punished me by staying behind. This I did not like very well," she wrote. After going their separate ways, they met in the woods on the other side of the field. "We penetrated the pleasant gloom and sat down upon the carpet of dried pine leaves. Then I clasped him in my arms in the lovely shade, and we laid down a few moments on the bosom of dear Mother Earth. OH, how sweet it was! And I told him I would not be so naughty again, and there was a very slight diamond shower without any thunder or lightning and we were happiest."

One of the things that Hawthorne liked most about the Old Manse was that it stood far enough from the road that drop-in visits like Margaret's were unlikely. He felt no need for socializing, but he made an exception in the case of Henry Thoreau, who was invited to dinner as a form of thanking him for planting the garden that was providing most of their food. On first acquaintance, Hawthorne found Thoreau to be "ugly as sin, long-nosed, queer-mouthed, and with uncouth and somewhat rustic, although courteous manners, corresponding well with such an exterior. But his ugliness is of an honest and agreeable fashion, and becomes him much better than beauty." Hawthorne's view of Thoreau began changing almost immediately when he consented to go for a row on the river in *Musketaquid* after dinner. Hawthorne was much impressed with Thoreau's boat-handling skills, which he claimed to have learned from Indians, and was surprised by the beauties to be seen on a river that he had thought to be a sluggish, dirt-colored watery wasteland. It was, for instance, lush with pond lilies, and he wanted to pluck them and bring them back to his beauty-loving bride. When he shared these sentiments with Thoreau, he was in for another surprise: how would Hawthorne like to buy the boat for seven dollars with instructions on seamanship thrown in for free? By the end of the voyage it was a done deal, and *Musketaquid* was renamed *Pond Lily*.

With a common ground in gardening and boating, and a fascination with the man's many faces—woodsman, craftsman, scholar, poet—Hawthorne entered into an easy friendship with Thoreau. Not so with the sage of Concord and his surrogate landlord, Ralph Waldo Emerson. In a letter to her mother, a somewhat baffled Sophia described this relationship: "Mr. Hawthorne's abomination of visiting still holds strong, be it to see no matter what angel. But he is very hospitable, and receives strangers with great loveliness and graciousness. Mr. Emerson says his way is regal, like a prince or general, even when at table he hands the bread. Elizabeth Hoar remarked that though his shyness was very evident, yet she liked his manner, because he always faced the occasion like a man, when it came to the point. Of what moment will it be, a thousand years hence, whether he saw this or that person? If he had the gift of speech like some others—Mr. Emerson, for instance—it would be different, but he was not born to mix in general society. His vocation is to observe and not to be observed. Mr. Emerson delights in him; he talks to him all the time, and Mr. Hawthorne looks answers. He seems to fascinate Mr. Emerson. Whenever he comes to see him, he takes him away, so that no one may interrupt him in his attack upon his ear. Miss Hoar says that persons about Mr. Emerson so generally echo him, that it is refreshing to him to find this perfect individual, all himself and nobody else."

Emerson was well aware of the difficulty he was having in getting through to Hawthorne, and he decided to try a rather daring experiment in view of the other man's attitude. A few days after Margaret Fuller left the Bush, Emerson called on Hawthorne and said, "I shall never see you in this haphazard way. We must take a long walk together. Will you go to Harvard and visit the Shakers?"

One of these communal communities of men and women who practiced celibacy and spartan living had been founded near the town of Harvard about twenty miles west of Concord. Emerson knew that Hawthorne had set some of his stories in a Shaker community and suggested that he would be an authoritative guide to a new experience for himself. However reluctantly, Hawthorne agreed to go. It was a round-trip walk with an overnight stay, and not even Hawthorne could keep silent that long. Indeed, Emerson noted in his report of the event that "we were in excellent spirits, had much conversation, for we were both old collectors who had never had the opportunity before to show each other our cabinets, so that we could have filled with matter much longer days." Despite disappointment at finding that the Temperance Society had "well nigh emptied the bar room" of a tavern at which they stopped along the way and Emerson's developing "a disgraceful barking cold," the walk served Emerson's purpose: he had made Hawthorne a participating member of Concord's intellectual community.

5

"A Beacon Fire of Truth"

No mean talker in any circumstances, Bronson Alcott was out-doing himself on a fall day in 1842 even though he was address-ing an audience of only one. He had just returned from being lionized in England by the disciples of Alcott House, two of whom had been so moved by his talk that they had pulled up roots and emptied their bank accounts to come to America with him. Pac-ing back and forth in the dim and quiet confines of Waldo Emer-son's book-lined study, Alcott was holding forth on the plans that he and his new English friends had formed for the creation of an ideal community. Seated by his work table, which was strewn with manuscripts that he was considering for the next issue of the *Dial*, now that Margaret Fuller had thrust the editor's job on him, Emerson politely feigned an interest in what his visitor was say-ing. If his bright eye occasionally strayed impatiently toward his work in hand, Alcott was in a flight too high to notice.

Their concept owed a lot to Brook Farm, as Alcott conceded, but their version of a rural retreat would provide for a more inti-mate, intense—above all, more innocent—experience. While they would create a livelihood by farming, they would not exploit animals for labor, as in plowing and hauling; or for food, as in eat-ing meats; or cover, as in wearing wool or leather. They would not even use products of the earth that were not in accord with their lofty aspirations. For instance, they would avoid cotton that could be traced back in any way to the labor of slaves, and they would eat only vegetables growing on plants above ground rather than the down-and-dirty root variety. Emerson had the good grace not to laugh at this, and Alcott went on to claim that they were ready to prove in practice the validity of the life they had in mind if somebody would come up with a gift of about a hundred acres "with good buildings, a good orchard, and grounds which admitted of being laid out with great beauty."

"You ask too much," Emerson said. "This is not solving the problem; there are hundreds of innocent young persons, whom, if you will thus stablish and endow and protect, will find it no hard matter to keep their innocency. I am more impressed by the person who there where he is, unaided, in the midst of poverty, toil, and traffic, extricates himself from the corruptions of the same and builds on his land a house of peace and benefit, good customs and free thoughts."

"How is this to be done? How can I do it who have a wife and family to maintain?" Alcott asked.

"Well, you are not the man to do it, or you would not ask the question," Emerson said.

A rebuke like this from the man whom he thought of as his best friend and benefactor sent Alcott scurrying back to Dove Cottage for consultation with Charles Lane and Henry Wright, his prospective British partners. They would have to do it on their own. While they were working this out, Lane and his son settled into the Alcotts' already overcrowded domicile as nonpaying guests, and Wright found other quarters. By taking over much of the instruction of the children, Lane eased life a bit for Bronson, who went back to hiring himself out. Since he was seeking to lead a spartan life for the sake of his spirit, Lane was not bothered by the fact that the presence of two more mouths to feed made the customary short rations at Dove Cottage seem shorter still.

In a letter to a friend in England, Lane reported on the meals at Dove Cottage, which were generally prepared by Bronson. Morning and evening, they would dine on bread, apples, and potatoes, served cold by the fireside without plates. The noon meal was served on the table, "there being generally some preparation which requires a plate." This preparation would not have anything to do with meat, fish, or fowl. Lane claimed to be very happy with what he was given and added, "I believe none of us would like to return to a more complicated diet of molasses, milk, butter, etc., all of which are given up. The discipline we are now under is that of abstinence." Lane carried this discipline further than his host. When invited, he declined to eat at Emerson's table, where both meat and wine were likely to be served. Alcott could not bear to miss the lively conversation at a dinner in the Bush, but he would pass on whatever food or drink he found offensive. Well aware of Alcott's opinions on food, his hosts were not bothered by his behavior at table. On one occasion, however, Alcott risked losing any future meal tickets when he heard Emerson start discussing the evils of cannibalism while carving a roast. "But, Mr. Emerson," Alcott said, "if we are to eat meat at all why should we not eat the best?"

If Lane had any doubts about Alcott's willingness to practice what he preached, they were laid to rest by observing him at home. Having heard during his daily rounds of a neighbor who had nothing in his house to eat, Alcott divided the Dove Cottage supper that night into eight portions, and took his own to the neighbor. Abba could overlook this kind of gesture but not his gift of the last of their wood to another neighbor on a cold winter's day. With their own fire sinking into gray ash, she gave voice to her anger as she had in the matter of the gold piece in Boston. Bronson tried vainly to soothe her by saying that the Lord would provide. Incredibly, his luck, or something more mysterious, held good. Toward sundown, a man headed for Boston with a wagonload of wood pulled into the yard of Dove Cottage and asked if he could leave it there for safekeeping in exchange for the use of whatever they needed until the weather improved enough for him to finish the journey. The fact that his host seemed blessed by providence as well as the ability to go hungry into the night was reassuring to Lane, who had offered to buy the farm they needed with the money he had brought from England. They would start looking for a place in the spring.

However spartan, life at Dove Cottage was never dreary, especially for the children. Education was child-centered in accord with Alcott's theories. In conversation, opinions of the young scholars were respected, and their interest was stimulated before instruction was applied. Teaching went on at all hours and in many ways. For instance, Abba invented a kind of game by creating what she called a household post office that served both as a learning exercise and a safety valve for emotions in the tight little community. She hung a basket in the entryway, and anyone wishing to communicate a grievance, a compliment, a plan of action, or whatever to another person would write a note, seal it, and drop it in the basket. Every evening after supper a postperson—one of the children on alternating days of duty—would empty the basket and pass the notes to addressees. As a result, there was very little friction in Dove Cottage, which could account for the kind of memories Louisa would later record of the experience. Allowing for a born writer's irresistible urge to fiddle with the facts, the essence of one anecdote is doubtless authentic:

> People wondered at our frolics, but enjoyed them, and droll stories are still told of the adventures of those days. Mr. Emerson and Magaret Fuller were visiting my parents one afternoon, and the conversation having turned to the ever interesting subject of education, Miss Fuller said:—
>
> "Well, Mr. Alcott, you have been able to carry out your methods in your own family, and I should like to see your model children."
>
> She did in a few moments, for as the guests stood on the door-steps a wild uproar approached, and round the corner of the house came a wheelbarrow holding baby May arrayed as a queen; I was the horse, bitted and bridled, and driven by my elder sister Anna; while Lizzie played dog, and barked as loud as her gentle voice permitted.

Amos Bronson Alcott was so often out somewhere carrying on a "conversation" or trying to raise a dollar by the sweat of his brow that it is a marvel he could be pictured behind a desk. But he did somehow read thousands of books and write thousands of pages, mostly in journals and unhappily unpublished manuscripts.

All were shouting wild with fun, which, however, came to a sudden end as we espied the stately group before us; for my foot tripped, and down we all went in a laughing heap; while my mother put a climax to the joke by saying, with a dramatic wave of the hand,—

"Here are the model children, Miss Fuller."

Whether from humility or poverty, the Alcotts left behind few pictures until daughter Louisa May began earning a measure of fame and fortune with a pen. Her letters and fact-based fiction provide some of the most vivid scenes of life among the intellectuals in Concord.

Abba Alcott's strong features are appropriate to the spirit of a woman who managed, as wife and mother, to work wonders with nothing at all in keeping her husband's head high in the clouds and her four daughters' feet firmly on the ground. Understandably, she was known to have a sharp tongue and a fiery temper to ease the strain when it sometimes became too much for her to bear.

Frolic would also have been the right word to describe much of the life that winter in the once somber Old Manse not far away from Dove Cottage. The Hawthornes were still enjoying what amounted to a prolonged honeymoon. With some help and advice from Elizabeth Hoar, Sophia had lightened up the study where they spent much of their time indoors. The once smoke-smudged walls were covered with gold-tinted paper; a Raphael Madonna and two small paintings of Lake Como were hung in place of dour ancestor portraits; vases refilled daily with fresh flowers, ferns, or whatever was in season stood on the tables; a statue of Apollo, god of sunshine, to whom Sophia compared her husband favorably, was a centerpiece. One aspect of the Old Manse that they were unable to change was the visitations by its ghosts. Hawthorne recorded deep sighs and rustlings "as of a minister's silk gown" in the parlor—sounds heard and confirmed on at least one occasion by guests—and midnight noises rising from the kitchen of "grinding coffee, cooking, ironing" that left no traces in the morning. Hawthorne interpreted these incidents as the return of souls still restless because of sermons unwritten or meals uncooked, and they made for entertaining small talk with their rare live visitors.

Ghosts or no, the Hawthornes were still living in their "Eden" enhanced by New England weather, as attested to by December letters from Sophia to her sister Mary, wife now of Horace Mann, a reforming educator inspired in part by Alcott's work. She reported that their maid "declared it did her heart good to see us as joyful as two children when we ran races down the avenue, or I danced before my husband to the measures of the great music box." Their outdoor activities were equally energetic and youthful. "Lately, we go on the river, which is now frozen, my lord to skate, and I to run and slide, during the dolphin death of day," she wrote. "I consider my husband a rare sight, gliding over the icy stream. For, wrapped in his cloak, he looks very graceful; perpetually darting from me in long, sweeping curves, and returning again—again to shoot away. Our meadow at the bottom of the orchard is like a small frozen sea, now; and that is the present scene of our heroic games. Sometimes, in the splendor of the dying light, we seem sporting upon transparent gold, so prismatic becomes the ice; and the snow takes opaline hues, from gems that float above as clouds. It is eminently the hour to see objects, just after the sun has disappeared. Oh, such oxygen as we inhale! Often other skaters appear,—young men and boys,—who principally interest me as foils to my husband, who, in the presence of nature, loses all shyness, and moves regally like a king. One afternoon, Mr. Emerson and Mr. Thoreau went with him down the river. Henry Thoreau is an experienced skater, and was figuring dithyrambic dances and Bacchic leaps on the ice—very remarkable, but very ugly, methought. Next him followed Mr. Hawthorne who, wrapped in his cloak, moved like a self-impelled Greek statue, stately and grave. Mr. Emerson closed the line, evidently too weary to hold himself erect, pitching headforemost, half lying on the air. He came in to rest himself, and said to me that Hawthorne was a tiger, a bear, a lion—in short, a satyr, and there was no tiring him out; and he might be the death of a man like himself. And then, turning upon me that kindling smile for which he is so memorable, he added, 'Mr. Hawthorne is such an Ajax, who can cope with him!'"

Sophia Hawthorne was relating a rare moment of relaxation for Emerson, who, along with editing the *Dial* and putting together a second volume of essays, was more often than ever away on the winter lecture tour. Still living at the Bush and filling in as paterfamilias, Thoreau tried to keep Emerson abreast of Concord affairs by letter. One of these was a quixotic but significant act by their mutual friend Bronson Alcott. Goaded by abolitionist friends and Lane, who reflected a rather smug, self-satisfied British attitude on the slavery question, Alcott decided that he should make a personal and public statement against the intention of the Tyler administration to annex Texas and thus extend slave territory. In January, he refused to pay his poll tax, was arrested and threatened with imprisonment until, unknown to him and unwelcome as well, Squire Hoar paid it for him. In a letter to Emerson, Thoreau wrote, "I suppose they have told you how near Mr. Alcott went to jail, but I can add a good anecdote to the rest. When Staples came to collect Mrs. Ward's taxes, my sister Helen asked him what he thought Mr. Alcott meant—what his idea was—and he answered, 'I vum, I believe it was nothing but principle, for I never heered a man talk honester.' There was a lecture on Peace by a Mr. Spear (ought he not to be beaten into a ploughshare?), the same evening, and, as the gentlemen, Lane and Alcott, dined at our house while the matter was in suspense, that is, while the constable was waiting for his receipt from the jailer—we three settled in that we, Lane and myself, perhaps, should agitate the State while Winkelried [a fourteenth-century Swiss martyr] lay in durance. But when, over the audience, I saw our hero's head moving in the free air of the Universalist Church, my fire all went out, and the State was safe as far as I was concerned." In her journal for January 17, 1843, Abba Alcott noted dryly, "A day of some excitement, as Mr. Alcott refused to pay his town tax and they had gone through the form of taking him to jail. After waiting some time to be committed, he was told it was paid by a friend. Thus we were spared the affliction of his absence and he the triumph of suffering for his principles."

Alcott's gesture was of great interest to Emerson in light of what he had written for his new book of essays. In advance, as it were, he had expressed considerable sympathy for the sort of thing that his friend would try to do. Two excerpts from an essay entitled "Politics" convey this message:

In this country, we are very vain of our political institutions, which are singular in this, that they sprung, within the memory of living men, from the character and condition of the people, which they still express with sufficient fidelity,—and we ostentatiously prefer them to any other in history. They are not better, but only fitter for us. We may be wise in asserting the advantage in modern times of the democratic form, but to other states of society, in which religion consecrated the monarchial, that and not this was expedient. Democracy is better for us, because the religious sentiment of the present time accords better with it. Born democrats, we are nowise qualified to judge of monarchy, which, to our fathers living in the monarchial idea, was also relatively right. But our institutions, though in coincidence with the spirit of the age, have not any exemption from the practical defects which have discredited other forms. Every actual State is corrupt. Good men must not obey the laws too well.

And:

Citizens of feudal states are alarmed by our democratic institutions lapsing into anarchy; and older and more cautious among ourselves are learning from Europeans to look with some terror on our turbulent freedom. It is said that in our license of construing the Constitution, and in the despotism of public opinion, we have no anchor; and one foreign observer thinks he has found safeguard in the sanctity of Marriage among us; and another thinks he has found it in our Calvinism. Fisher Ames expressed the popular security more wisely when he compared monarchy to a republic, saying, "that a monarchy is a merchantman, which sails well, but will sometimes strike a rock, and go to the bottom; whilst a republic is a raft, which would never sink, but then your feet are always in water."

Come spring, Lane, often accompanied by an enthusiastic Abba Alcott, who had tired of the cramped living in Dove Cottage, set out in search of a suitable property for the new community. Alcott wanted it to be in sight of, and easy walking distance from, Concord to continue his almost daily contact with Emerson and Thoreau. Lane considered the meat-eating, wine-drinking, sometimes cigar-smoking Emerson a bad influence on Alcott and searched in the neighborhood of Harvard where they would have the influence of the Shakers, whose asceticism he admired. Lane shared the Shakers' belief in celibacy, and he felt that he was on his way to converting the Alcotts to that belief. As he had noted in that glowing letter about life in Dove Cottage, "We are learning to hold our peace, and to keep our hands from each other's bodies." They did find a farm and buildings on Prospect Hill near Harvard that very nearly matched Alcott's description of what they wanted. Although Wright had dropped out, the cost fell within Lane's means, and he had enough left over to pay off the three hundred dollars in debts accumulated by Alcott in Concord. With minimum bag and baggage, they all departed Dove Cottage in June and settled in the new home that they christened Fruitlands.

Meanwhile, with the lecture season over, Emerson took charge at the Bush and arranged for Thoreau to live with brother William, now a judge, in Staten Island as tutor to his nephew, Willie. Thoreau's duties there would be less arduous than they were at the Bush, and he would have a chance to widen his horizons and become acquainted with the New York literary scene. Neither Thoreau nor Lidian Emerson, who had come to rely on him for help in running the household, was happy about the arrangement. Homesick almost from the start of his new job, Thoreau began writing plaintive letters to Lidian in which he revealed an emotional attachment that he was too shy to talk about. In one, for instance, he wrote that he thought of her as "some elder sister of mine whom I could not have avoided,—a sort of lunar influence,—only of such age as the moon, whose time is measured by her light. You must know that you represent to me woman." He went on to explain that he liked to deal with her because she did not lie or steal—"very rare virtues"—and thanked her for her influence on him. "You always seemed to look down on me as from some elevation—some of your high humilities—and I was better for having to look up. I felt taxed not to disappoint your expectations."

In responding to a letter from Lidian, Thoreau gushed, "Your voice seems not a voice, but comes as much from the blue heavens, as from the paper. The thought of you will constantly elevate my life." Having been informed that Lidian was suffering from her usual indispositions, he wrote that "I could hope that you will get well soon, and have a healthy body for this world, but I know that cannot be—and the Fates, after all, are the accomplishers of our hopes. Yet I do hope you may find it a worthy struggle, and life seems good still through the clouds." Knowing how Henry must have been missed by his family, Lidian offered to show his letters to his mother with a warning that Henry had heaped "undeserved praise" on her head. Uncowed by the Emersons, tart-tongued Mrs. Thoreau said, "Oh, yes, Henry is very tolerant."

Thoreau missed the town itself as much as he did Lidian and inquired in his letters about the "dear hills" and whether the river was "still drinking the meadows." He was happy, however, to miss the sight of the Irish labor gangs cutting into his beloved woods to lay tracks for the coming of the railroad right along the edge of Walden Pond where he delighted in fishing and swimming. Not given to general socializing much more than Hawthorne, Thoreau also did not miss dealing with the transcendentalists and would-be transcendentalists who swarmed into town when Emerson was in residence and the weather favored travel, hoping to confer with, or at least get a glimpse of, the sage of Concord. Observing this phenomenon for the first time, Hawthorne was moved to write of it:

> There were circumstances around me which made it difficult to view the world precisely as it exists; for, severe and sober as was the Old Manse, it was necessary to go but a little way beyond its threshold before meeting with stranger moral shapes of men than might have been encountered elsewhere in a circuit of a thousand miles.
>
> These hobgoblins of flesh and blood were attracted thither by the wide-spreading influence of a great original

thinker, who had his earthly abode at the opposite extremity of our village. His mind acted upon other minds of a certain constitution with wonderful magnetism, and drew many men upon long pilgrimages to speak with him face to face. Young visionaries—to whom just so much of insight had been imparted as to make life all a labyrinth to them—came to seek the clue that should guide them out of their self-involved bewilderment. Grey-headed theorists, whose systems, at first air, had finally imprisoned them in an iron frame-work, travelled painfully to his door, not to ask deliverance, but to invite the free spirit into their own thraldom. People that had lighted onto a new thought, or a thought that they fancied new, came to Emerson, as the finder of a glittering gem hastens to a lapidary to ascertain its quality and value. Uncertain, troubled, earnest wanderers through the midnight of the moral world beheld his intellectual fire as a beacon burning on a hill-top, and, climbing the difficult ascent, looked forth into the surrounding obscurity more hopefully than hitherto. The light among the chaos—but also, as were unavoidable, it attracted bats and owls, and the whole host of night-birds, which flapped their dusky wings against the gazer's eyes, and sometimes were mistaken for fowls of angelic feather. Such delusions always hover nigh whenever a beacon fire of truth is kindled.

For myself, there had been epochs of my life when I too might have asked of this prophet the master-word that should solve me the riddle of the universe. But now, being happy, I felt as if there were no question to be put, and therefore admired Emerson as a poet of deep beauty and austere tenderness, but sought nothing from him as a philosopher. It was good nevertheless, to meet him in the wood-paths, or sometimes in our avenue, with that pure intellectual gleam diffused about his presence like the garment of a shining one; and he, so quiet, so simple, so without pretension, encountering each man alive as if expecting to receive more than he could impart. But it was impossible to dwell in his vicinity without inhaling, more or less, the mountain atmosphere of his lofty thought, which, in the brains of some people, wrought a singular giddiness—new truth being as heady as old wine.

Because of an event that took place on the first anniversary of his marriage—July 9, 1842—Hawthorne would have good reason to be wary of what new truth and lofty aspirations can do to the mind. Answering a surprise knock at the door of the Old Manse that evening, he found a new neighbor, Ellery Channing, aflutter with excitement. A nephew and namesake of the great Unitarian minister and husband of Margaret Fuller's sister, Channing had just recently moved into a small house near the Bush. Described as a poet's poet by Emerson, Channing had in some ways stepped into the shoes of the absent Alcott as a walking, talking, swimming companion to both Hawthorne and Emerson. On this night, Channing was not seeking pleasure but the use of *Pond Lily* with Hawthorne as steersman to search the river for a young woman who apparently had drowned herself. One of ten children of a local farmer, Martha Hunt had been educated in a good academy and had risen at the age of nineteen to be superintendent of one of the Concord schools. Instead of taking pride in her accomplishments, she had, as Hawthorne put it, "cultivated and refined herself out of the sphere of natural connections" and was desperately lonely. A sister had talked her out of walking into the river on another occasion, and this night her bonnet, shoes, and handkerchief had been found at a place on the bank where she had been seen walking between five and seven that morning. She had evidently used her keen intelligence to pick her spot, since there was a twenty-foot drop-off—the deepest hole in the river—just steps from the bank where she left her clothing.

With Channing rowing, Hawthorne steered downstream until they saw a small gathering of men on the bank. They pulled in close to shore and two men with hooks fixed to long poles scrambled aboard *Pond Lily*. They tried to position the boat over the deep spot, but, as Hawthorne wrote later, "holding a lantern over it, it was black as midnight, smooth, impenetrable, and keeping its secrets from the eye as perfectly as mid-ocean would." For a seeming eternity, they rowed upstream and drifted down past the place where the clothes were found, probing the bottom and picking up nothing but weeds. Then suddenly something struck the hook of the man sitting on a thwart just in front of Hawthorne. When he brought the strike to the surface, it turned out to be the body of the girl, and Hawthorne recalled that "I never saw or imagined a spectacle of such perfect horror. Her arms had stiffened in the act of struggling, and were bent before her, with hands clenched. She was the very image of death-agony. That rigidity!— it is impossible to express the effect of it; it seemed as if she would keep the same position in the grave, and that her skeleton would keep it too, and that when she rose at the Day of Judgment, it would be in the same attitude. So horribly did she look that a middle aged man absolutely fainted away, and was found lying on the grass at a little distance, perfectly insensible. It required much rubbing of hands and limbs to restore him." Hawthorne would remain almost too sensible and retain the horrible image until he could turn it into art.

A much pleasanter occurrence within a day of this tragedy was Waldo Emerson's visit to Fruitlands. Alcott was enough of a farmer to realize that June was very late for planting, and he had persuaded Lane to compromise to the extent of hiring a man who quaintly teamed an ox with a cow to plow the garden area and to plant some "impure" vegetables like potatoes, carrots, and turnips. The compromises did not affect the harmony of the group. Emerson was able to report in his journal that "the sun and the evening sky do not look calmer than Alcott and his family at Fruitlands. They seemed to have arrived at the fact, to have got rid of the show, and so to be serene. Their manners and behavior in the house and in the field were those of superior men,—of men at rest. What had they to conceal? what had they to exhibit? and it seemed so high an attainment that I thought, as often before, so now more because they had a fit home, or the picture was fitly framed, that these men ought to be maintained in their place by the country for its culture. Young men and young maidens, old men and women should visit them and be inspired. I think there is much merit in beautiful manners as in hard work. I will not pre-judge them successful. They look well in July. We will see them in December. I know they are better for themselves, as partners. One can easily see that they have yet to settle several things. Their saying that things are clear and they sane, does not make them so. If they will in very deed be lovers and not selfish; if they will serve the town of Harvard, and make their neighbors feel them as bene-factors, wherever they touch them, they are as safe as the sun."

Emerson's reservations were well taken. The late planting at Fruitlands did not do well. The compromises had not extended to enriching the soil with manure, and cultivation suffered severely from the fact that Lane and Alcott were often away in tandem preaching their message rather than keeping their hands on a hoe. When an early and unanticipated frost struck the crops, Abba Alcott had to organize a salvage operation with a crew consisting of her three oldest daughters, ranging downward in age from thir-teen to seven, and ten-year-old William Lane. They were not able to rescue enough food to see them through the winter. In a way, it was the hand of providence at work, since the cool and celibate Lane and the warm and affectionate Alcott were turning out to be as mismatched as the cow and ox that broke the ground. Lane had been trying to separate the loving Alcotts, and they were glad to see him go when he decided to desert an obviously dying enter-prise and move with his son into the Shaker village. With his family facing starvation and possibly freezing, Alcott reacted much as he had done after the failure of his Temple School. He stretched out in bed, turned his face to the wall, and tried to die. Sometime in December, he responded enough to the pleading of his wife and daughters to move in with a nearby farm family, an arrangement provided by Abba's brother. It would be a winter's way station on the road back to Boston.

Another living experiment that failed because of an attempt to blend psychological oil and water was Thoreau's stint in Staten Island. Kindly as William Emerson and his wife, Susan, were, Thoreau could not view them as "kith and kin" in the way he could Waldo and Lidian. As a judge and businessman, William's interests were urban and practical whereas Thoreau's could be called natural and poetic. There was considerable irony in the ongoing financial relief that the transcendental Waldo had to provide for supposedly hardheaded William. In any event, Emerson conceded that William and Henry could not get along together and summoned Thoreau back to Concord in time to give a Thanksgiving lecture at the Lyceum. Although denying that he had been homesick, Thoreau told his mother prophetically that he would be content to sit in her backyard forever.

Early in 1844, romance evolved into domesticity at the Old Manse with the arrival of a daughter named Una. Reporting on this event to a friend, Hawthorne wrote, "I find it a very sober and serious kind of happiness that springs from the birth of a child. It ought not to come too early in a man's life—not till he has fully enjoyed his youth—for methinks the spirit can never be thoroughly gay and careless again, after this great event. We gain infinitely by the exchange; but we do give up something nevertheless. As for myself, who have been a trifler preposterously long, I find it necessary to come out of my cloud-region, and allow myself to be woven into the sombre texture of humanity. There is no escaping it any longer. I have business on earth now, and must look about me for the means of doing it."

Actually, a combination of sobering circumstances—the coming on of what Hawthorne thought of as writing weather, Sophia's pregnancy, and a rapid dwindling of their funds—had brought Hawthorne down from his cloud well before the baby appeared. Emerson reported that "Hawthorne remains in his seat and writes very actively for all the magazines." With the help of a high-powered agent and people like his sister-in-law, Elizabeth Peabody, he was achieving publication, but unfortunately publication did not mean profit. In a typical letter to a friend in the city that winter, he wrote, "I wish at some leisure moment you would give yourself the trouble to call on Munroe's bookstore and inquire about the state of my 'Twice-told Tales.' At the last accounts (now about a year since) the sales had not been enough to pay the expenses; but it may be otherwise now—else I shall be forced to consider myself a writer for posterity; or at all events not for the present generation. Surely the book was puffed enough to meet with a sale. What the devil's the matter?" The Hawthornes had been on short rations since Christmas, when they had "a paradisaical dinner of preserved quince and apple, dates, and bread and cheese, and milk." Only as the garden began to produce again would their dining improve.

To that end a once more carefree Thoreau pitched in with planting at the Old Manse as well as at the Bush. He also helped his father in the pencil-making business and in building a new house and did surveying jobs when in need of cash. Thoreau had no literary work to do since Emerson had closed down his only outlet, the *Dial*, for lack of subscribers, and he even neglected his journal. In April of that year, Thoreau went through a shattering experience that had started out to be a pleasant river trip with Elizabeth Hoar's younger brother, Edward, a student at Harvard. They caught a mess of fish during the first day's row and beached the boat at Fair Haven to cook and camp. It had been uncommonly dry for that time of year, and a spark from their fire ignited the surrounding grass. The flames spread faster than they could stomp them out and eventually caused a dramatic conflagration that burned out some three hundred acres and set the alarm bells clanging in surrounding settlements, including their hometown of Concord. Even though sparks from the locomotives on the new railroad spread as much fire, the Fair Haven event was a source of such embarrassment to Thoreau, the supposedly accomplished woodsman, that he could not bring himself to talk or write about it for six years. Of as much concern to Thoreau at the time was the health of Lidian Emerson, who, despite her usual complement of ailments, was going through a difficult late pregnancy, but on July 10 all hands at the Bush rejoiced in the arrival of a boy who would be named Edward.

If things were going well for Emerson on a personal level, he thought that they were going badly in the public arena in that election year of 1844. The ferment over the extension of slavery through the annexation of Texas had grown greater since Alcott's seemingly futile gesture of risking imprisonment to protest President Tyler's policies. It had become the dominant issue at the spring nominating conventions of both parties. In an orderly gathering at Baltimore, the Whigs had unanimously chosen as their candidate Henry Clay of Kentucky, who opposed annexation. Meeting in the same city a few days later, the Democrats were divided by a floor fight between adherents to former president Martin Van Buren, who like Clay opposed annexation, and delegates from the slave states. It took nine ballots before they chose a virtually unknown politician from Tennessee named James K. Polk, who subscribed to a platform calling for "reoccupation of Oregon and the reannexation of Texas." A sizable splinter group of Democrats moved to another hall in Baltimore and renominated President Tyler.

Following all this wrangling over the way that the nation ought to go, Waldo Emerson decided that the time had come for him to speak out. It so happened that August 1, 1844, would be the tenth anniversary of Britain's emancipation of slaves in the West Indies, and Emerson seized the occasion to advertise in some thirteen towns around Concord his intention to give an address on that subject on that date. Somewhat surprisingly in view of Emerson's standing in the town and the mild, scholarly title of his address—"On the Anniversary of the Emancipation of the Negroes in the British West Indies"—he had trouble finding a hall. When all the Concord churches closed their doors to him, an indignant Henry Thoreau managed to get permission from authorities to use the town hall. His abolitionist mother was the wind under Thoreau's wings as he went from door to door urging his fellow citizens to attend the event. When the time came for the hall to open, Henry had to wrestle aside the sexton of the First Parish Church, who refused to announce the event by ringing the bell as was customary on such occasions. Grabbing the rope himself, he "rang it merrily," until a crowd had gathered.

As usual, Emerson did not tell his audience what to think but gave them what he considered to be ample grounds for making up their own minds in the right way. He presented in rich detail and with evident approval the progress of emancipation in what not too long before had been the mother country. It had begun, in fact, during colonial times with a decree outlawing slavery in England proper in 1772. Fifteen years later Britain abolished the slave trade, and by 1834 was ready to free all the slaves in its island colonies. He hailed that August day as one "which gave the immense fortification of a fact of gross history, to ethical abstractions." Conscious of the Yankee concern about losing commerce in the event of abolishing slavery in America, Emerson slyly pointed out the argument that enlightened British businessmen had made for emancipation: freed slaves would become paying customers for their goods. Although Emerson kept his cool throughout, nobody left the hall in any doubt of his belief that slavery was a moral, political, and economic abomination in a democratic nation.

There was no way of knowing how many, if any, votes Emerson might have swayed. It was a close election and indecisive as to the true temper of the country. With his mind more on romance as the first president to marry in office, Tyler elected not to run. Polk won only 49.3 percent of the popular vote, but because an abolitionist candidate split the Democrat vote in New York he won 61.9 percent of the electoral vote. Emerson did not take this lightly. Although he may have held his tongue in public, he let himself go in his journal noting that the Whigs, whom he called "the real life and strength of the American people," had been "defeated everywhere by the hordes of ignorant and deceivable natives and the armies of foreign voters who fill Pennsylvania, New York, and New Orleans. The creators of wealth, and conscientious, rational and responsible persons find themselves degraded into observers, and violently turned out of all share in the actions and counsels of the nation." In this frame of mind, Emerson was evidently more determined than ever to create an American Athens in Concord, or, as he had said of the Bush when he bought it, to "crowd so many books and papers, and, if possible, wise friends into it, that it shall have as much wit as it can carry." He started something he called the Monday Night Club to meet for discussion in his parlor. Some such device seemed needed to put heart into the disenfranchised "rational and responsible" people by reminding them that they were not alone.

Emerson was particularly eager to entice Hawthorne into his cultural circle for the sake of the fresh thinking that he might stimulate. Hawthorne was certainly no transcendentalist, no Unitarian or known adherent to any religious tradition, no Whig, no poet. Although it was not to Emerson's taste, Hawthorne's writing revealed him to be a keen observer, but his personal convictions about the events and characters that he rendered so vividly into fiction remained a mystery, as they did in social conversation. The man was almost pathologically shy. With their interest in children and their own brood to amuse, the Emersons staged outdoor entertainments for children of the neighborhood in good weather. At one of these, Hawthorne, the new father, was discovered hiding behind a tree to play his observer's role unnoticed. Nevertheless, Emerson invited Hawthorne to his Monday Night Club and was pleasantly surprised to see him walk through the door. But, according to an eyewitness account of the meeting, Hawthorne, "a statue of night and silence, sat, a little removed, under a portrait of Dante, gazing imperturbably upon the group" engaged in rapid repartee. This witness was so mesmerized by Hawthorne's total silence that he himself lost the thread of discussion. After a still silent Hawthorne left the house, Emerson said, "Hawthorne rides well his horse of the night."

Hawthorne's behavior could have been a factor in Emerson's disbanding his club after a few more meetings. More likely, it was simply that he had more to do than he had time for, what with adding more stops on a new fall and winter lecture tour to meet the needs of a growing family. He was also adding property demanding care, as he reported to brother William in a letter dated October 4, 1844: "I have lately added an absurdity or two to my usual ones, which I am impatient to tell you of. In one of my solitary wood-walks by Walden Pond, I met two or three men who told me that they had come thither to sell & buy a field, on which they wished me to bid as purchaser. As it was on the shore of the pond, & now for years I had a sort of daily occupancy in it, I bid on it, & and bought it, eleven acres for $8.10 per acre. The next day I carried some of my well beloved gossips to see the same place & they deciding that the field was not good for anything, if Heartwell Bigelow should cut down his pine grove, I bought for 125 dollars more, his pretty wood lot of 3 or 4 acres, and so am landlord & waterlord of 14 acres more or less, on the shore of Walden, & can raise my own blackberries."

Although there had been little public reaction to his address on emancipation and although he had folded up the *Dial*, Waldo had heartening news toward the end of that year that would help justify Hawthorne's description of him as "a beacon fire of truth." Emerson could not know then what his silent neighbor thought of him; it would not be published for years. Given his humility, such extravagant language would embarrass him, but it was a good metaphor for what he aspired to be. In this instance, he had taken a risk as editor of the *Dial* by publishing Margaret Fuller's article entitled "The Great Lawsuit: Man vs. Men and Woman vs. Women." The young crusading editor of the *New York Tribune* liked it so much that he hired Fuller to work for him and persuaded her to turn her article into a book called *Woman in the Nineteenth Century*. The truth and power of what she had to say was reflected in Horace Greeley's reaction: "If not the clearest and most logical, it was the loftiest and most commanding assertion yet made of the right of Woman to be regarded and treated as an independent, intelligent, rational being, entitled to an equal voice in framing and modifying the laws she is required to obey, and in controlling and disposing of the property she has inherited or aided to acquire—hers is the ablest, bravest, broadest assertion yet made of what are termed Woman's Rights." Not only was Emerson the first to publish this kind of challenge to accepted and historic male dominance, but he well knew how much of it had evolved during the many talks and walks he and Margaret had shared.

Margaret's success was not the only development among his friends that brightened the end of the year for Waldo. Abba Alcott's inheritance finally filtered through the legal system and provided enough money that, sweetened by a five-hundred-dollar loan from Emerson, the Alcotts were able to buy a suitable house in Concord. Because of the land's topography, they called it Hillside, and it would provide enough space both inside and out for four rambunctious daughters and the guests they liked to entertain. Always concerned about the welfare of the Alcott family and always stimulated by Bronson's conversation, Emerson was glad to have them within walking distance once more. The five hundred dollars that he would probably never see again was money well spent. He was reasonably sure of having the Alcotts as good neighbors for the rest of all of their lives, now that Bronson had Fruitlands out of his system.

6

A Parting of the Ways

EARLY IN 1845, A SERPENT in the form of the Reverend Samuel
Ripley slithered into the Eden that Nathaniel and Sophia Hawthorne were making of the Old Manse in Concord. Ripley noti-
fied the Hawthornes that he wished to occupy the property that
he had inherited from his late father, the Reverend Ezra Ripley.
As his tenants, the Hawthornes were in no position to protest
what amounted to an eviction notice. Relying on Emerson, acting
as his uncle's agent, they had no signed rental agreement, and
they were several months in arrears on rental payments. They had
accumulated other debts as well, but since they had more money
owing to them from Nathaniel's investment in Brook Farm than
they owed, they were taking it all lightly. As Sophia wrote to her
mother, "The other day, when my husband saw me contemplating
an appalling vacuum in his dressing gown, he said he was 'a man
of the largest rents in the country, and it was strange he had not
more ready money.' Our rents are certainly not to be computed;
for everything now seems to be wearing all at once, and I expect
the dogs will begin to bark soon, according to the inspired dictum
of Mother Goose. But, somehow or other, I do not care much,
because we are so happy."

Embarrassed by not being able to pay his rent, Hawthorne discussed his financial situation with Emerson, including the fact

that the Brook Farm management owed him $524.05 on a note they had given him when he put the money down for construction of a cottage that was never built. The sage of Concord's lighthearted response was something of a surprise, as Sophia noted in a letter to her mother. This time she called Ripley "that most anti-angelic man" for driving them out of "Paradise" and added that Hawthorne was in difficulties because he "put too great a trust in the honor and truth of others. There was owing to him, twice more than money enough to pay all his debts—and he was confident that when he came to a pinch like this, it would not be withheld from him. It is so wholly new to him to be in debt that he cannot 'whistle for it' as Mr. Emerson advised him to, telling him that everybody was in debt, and they were all worse than he was."

An unanticipated visit from two of Nathaniel's college mates—Horatio Bridge, a successful businessman, and Franklin Pierce, who had returned to the practice of law in New Hampshire after a term as one of the state's senators in Washington—gave Sophia, as she reported to her mother, "solid hope. I had never seen Mr. Pierce before. As the two gentlemen came up the avenue, I immediately recognized the fine, elastic figure of the 'Admiral.' When he saw me, he took off his hat and waved it in the air, in a sort of playful triumph, and his white teeth shone in a smile. I raised the sash, and he introduced 'Mr. Pierce.' I saw at a glance that he was a person of delicacy and refinement. Mr. Hawthorne was in the shed, hewing wood. Mr. Bridge caught a glimpse of him, and began a sort of waltz towards him. Mr. Pierce followed; and when they reappeared, Mr. Pierce's arm was circling my husband's old blue frock. How his friends love him! Mr. Bridge was perfectly wild with spirits. He danced and gesticulated and opened his round eyes like an owl. He kissed Una so vehemently that she drew back in majestic displeasure, for she is very fastidious about giving and receiving kisses. They all went away soon to spend the evening and talk of business. My impression is very strong of Mr. Pierce's loveliness and truth of character and natural refinement. My husband says that Mr. Pierce's affection for him and reliance upon him are perhaps greater than any other person's. He called him 'Nathaniel,' and spoke to him and looked at him with peculiar tenderness." In a more practical form of support that Sophia may not have known about, Bridge loaned Hawthorne a hundred dollars before they left.

Also planning to make a move that spring was the Concord neighbor closest to Hawthorne's heart, Henry Thoreau. Seeking to escape his boardinghouse home, where mixing with the guests and his garrulous mother made concentration difficult, Thoreau asked Emerson's permission to build a "house" on the property that he had just acquired bordering Walden Pond. Thoreau's intent was to turn his notes and memory of the river trip with his late brother John into a book. Emerson was enthusiastic and encouraging about the project. So was Alcott, who loaned Thoreau an axe with which he began clearing brush and felling pine trees on a hillside overlooking the pond about two miles from town. The axe was something of a magic weapon, and Thoreau would later write of it that "the owner of the axe, as he released his hold on it, said that it was the apple of his eye; but I returned it sharper than I received it." Having helped build his family's new home, Thoreau was well equipped for the job he took on. He used the sharp axe to shape timbers for the studs and rafters but decided to take a shortcut by acquiring the shanty of James Collins, an Irish worker on the Fitchburg Railroad that ran along the pond's west end, in a deal that he thought wisely was worth reporting in detail:

> When I went to see it, he was not at home. I walked around the outside, at first unobserved from within, the window was so deep and high. It was of small dimensions with a peaked cottage roof, and not much else to be seen, the dirt being raised five feet all around as if it were a compost heap. The roof was the soundest part, though a good deal warped and made brittle by the sun. Door-sill there was none, but perennial passage for the hens under the door board. Mrs. C. came to the door and asked me to view it from the inside. The hens were driven in by my approach. It was dark, and had a dirt floor for the most part, dank, clammy, and aguish,

only here a board and there a board which would not bear removal. The bargain was soon concluded, for James had in the meanwhile returned. I to pay four dollars and twenty five cents tonight, he to vacate at five tomorrow morning, selling to nobody else meanwhile. I to take possession at six. It were well, he said, to be there early and anticipate certain indistinct but wholly unjust claims on the score of ground rent and fuel. This he assured me was the only encumbrance. At six I passed him and his family on the road. One large bundle held their all,—bed, coffee-mill, looking-glass, hens,—all but the cat; she took to the woods and became a wild cat, and, as I learned afterward, trod in a trap set for woodchucks, and so became a dead cat at last.

Thoreau took the shanty apart board by board, nail by nail, and transported the pieces to his building site where he had dug a cellar into the hillside. When he was ready, he held a house-raising party with Emerson, Alcott, Ellery Channing, philosopher-farmer Homer Hosmer and his sons participating. It was a small hut, deliberately intended for only one, and called by Channing "a wooden ink stand." He did build a fireplace and add a wood-shed and privy. Furnishings consisted of a bed, table, lamp, looking glass, and three chairs, one of which he would set outside to let people know he was open to company. The total cost of this dwelling was $28.12. To provide food for himself, Thoreau cleared and planted some two acres around the hut. By July 4, the work was far enough advanced that he was able to move in. Whether intentional or not, there was an almost eerie symbolism in his withdrawing from his fellow townsmen on a day when they were staging a patriotic celebration and calling for support in the clearly oncoming war with Mexico.

Thoreau had no intention of becoming a hermit, but he did want to discover the degree to which he could become self-sufficient. In a journal entry two days after the move, he crafted a rather lofty statement of intent: "I wish to meet the facts of life—

the vital facts, which are the phenomena of actuality the gods meant to show us—face to face, and so I came down here. Life! who knows what it is, what it does? If I am not quite right here, I am less wrong than before; and now let us see what they will have." Few who knew Thoreau had any doubt that he would survive—perhaps even thrive—in his surroundings. Whether living in the woods would enable him to meet his other goal of writing a book was another matter. Hawthorne wrote to an editor who was interested in the possibility of using it in a planned American book series: "As for Thoreau, there is one chance in a thousand that he might write a most excellent readable book; but I should be sorry to take responsibility, either toward you or him, of stirring him up to write anything for the series. He is the most unmalleable fellow alive—the most tedious, tiresome, and intolerable—the narrowest and most national—and yet, true as all this is, he has great qualities of intellect and character. The only way, however, in which he could ever approach the popular mind, would be by writing a book of simple observation of nature."

While Thoreau was isolating himself to concentrate, the events of that year of decision were disrupting Emerson's concentration with what he viewed as his duty to participate in public affairs. Always active in the civic life of Concord, he was discovering the extent to which it was affected by issues troubling the nation. As a curator of the Concord Lyceum, he devised an argument that persuaded his somewhat reluctant colleagues to open the doors to a lecture on slavery by the celebrated abolitionist Wendell Phillips. He cited two reasons for doing so: "*First*, because the Lyceum was poor, and should add to the length and variety of the entertainment by all innocent means, especially when a discourse from one of the best speakers in the common-wealth was volunteered. *Second*, because I thought, in the present state of the country, the particular subject of slavery had a commanding right to be heard in all places of New England, in season and out of season. The people must be content to be plagued with it from time to time until something was done and we had appeased the negro blood so."

WALDEN;

OR,

LIFE IN THE WOODS.

By HENRY D. THOREAU,

AUTHOR OF "A WEEK ON THE CONCORD AND MERRIMACK RIVERS."

I do not propose to write an ode to dejection, but to brag as lustily as chanticleer in the morning, standing on his roost, if only to wake my neighbors up. — Page 92.

BOSTON:
TICKNOR AND FIELDS.
M DCCC LIV.

The title page of Henry Thoreau's *Walden* features an illustration after a sketch that Sophia Thoreau drew of her brother's hut, which he built to overlook Walden Pond. Situated on a piece of land that Emerson had recently acquired, the hut served as Thoreau's home for some two years and the experience as the book that would one day make him famous.

In later years, Thoreau wore a beard, perhaps to distinguish himself from the clean-shaven Emerson. Except as a boy, Thoreau never shared Emerson's sunny view of life. He was unlucky in love and, as it turned out, unlucky in health—"facts of life," as he would have called them, that he learned to accept during his isolation at Walden.

The slavery issue came closer to home when Concord's leading citizen, Samuel Hoar, was driven by a mob out of South Carolina where he had been sent by Massachusetts to protect the rights of the state's colored citizens. Emerson was part of a committee staging a meeting at the Concord Court House to discuss this affront to Judge Hoar, and he helped draft a resolution that cautioned against letting such incidents dissolve the Union.

By September the focus had shifted both nationally and locally to the new administration's ongoing policy of expansion in the West. President Polk was as good as his campaign promise to press for annexation of Texas and occupation of Oregon. A Washington editor, John O'Sullivan, a friend and agent for Hawthorne, had coined the term "Manifest Destiny" to describe what seemed to be the national need and will to expand at whatever cost. By the time a gathering was held in Concord to decide what stand to take on annexation, the United States Congress and a convention in the Republic of Texas had agreed upon annexation, but Mexico opposed it. In June Polk had sent an army under the command of General Zachary Taylor to the Nueces River on the southern border of the proposed state to prevent a Mexican attack. Throughout the northern states and especially in New England there was strong opposition to the move since Texas had been free of slavery under Mexican rule and was likely to become a slave state when annexed. But Emerson came close to endorsing the concept of Manifest Destiny—for good or ill—in a speech he prepared for the Concord meeting: "The great majority of the Massachusetts people are essentially opposed to the annexation, but they have allowed their voice to be muffled by the persuasion that it is of no use. This makes the mischief of the present juncture,—our timorous and imbecile behavior, and not the circumstance of the public vote. The event is of no importance; the part taken by Massachusetts is of the last importance. The addition of Texas to the union is not material; the same population will possess her in either event, and similar laws; but the fact that an upright community have held fast their integrity,—that is the great and commanding event. I wish that the private position of the men of this neighborhood, of this county, of this State, should be erect in this matter. If the State of Massachusetts values the treaties with Mexico, let it not violate them. If it approves of annexation, but does not like the authority by which it is made, let it say so. If it approves the act and the authority, but does not wish to join hands with a barbarous country in which some men propose to eat men or to steal them, let it say that well. If on any or all of these grounds it disapproves the annexation, let it utter a cheerful and peremptory No, and not a confused, timid, and despairing one."

A sometime Concord citizen with other than national problems on his mind, Nathaniel Hawthorne managed to find a temporary solution to some of his own at about the time of that meeting. He borrowed another hundred and fifty dollars from his friend Bridge and used it to move with his wife and child into a few rooms in his mother's Salem house. Despite the efforts that Emerson made, the Hawthornes had never quite meshed with Concord society. It was not only Nathaniel's silence, but also Sophia's social ineptness that set them apart. An instance of this was related by Ellen Emerson: "Mother, also, more & more shocked at Mrs. Hawthorne's asking Father several times to her house when there were other ladies and omitting her altogether, finally asked her, 'Why do you so?' and Mrs. Hawthorne answered 'you are such a great invalid it never occurred to me that you *could* come.' 'Yet I have often invited you and you have seen that the company was sometimes large. If I am able to have much company, why should you suppose me unable the refreshment of going out?'"

Quite possibly the happiest residents of Concord in 1845 were the people in Hillside. Recovering rapidly from the disaster of Fruitlands, the Alcotts fairly wallowed in domestic bliss. It was the first time that they had owned a home of their own, and they gloried in it. One prized item of furniture was a piano on which the third girl down, ten-year-old Elizabeth, was already demonstrating her talent for music. Like her sisters, she was also quite literally a journalist. Her entries for the spring of 1845 provide an inside look at the Alcott family at Hillside, as Anna's did at Dove Cottage:

Concord, April 27, 1845: It was a sunny morning. I carried my dollies on the hill, then went to the village. I sat in a cherry tree and wrote my Journal. I read to Abba about Oliver Twist and she cried because he was so poor.

May 1st, Father took us to Mr. Emerson's in Mr. Watt's hay cart. We danced around the May pole, and I had a very pleasant time. Mr. Emerson said he would take us to ride in the woods. But it rained so we came back home. After the shower Abba and I played in the barn. We made dirt cakes and a little wagon to draw our dollies in.

May 2nd, I made my bed and read in Fireside stories until school time. I wrote my Journal and did two sums with two figures. Anna helped me before Father came to the schoolroom. He asked me to write the order for the day's doings and I put it down on the next page.

A DAY'S ORDER

Rise at half past five dress and bathe. Breakfast at half past six. Sing and make my bed. Play till ten. Study in the schoolroom till twelve. Dinner. Wash the dishes and sweep the kitchen. Play till three. Sew till five. Supper. Read or play with Abba—I write my journal first when I come to school.

Father took us in the woods with him to get some trees. The dog went with us. It was very pleasant. While Father was digging the pretty Larch and Spruce trees, I picked some handsome green mosses for my attic chamber. Father gave me some little pines and larches to put in my garden. Father and I walked up the hill coming home to lighten the load for the horse. After dinner, I washed the dishes. We thought of going to Waldron [sic] Water for some hemlocks, but did not. I read in "Undine" a while, then went to the brook and got white violets and snow drops.

Transplanting trees and bushes would have been a typical day for Bronson, whose pride in ownership was causing him to devote most of his time and energy to improvements on the property. He accomplished many interior repairs required by an aging house, and then built a bathing pavilion and arbor on the hillside. He went at gardening so enthusiastically that he spent seventy-five dollars of what was probably somebody else's money to add three acres for an apple orchard. Alcott's industriousness came as a presumably pleasant surprise to Emerson. He knew his friend mostly as a world-class talker, about whom he once said that "I know no man who speaks such good English as he." However much he appreciated it, Emerson complained that Alcott could let talk get in the way of other worthy activities, as he noted in his journal: "He takes such delight in the exercise of this faculty that he will willingly talk the whole of a day, and most part of the night, and then again tomorrow, for days successively, and if I, who am impatient of much speaking, draw him out to walk in the woods or fields, he will stop at the first fence and very soon propose either to sit down or to return."

In the first month of 1846, President Polk ordered General Taylor to move from the Nueces River to the left bank of the Rio Grande. Since the Nueces had been the southern boundary of Texas for a century, Taylor was committing an act of war. One of few congressmen who had the temerity to rise to his feet and accuse the president of making a false claim to Mexican territory was a young man from Illinois named Abraham Lincoln who feared what would happen next. His fears came true on April 25 when a scouting party of Taylor's forces was surrounded by Mexican cavalry and eleven Americans were killed. Charging that the Mexicans had "invaded our territory and shed American blood upon American soil," Polk asked for and got a declaration of war from Congress. Although he did not have a platform like Lincoln's to express it, Henry David Thoreau shared the Illinois man's point of view. After brooding over the matter in his hut by the pond, Thoreau decided that he was doing his part by simply not participating in a government he deplored as long as it tolerated slavery

and instituted war. He had never voted and, in 1843, had followed in Alcott's footsteps and stopped paying his poll tax. So far
nobody had bothered him about it, but on an ordinary July afternoon when he went into town to pick up a shoe he had left at the
cobbler's, the Concord tax collector, Sam Staples, possibly moved
by wartime patriotism, clapped him in jail. His own written
account of this surprise development reads in part:

> As I stood considering the walls of solid stone, two or
> three feet thick, the door of wood and iron a foot thick,
> and the iron grating which strained the light, I could not
> help being struck with the foolishness of that institution
> which treated me as if I were mere flesh and blood and
> bones, to be locked up. I wondered that it should have
> concluded at length that this was the best use it could put
> me to, and never thought to avail itself of my services in
> some way. I saw that, if there was a wall of stone between
> me and my townsmen, there was a still more difficult one
> to climb or break through before they could get to be as
> free as I was. I did not for a moment feel confined, and the
> walls seemed a great waste of stone and mortar. I felt as if
> I alone of all my townsmen had paid my tax. I could not
> but smile to see how industriously they locked the door on
> my meditations, which followed them out again without let
> or hindrance, and *they* were really all that was dangerous.
>
> It was like travelling into a far country, such as I had
> never expected to behold, to lie there for one night. It
> seemed to me that I never had heard the town clock strike
> before, nor the evening sounds of the village; for we slept
> with the windows open, which were inside the grating. It
> was my native village in the light of the Middle Ages, and
> our Concord was turned into a Rhine stream, and visions
> of knights and castles passed before me. They were the
> voices of old burghers that I heard in the streets. I was an
> involuntary spectator and auditor of whatever was done
> and said in the kitchen of the adjacent village inn—a

wholly new and rare experience for me. It was a closer view of my native town. I was fairly inside of it. I never had seen its institutions before. This is one of its peculiar institutions; for it is a shire town I began to comprehend what its inhabitants were about.

In the morning, our breakfasts were put through the hole in the door, in the small oblong-square tin pans, made to fit, and holding a pint of chocolate, with brown bread, and an iron spoon. When they called for the vessels again, I was green enough to return what bread I had left; but my comrade seized it, and said that I should lay up for lunch or dinner.

Thoreau did not need food for dinner since his aunt Maria Thoreau bailed him out by paying his tax before the morning was far advanced. Angry rather than thankful to be thus sprung, he went about his interrupted business by picking up his shoe and setting off on the berrying expedition that he had planned for the day. Soon he was "on one of our highest hills two miles off, and then the State was nowhere to be seen." But Thoreau could not forget his incarceration, nor could his friends and neighbors. A week or so later on one of their frequent walks, Alcott and Emerson discussed it, as reported in Alcott's journal: "Had an earnest talk with Emerson dealing with civil powers and institutions, arising from Thoreau's going to jail for refusing to pay his tax. E. thought it mean and skulking, and in bad taste. I defended it on the grounds of a dignified non-compliance with the injunction of civil powers." Emerson was either misquoted or changed his mind upon reflection. His real feeling about the incident comes through in a comment about the war with Mexico:

These—rabble—at Washington are really better than the snivelling opposition. They have a sort of genius of bold and manly cast, though Satanic. They see, against the unanimous expression of the people, how much a little well-directed effrontery can achieve, how much crime the people will bear, and they proceed from step to step, and it seems they have calculated but too justly upon your Excellency, O Governor Briggs. Mr. Webster told them how much the war cost, that was his protest, but voted the war, and sends his son to it. They calculated rightly on Mr. Webster. My friend Mr. Thoreau has gone to jail rather than pay his tax. On him they could not calculate. The Abolitionists denounce the war and give much time to it, but they pay the tax.

The only one of the Concord writers who did not weigh in on the Mexican War or on slavery was Nathaniel Hawthorne. His disinterest in political affairs—at least in current ones—was very nearly total. He once said that he could not understand a newspaper less than a hundred years old and almost boasted while in Concord of having voted only twice. As for politicians, he claimed that "their hearts wither away, and die out of their bodies. Their consciences are turned to India-rubber—or to some substance as black as that, and which will stretch as much." But, having arrived back in Salem with only ten dollars to his name, he decided to apply for a government job—as surveyor at the local Custom House, where his Boston experience would come in handy. More important than experience in getting such a job was political preference, and Hawthorne was fortunate in that his father and uncle had been well-known Democrats, the party then empowered to dispense federal jobs. While awaiting an appointment, Hawthorne spent the first part of 1846 putting together some of his writings to make up a volume he entitled *Mosses from an Old Manse*.

The long introduction he wrote to the collection virtually sang with the sweetness of the Hawthornes' honeymoon days in Concord. Only at the very end did he hint at the less than happy nature of their departure. Despite a last-minute windfall when John O'Sullivan happened by with a hundred dollars for some Hawthorne pieces he had used in his Washington magazine, which enabled them to pay off local merchants, they were still owing months of rent when they passed through the stone gateposts for the last time. Hawthorne may not have suffered much regret over that in view of this passage in his introduction: "In fairy-land, there is no measurement of time; and, in a spot so sheltered from the turmoil of life's ocean, three years hastened away with a noiseless flight, as the breezy sunshine chases the cloud-shadows across the depths of a still valley. Now came hints, growing more and more distinct, that the owner of the old house was pining for his native air. Carpenters next appeared, making a tremendous racket among the out-buildings, strewing the green grass with pine-shavings and chips of chestnut joints, and vexing the whole antiquity of the place with their discordant renovations. Soon, moreover, they divested our abode of the veil of woodbine, which had crept over a large portion of its southern face. All the aged mosses were cleaned unsparingly away; and there were horrible whispers about brushing up the external walls with a coat of paint—a purpose as little to my taste, as might be that of rouging the venerable cheeks of one's grandmother. But the hand that renovates is always more sacrilegious than that which destroys."

Hawthorne had very nice things to say about Emerson in his introduction, but Emerson, never a fan of Hawthorne's writing, acknowledged the book in his journal by noting that Hawthorne "invites his readers too much into his study, opens the process before them. As if the confectioner should say to his customers Now let us make a cake." Undoubtedly, Emerson's tart remark was inspired by Hawthorne's writing that "the treasure of intellectual gold, which I hoped to find in our secluded dwelling, had never come to light. No profound treatise of ethics—no philosophical history—no novel, even, that could stand, unsupported, on its edges. All that I had to show as a man of letters, were these few tales and essays, which had blossomed like flowers in the calm summer of my heart and mind. With these idle weeds and withering blossoms, I have intermixed some that were produced long ago—old, faded things, reminding me of flowers pressed between the leaves of a book—and now offer the banquet, such as it is, to any whom it may please. These fitful sketches, with so little of external life about them, yet claiming no profundity of purpose,—so reserved, even while they sometimes seem so frank,—often but half in earnest, and never, even when most so, expressing satisfactorily the thoughts which they profess to image—such trifles, I truly feel, afford no solid basis for a literary reputation. Nevertheless, the public—if my limited number of readers, whom I venture to regard rather as a circle of friends, may be termed a public, will receive them more kindly, as the last offering, the last collection of this nature."

Emerson was kinder about another book being written that spring. On a visit to Thoreau's retreat, he was treated to a reading of Thoreau's work in progress about his river trip while they sat "under an oak on the river bank." Emerson found it to be "pastoral as Isaak Walton, spicy as flagroot, broad and deep," and he claimed that "it invigorated me." As a frequent visitor to the hut in the woods, Alcott, too, heard readings from the book and noted in his journal that it "is purely American, fragrant with the lives of New England woods and streams, and could have been written nowhere else. There is a toughness, too, and a sinewy vigor, as of roots and strength that comes of feeding on wild meats, and the moist lustres of the fishes in the bed below. It has the merit, moreover, that somehow despite all presumptions to the contrary, the sod and sap and fibre and flavor of New England have found at last a clear relation to the literature of other and classic lands." Although Emerson thought it ready for publication, Thoreau would find it necessary to put it through many rewrites before that event.

Apparently out of feelings of guilt about his own comfortable life in contrast to the struggles of his colleagues, Emerson was trying once more his idea of sharing his good life with others. With Lidian agreeing in the hope of easing her housekeeping burden, they turned over all but four rooms of the house to a Mrs. E. C. Goodwin with an arrangement that would allow her to run the Bush as a boardinghouse. The Emersons became, in effect, boarders in their own home as Mrs. Goodwin brought in her own four children and rented several rooms to paying guests. As if the arrangement did not make full enough use of the house, the Emersons hired a live-in tutor for the children named Sophia Foord and created a space in the barn for a schoolroom where several neighbor children, including the two youngest Alcott girls, joined their own brood as pupils.

Despite occasional claims that he was antisocial, Emerson liked having a variety of people around him, especially children. In her book about growing up in the Bush, daughter Ellen wrote,

> His interest and sympathy about every detail of school affairs, school politics and school pleasures were unbounded. We told him every word as we should have told our mates, and I think he had as much enjoyment out of it as we. He considered it as our duty to look after all the strangers that came to the school; at his desire we had large tea-parties every year, to be sure to have all the out-of-town boys and girls come to the house. He used to ask me, "Did you speak to her?" "No, I hadn't anything to say." "Speak, speak, if you haven't anything to say. Ask her, 'Don't you admire my shoe-strings?'" And he was always kind and friendly to them when they came to tea; made them talk and entered into what they said.
>
> On Sunday afternoons he came to the front entry at four o'clock, and whistled or said, "Four o'clock," and we all walked with him, from four to eight miles, according to the walking and the flowers we went to see as, when a rare flower was in bloom, we went to find it, in Becky Stowe's Hole, or Ledum Swamp, or Copan, Columbine Rock or Conantum. Mr. Channing often gave the name to the spots, and showed them to father in their glory; then he would conduct us to see the show, or take us to places he had found beautiful in the course of the week; full of pretty speeches about what we were to see, making it a

great mystery. Once I expressed fear that he would cut down his Walden grove or sell it; he answered, "No, it is my camel's hump. When the camel is starving in the desert and can find nothing else, he eats his own hump. I shall keep these woods till everything else is gone." One day when he saw smoke in the direction of the grove, he cried out with such love and fear in is voice, "My woods, my beautiful woods!" and hurried off to the rescue. A baby could not be too young or small for him to take into his arms. Children were always in his study.

In the midst of what some writers would regard as chaos, Emerson managed to create a book of poetry before he embarked on the fall lecture circuit. Published in the last month of 1846, it bore the simple title *Poems*. He called the first poem "The Sphinx," and his editors held it to be as inscrutable as the statue itself and moved it to a less prominent place in the volume. In the poem are many of the themes that sound throughout all of his work. One stanza, for instance, deals with his belief in the evolutionary nature of a human being's spiritual life:

> To vision profounder,
>   Man's spirit must dive;
> His aye-rolling orb
>   At no goal will arrive;
> The heavens that now draw him
>   With sweetness untold,
> Once found,—for new heavens
>   He spurneth the old.

With his book of poetry out and on the market, Emerson found himself at loose ends in the early part of 1847. He had no major project under way and had lost two people whose society he most enjoyed and found stimulating. After a failed romance in New York where she was working for Horace Greeley, Margaret Fuller had persuaded the editor to send her to Europe as a correspondent.

The house that Emerson bought just before his marriage and christened the Bush became the center of transcendentalism. But it was also a happy home for a family in which Emerson took great pleasure. When it was badly damaged by fire in 1872, friends and admirers raised funds to restore it in every detail while Emerson traveled abroad with his daughter Ellen.

Lidian Emerson cradles the couple's second son, Edward. The only great tragedy of their lives was the early death of their first son, Waldo. When Emerson was away, Thoreau lived at the Bush, serving as a surrogate father to the children and brother to Lidian, with overtones of romance.

Emerson had a close and lasting relationship with all of his children. He is shown here with Edward, who became a physician and was on hand to help him through his final hours, and Edith, whose marriage to the wealthy Forbes family enabled the Emersons to enjoy some of the delights of the "Gilded Age."

Ironically, Emerson's book alienated an attractive young lady named Caroline Sturgis, who shared his deep interest in poetry and with whom he had been conducting an intellectual flirtation. Miss Sturgis was put off by what she detected as veiled references to herself and their relationship in some of the poems. Even his role as lord of a small manor began to pall, as a journal entry of that period attests:

> In an evil hour I pulled down my fence and added Warren's piece to mine; no land is bad but land is worse. If a man own land, the land owns him. Now let him leave home if he dare! Every tree and graft, every hill of melons, every row of corn, every hedge-shrub, all he has done, and all he means to do—stand in his way, like duns, when he so much as turns his back on his house. Then the devotion to these vines and trees and corn hills I find narrowing and poisonous. I delight in long, free walks. These free my brain and serve my body. Long marches would be no hardship to me. My frame is fit for them. I think I compose easily so. But these stoopings and scrapings and fingertips in a few square yards of garden are dispiriting, drivelling, and I seem to have eaten lotus, to be robbed of all energy, and I have a sort of catalepsy or unwillingness to move, and have grown peevish and poor-spirited.

Possibly sensing their friend's malaise, Alcott and Thoreau teamed up to build a summer house about a hundred feet from the Bush that Emerson could use as a study. Alcott appointed himself architect, and Thoreau offered to help with the heavy lifting and nail driving. Alcott wanted to create a fanciful structure with peristyle gables and dormer windows out of a strange assortment of materials like gnarled pine limbs and knotty oak. There was hardly a straight line in the lot. Although he worked with a will, Thoreau found the project so confusing that he complained of feeling "as if I were nowhere doing nothing." It was, however, interesting and attracted crowds of bemused onlookers. Writing to his wife, who was away in Maine, Emerson said that "Mr. Alcott and Henry are laboring at the summer house, which, in spite of their joint activity has not yet fallen. A few more spikes would to all appearances shatter the supporters. I think to call it Tumble-down Hall." When she saw it on her return, Lidian came up with a briefer, more descriptive name—"The Ruin." Open to the air, it was soon infested with so many mosquitoes that Emerson could never use it, and it gradually returned to nature.

However he felt about personal affairs, Emerson was cheered that season to learn that the Massachusetts legislature declared the ongoing war with Mexico to be "wanton, unjust and unconstitutional." Nevertheless, the war went on, and either by reading the papers or through talk at work in the Salem Custom House where he had finally landed a job, Nathaniel Hawthorne was intrigued to learn that General Franklin Pierce had arrived with an army under his command to reinforce General Winfield Scott's troops in their advance on Mexico City. Hawthorne had no yen to go to war himself. By then, his still happy and passionate marriage had produced what he called "a small troglodyte," a boy who would be named Julian. His job that promised an income of some eighteen hundred dollars a year took only three hours a day, leaving him ample time to start work on a novel he had in mind. But it would be a long time, if ever, before he climbed out of debt. He had filed suit for eight hundred dollars to recover his investment in Brook Farm and won a judgment of six hundred dollars on which he was unable to collect a penny since the institution's new management was going bankrupt. Nevertheless, the hopeful Hawthornes, relying on the prospect of regular income, rented a bigger house on Mall Street into which they could move their expanding family and Hawthorne's mother and sisters, with a room left over for the author's study.

While they were making this small move, the restless Mr. Emerson accepted an invitation to lecture in England and made plans for a sailing in the fall. He only felt free to do so when, at Lidian's request, Thoreau agreed to give up his hermit's life and move once more into the bedroom at the head of the stairs in the Bush.

Thoreau had done what he had hoped to do. He had completed a book, still circulating among publishers with as yet no takers, and he had proved that he could live on as little as twenty-seven cents a day. When he moved into Emerson's house again, he responded to a request from the secretary of his class of 1837 for news on what he was up to ten years out of college:

> I don't know whether mine is a profession, or a trade, or what not. It is not yet learned, and in every instance has been practised before being studied. The mercantile part of it was begun *here* by myself alone.
>
> —It is not one but legion. I will give you some of the monster's heads. I am a Schoolmaster—a Private Tutor—a Gardener, a Farmer—a Painter, I mean a House Painter, a Carpenter, a Mason, a Day-Laborer, a Pencil-Maker, a Glass-paper Maker, a Writer, and sometimes a Poetaster. If you will act the part of Iolas, and apply a hot iron to any of these heads, I shall be greatly obliged to you.
>
> My present employment is to answer such orders as may be expected from so general an advertisement as the above—that is, if I see fit, which is not always the case, for I have found a way to live without what is commonly called employment, if such it can be called, to keep myself at the top of my condition and ready for whatever may turn up in heaven or on earth. For the last two or three years I have lived in Concord woods alone, something more than a mile from any neighbor, in a house built entirely by myself.

Reflecting on the economy of his stay by the pond, Thoreau added a postscript to say that if any classmates "are in want of pecuniary assistance, and will make known their case to me, I will engage to give them some advice of more worth than money." In early October, Thoreau accompanied a family party to Boston to see Emerson off on the *Washington Irving* bound for Liverpool. Not long afterwards, Thoreau was using his writing skills to keep

Emerson posted on doings in the family. "Lidian and I make very good housekeepers," he reported. "She is a very dear sister to me. Ellen and Edith and Eddy and Aunty Brown keep up the tragedy and comedy and tragic-comedy of life as usual. Eddy occasionally surveys mankind from my shoulders wisely as ever Johnson did. I respect him not a little, though it is I that lift him up so unceremoniously. He very seriously asked me the other day, 'Mr. Thoreau, will you be my father?' I am occasionally Mr. Rough and Tumble with him that I may not miss *him*, and lest he should miss *you* too much. So you must come back soon, or you will be superseded." Almost as an afterthought he reported a proposal for marriage by letter from Miss Foord, the tutor he had met at the Bush in his earlier stay, to which he had responded with a definite no.

Another young person in Concord who would certainly miss Emerson was Louisa May Alcott. As she later recalled for a friend, "My romantic period began at fifteen, when I fell to writing poetry, keeping a heart-journal, and wandering by moonlight instead of sleeping quietly. About that time in browsing over Mr. Emerson's library, I found Goethe's 'Correspondence with a Child,' and at once was filled with the desire to be a Bettine, making my father's friend my Goethe. So I wrote letters to him, but never sent them; sat in a tall cherry-tree at midnight, singing to the moon till the owls scared me to bed; left wild flowers on the doorstep of my 'Master,' and sung Mignon's song under his window in very bad German."

In that mood, Louisa May was nearly devastated when, shortly after Emerson's return from England in the summer of 1848, her parents announced plans to move to Boston. It was Abba's doing, not her father's. Abba had finally had enough of Bronson's inability to earn any money. Quite apart from the trials of doing without—there were times, for instance, when Louisa May had to forgo running in the fields because her shoes were virtually soleless—and the embarrassment of debt, Abba thought that Concord society scorned her because of her husband's idiosyncracies. For whatever reason, Hawthorne, for one, was on record as disliking both

Alcotts. But in a letter to her brother, Abba did not single out Hawthorne or anybody else; she branded the whole town as "cold, heartless, brainless, soulless." With his wife in such a temper, Alcott agreed to rent Hillside and move to lodgings in Boston. He took the change in stride with his usual optimism and rented a room of his own at 12 West Street, where he would hold his "conversations" about "Man: His History, Resources, and Expectations" for whatever the traffic would bear. Abba took on the task of being what they called a missionary to the poor by acting as a paid agent for a group of wealthy donors and distributing used clothing and provisions in all kinds of weather throughout the city's slum tenements. The two older girls were farmed out, as it were—Anna to a teaching job in Roxbury and Louisa May to a house-helping job for a wealthy Boston family. Back in Concord, Bronson would be missed, as Emerson indicated in his journal: "My friends begin to value each other, now that Alcott is to go; and Ellery declared, 'that he never saw that man without being cheered,' and Henry says, 'He is the best natured man I ever met. The rats and mice make their nests in him.'"

Emerson had arrived home in time to endure the 1848 election. With the war ended by Scott's successful invasion of Mexico and Polk's decision not to run because of ill health, the parties chose popular military men as their candidates. The Democrats doubled the draw of patriotism by putting General Lewis Cass of Michigan, a known pro-slavery man, on the ticket as president and Mexican War general William O. Butler of slaveholding Kentucky as vice president. Their platform praised the war and rejected any effort to halt slavery. Since the North was divided on slavery, the cautious Whigs chose "Old Rough and Ready"—General Zachary Taylor, who rivaled Scott as a war hero—for president, and an unknown lawyer, Millard Fillmore of New York, for vice president. Since the Whig platform took no stand on slavery, a radical Democrat group called the "Barnburners" who opposed extending slavery held a convention at which they nominated former president Martin Van Buren, with Charles Francis Adams, a son of John Quincy Adams, as his running mate. Emerson, who didn't even bother to vote, recorded his reason: "Here has passed an election, I think, the most dismal ever known in this country. Three great parties voting for three candidates whom they disliked."

Taylor won. Had Emerson been in the shoes of his erstwhile fellow townsman Nathaniel Hawthorne he might have had a different attitude about the event. The outcome of that election would change Hawthorne's life in more ways than the eviction from Eden by the Reverend Samuel Ripley.

7

A President's Man

IF HENRY DAVID THOREAU HAD BEEN ASKED to report to his Harvard College classmates in 1849 instead of 1847, he could have described himself simply as an author. In the early part of that year Monroe and Co. in Boston published his first book, *A Week on the Concord and Merrimac Rivers*, and Elizabeth Peabody ran his essay entitled "Resistance to Civil Government" in the first and only issue of a magazine that she called *Aesthetic Papers*. Both were works of nonfiction growing out of his personal experiences—his river trip in 1839 with his late brother, John, and his incarceration for failing to pay his poll tax in 1846. But they were no bare-bones accounts of the events; they were fleshed out with his thoughts about everything under the sun. For instance, there was a long section on friendship in the book in which he claimed that "friendship is evanescent in every man's experience, and remembered like heat lightning in past summers. All men are dreaming of it, and its drama, which is always a tragedy, is enacted daily."

This passage was prophetic, for the book itself played a part in a rift between Emerson and Thoreau. Instead of hailing publication of the book that he had so highly praised while it was in progress, Emerson apparently greeted it with some critical remarks that went unrecorded. The nature of what he said can be judged from Thoreau's reaction: "I had a friend. I wrote a book. I asked my friend's criticism. I never got but praise for what was good in it—my friend became estranged from me and then I got blame for all that was bad. While my friend was my friend he flattered me, and I never heard the truth from him—but when he became my enemy he shot it to me on a poisoned arrow."

There was more than the criticism of the book involved in the estrangement. Emerson's return from England dislodged Thoreau from the Bush, where he was happy in his relationships with Lidian and the Emerson children. With his fixation on Concord as universe enough, Thoreau was annoyed by Emerson's happy talk about his foreign travels. Thoreau's feelings in this regard took form in a poem:

> Though all the fates should prove unkind,
> Leave not your native land behind.
> The ship, becalmed at length stands still;
> The steed must rest beneath the hill;
> But swiftly still our fortunes pace
> To find us out in every place.
>
> The vessel, though her masts be firm,
> Beneath the copper bears a worm;
> Around the cape, across the line,
> Till fields of ice her course confine;
> It matters not how smooth the breeze,
> How shallow or how deep the seas,
> Whether she bears Manila twine,
> Or China teas, or Spanish hides,
> In port or quarantine she rides;
> Far from New England's blustering shore,
> New England's worm her hull shall bore,
> And sink her in the Indian seas,
> Twine, wine, and hides, and China teas.

On his part and perhaps motivated by memories of sophisticated companionship abroad, Emerson found himself put out by Thoreau's provincialism and cold reserve. "As for taking Thoreau's arm, I should as soon take the arm of an elm tree," he noted. "It is a misfortune of Thoreau's that he has no appetite. He neither eats nor drinks. What can you have in common with a man who does not know the difference between ice cream and cabbage and who has no experience of wine or ale?" But, in fact and down deep, the two men had a great deal in common, and they soon reconciled. A factor in reminding them of the true values that they shared was Thoreau's praiseworthy essay on civil disobedience inspired by their joint hatred of slavery and the war with Mexico. The essay was a long, carefully reasoned, and often passionate argument in favor of putting the individual conscience above the law. Like Emerson, his most-times friend and mentor, Thoreau peppered his piece with pithy passages:

"Must the citizen ever for a moment, or in the least degree, resign his conscience to the legislator? Why has every man a conscience then? I think that we should be men first, and subjects afterward. It is not desirable to cultivate a respect for the law, so much as for the right."

Or: "How does it become a man to behave toward this American government today? I answer, that he cannot without disgrace be associated with it. I cannot for an instant recognize that political organization as *my* government which is the *slave's* government also."

Or: "If I have unjustly wrested a plank from a drowning man, I must restore it to him though I drown myself. This would be inconvenient. But he that would save his life, in such a case, shall lose it. This people must cease to hold slaves, and to make war on Mexico, though it cost them their existence as a people."

Or: "I do not hesitate to say, that those who call themselves Abolitionists should at once effectually withdraw their support, both in person and property, from the government of Massachusetts, and not wait till they constitute a majority of one, before they suffer the right to prevail through them. I think it is enough if they have God on their side, without waiting for the other one. Moreover, any man more right than his neighbors constitutes a majority of one."

Although Thoreau had served his own conscience by publishing his views, the failure of Peabody's magazine meant that very few people would be inspired by his effort and that he would not be at all enriched by it. If there was any outreach or monetary reward from the work, it came from a lecture on which it was based. Ironically, Thoreau owed what was becoming a very modest lecturing career to that very unpolitical and departed friend, Nathaniel Hawthorne. As a board member of the Salem Lyceum, Hawthorne arranged to have Thoreau invited to its platform and to his home as a guest on a couple of occasions. Considering remarks made about him by Hawthorne, it is surprising that Alcott was also a guest in the Hawthornes' Salem home, probably at the insistence of Sophia, who had good memories of working with him in Boston. In Salem, Alcott held a "conversation," as described by Sophia in a letter to her sister Mary Mann: "Mr. Alcott said he would commence with the Nativity, and first read Milton's Hymn. Then he retreated to his corner, and for about an hour and three quarters kept up an even flow of thought, without a word being uttered by any other person present. Then Mr. Stone questioned him upon his use of the word 'artistic'; which provoked a fine analysis from him of the word 'artist' as distinguished from 'artisan.' I thought the whole monologue very beautiful and clear. This evening Mr. Thoreau is going to lecture, and will stay with us. His lecture before was so enchanting; such a revelation of nature in all its exquisite details of wood-thrushes, squirrels, sunshine, mists and shadows, fresh vernal odors, pine-tree ocean melodies, that my ear rang with music, and I seemed to have been wandering through copse and dingle! Mr. Thoreau has risen above all his arrogance of manner, and is as gentle, simple, ruddy, and meek as all geniuses should be; and now his great blue eyes fairly outshine and put into shade a nose which I once thought must make him uncomely forever."

Their guests could not have failed to see that the Hawthorne marriage was as loving as it had been during their time at the Old Manse. The kind of affection Hawthorne exhibited in a letter to

Sophia when she was away visiting relatives—"And then our great, lonesome bed at night—the scene of so many blissful intercourses—now so solitary"—shone in their faces. But soon they would again be in deep financial trouble. Just months after General Taylor's Whig administration took office in March 1849, Hawthorne, the Democrat by inheritance, was fired from his job at the Custom House. As usual Sophia put a good face on the event in a letter to her mother: "I have not seen my husband happier than since this turning out. He has felt in chains for a long time, and being a MAN, he is not alarmed at being set upon his own feet again,— or on his *head*, I might say,—for that contains the available gold, of a mine scarcely yet worked at all. As Margaret [Fuller] truly said once, 'We have had but a drop or so from that ocean.' We are both perfectly well, too, and brave with happiness, and 'a credence in our hearts, and esperance so absolutely strong, as doth outview the attest of eyes and ears.' (So Shakespeare somewhere speaks for us, somewhat so—but not verbatim, for I forget one or two words.) Above all, it has become in the way of an inevitable Providence to us (whatever knavery some people may have to answer for, who have been the agents in the removal), and I never receive inevitable Providence with resignation merely; but with *joy*, as certainly, undoubtedly, the best possible events can happen for me—and immediately I begin to weave the apparent straw into gold, like the maiden in the fairy tale."

The straw did turn into gold for the Hawthornes. Nathaniel used the present of time from his dismissal to finish what he called his "fourteen-mile-story with one end being in press in Boston, while the other was in my head here in Salem" in time for publication early in 1850 under the title *The Scarlet Letter*. It could not have been finished without another present—a check for five hundred dollars from his friend George Hilliard, who said it came from a group of unnamed admirers and added, "I know the sensitive edge of your temperament; but do not speak or think of obligation. It is only paying, in a very imperfect measure, the debt we owe you for what you have done for American Literature." The book represented a daring gamble by all concerned—the author, his publisher James Fields, and his admirers—since it dealt quite frankly with the delicate subject of adultery, involving a pure-in-heart young woman and a minister of the gospel.

Hawthorne was acutely conscious of the risk that they were taking. It could make or break him emotionally as well as financially. This is quite clear from these words in his letter of thanks to Hilliard: "It is something else besides pride that teaches me that ill-success in life is really and justly a matter of shame. I am ashamed of it, and I ought to be. The fault of a failure is attributable—in a great degree, at least—to the man who fails. Nobody has a right to live in this world unless he be strong and able, and applies his ability to good purpose. The only way in which a man can retain his self-respect, while availing himself of the generosity of his friends, is, by making it an incitement to his utmost exertions, so that he may not need their help again." On top of shame, Hawthorne was working under the strain of turbulent emotions induced by his firing, the death of his mother, and his usual doubts as to his own ability. But in a letter to Horatio Bridge, he revealed a curious cause for hope. When he had read the last chapters of the book to Sophia, "it broke her heart and sent her to bed with a grievous headache, which I look upon as a triumphant success."

The Scarlet Letter was, in fact, a triumphant success, both critically and commercially. Most critics within the literary establishment hailed it; only those in the religious establishment deplored it. One of the latter, Arthur Cleveland, an Episcopal bishop, writing in *Church Review*, berated Hawthorne for choosing as a subject "the nauseous amour of a Puritan pastor, with a frail creature of his charge, whose mind is represented as far more debauched than her body. Is the French era actually begun in our literature?" What had begun, as the healthy sales of the book attested, was an era of new freedom for authors. Although he attributed it to "an unsound state of public morals," Orestes Brownson said rightly that "the novelist is permitted, without scorching rebuke, to select such crimes and invest them with all the fascination of genius and all the charms of a highly polished style." One good friend and literary figure who would have personally and professionally admired and lauded *The Scarlet Letter* was sadly gone. That summer Margaret Fuller, returning to America, was drowned along with the Italian nobleman she loved, Giovanni Angelo Ossoli, and their young son when a storm drove their ship onto a sandbar off Fire Island.

Despite Emerson's criticism of the device he used in *Mosses from an Old Manse*, Hawthorne wrote an autobiographical preface to *The Scarlet Letter* in which he settled some old scores by providing acid portraits of fellow workers at the Custom House and the political opponents who had engineered his firing. It did not make him popular in Salem, but he could not have cared less. Provided a flow of cash from the book, buoyed by Fields's promise to publish his works "a-la-Steam Engine," relieved of family responsibilities by his mother's death, and in search of diversion, Hawthorne decided to move. Sophia not only agreed with him but, through the Peabody clan's contacts, found a place to alight. It was a small, story-and-a-half red house on an estate at Lenox, Massachusetts, that the William Aspinwall Tappans were renting. Mrs. Tappan was Caroline Sturgis, whose marriage into a wealthy New York family may have represented a rebound from her failed flirtation with Emerson. Although the house was a warren of small rooms, it provided magnificent Berkshire views, clean mountain air, and the society of a literary community, as would be expected of any habitat of Caroline Sturgis Tappan.

In a burst of creative energy, Hawthorne completed another novel, *The House of the Seven Gables*, and sent it off to Fields in early 1851. Weary and depleted, he gave himself over to the pleasures, and sometimes pains, of family life and more socializing than he normally liked. Son Julian later recalled thrilling rides on a big sled with father and sister Una down "a long declivity towards Tanglewood and the lake" and playful pranks with which his father entertained them. In a typical one of these Hawthorne told the children to turn around and shut their eyes until they heard him shout. When called to look, they saw him "swaying and soaring" in a treetop—"a delightful mystery and miracle." In the not so merry month of May, a small sister to be named Rose arrived on the scene. In the confines of the small house, Hawthorne could not escape being aware of the pangs of childbirth, an awareness that neither party to a marriage that they had tried to keep on a high romantic plain appreciated. Hawthorne was so profoundly affected by the experience that he pledged himself at age forty-seven to a life of celibacy. Though never written nor announced, that pledge sets the tone of his letter about Rose to his sister-in-law, Elizabeth Peabody.

"Sophia and the baby are getting on bravely. She gazes at it all day long, and continually discovers new beauties. As for me, who look at it perhaps half a dozen times a day, I must confess that I have not yet discovered the *first* beauty. But I think I never have had any natural partiality for my children. I love them according to their desserts [sic]—they have to prove their claim to all the affection they can get; and I believe I could love other people's children better than mine, if I felt they deserved it more. Perhaps, however, I should not be quite a fair judge on which side the merit lay. It does seem to me, moreover, that I feel a more decided drawing of the heart strings towards this baby than either of the other two, at their first appearance. This is my last and latest, my autumnal flower, and will be still in her gayest bloomage when I shall be most decidedly an old man—the daughter of my age, if age and decrepitude are really to be my lot."

Hawthorne's uncharacteristically active social life in the Berkshires began when a young writer named Herman Melville arrived at the door of the snow-covered red house in a horse-drawn sleigh. Melville had married the daughter of the chief justice of the Massachusetts Supreme Court and was living in a large house in Pittsfield at the courtesy of his in-laws. At work on a book about whaling, he was anxious to meet a now famous fellow writer. The attraction turned out to be mutual, and they had several meetings in each other's homes "discussing the Universe with a bottle of brandy and cigars," as Melville reported, when their wives were elsewhere or otherwise engaged. Strong drink was the lubrication of good talk throughout the literary community. On one occasion, both Hawthorne and Melville were part of a summer party organized by publisher James Fields that included Dr. Oliver Wendell Holmes, three attractive young ladies, and some lesser lights in publishing. Written up in detail by several of the participants, the event began with a morning hike to Monument Mountain, iced down with champagne; continued with a dinner at Fields's house described as "a three hour's business from turkey to ice cream, well moistened by the way"; and ended with an afternoon visit to a gorge called Ice Glen that looked, in Hawthorne's words, "as if the Devil had torn his way through a rock & left it all jagged behind him." The usually tongue-tied Hawthorne led an exploration into this eerie place, and Fields said that he was "among the most enterprising of the merrymakers; and being in the dark much of the time, he ventured to call out lustily and pretend that certain destruction was inevitable to all of us."

There apparently was little concern among the merrymakers in the mountains about events in Washington that would bring certain destruction upon the nation in the view of their counterparts in Boston and Concord. Passed by Congress and signed by President Fillmore, who had taken over the White House after General Taylor died suddenly of cholera morbus, the laws that constituted the Compromise of 1850 were to become effective in 1851. The law that most disturbed the peace of Concord was a strengthened Fugitive Slave Law. Before moving to Boston, the Alcotts had made of Hillside a station on the Underground Railway. This activity was reflected in a rather despairing entry in Bronson's journal: "The hunters are astir these sunny days, and from this my espial I hear every now and then the bolt dealt sure from the fowler's gun. Man is harried by his propensities. Everywhere in Nature I find the old felon, Murder, dogging Mercy. I cannot step upon my hill-top or plunge into the pine woods behind my house without encountering this huntsman. I am upon his track, he on mine—I in quest of my game, he of his. One cannot escape these Nimrods anywhere. And now, as if to domesticate this wolf in my fancy, there arrives from the Maryland plantations a fugitive to sit at my table and fireside, whom yet another Nimrod will seize and hurry swiftly into bondage or death if he can." The Thoreau household was another station, and Henry reported in his journal that one Henry Williams, a fugitive from Virginia, was staying with them after the new law was in effect. Thoreau collected money for train fare from friends and neighbors, one of whom was Emerson, and personally saw the man safely aboard the cars for Canada.

Emerson's contribution was to be expected in view of his most succinct comment on the Fugitive Slave Law: "This filthy enactment was made in the nineteenth century, by people who could read and write. I will not obey it, by God." Emerson shared his feelings about the law with the people of Concord in a speech and wrote a diatribe about it in his journal, in which he said of a political figure whom he had once admired, "The word *liberty* in the mouth of Mr. Webster sounds like the word *love* in the mouth of a courtezan." In an impassioned speech to the Senate, Daniel Webster had supported the compromise devised by Kentuckian Henry Clay on the grounds that preserving the Union was more important than restricting slavery. "The Union! Oh, yes, I prized that, other things being equal," Emerson told his journal, "but what is the Union to a man self-condemned, with all sense of self-respect and chance of fair fame cut off,—with the names of conscience and religion become bitter ironies, and liberty the ghastly nothing which Mr. Webster means by that word? The worst mischiefs that could follow from Secession and new combination of the smallest fragments of the wreck were slight and medicable to the calamity your Union has brought us. Another year, and a standing army, officered by Southern gentlemen to protect the Commissioners and to hunt the fugitives will be illustrating the new sweets of Union in Boston, Worcester, and Springfield." Webster was rewarded for his stance by President Fillmore's appointing him secretary of state, making him look even worse in the eyes of former supporters like Emerson.

Although Alcott's head was in Boston, his heart remained in Concord; throughout the year of 1851, his body was often there, too, as his journal jottings attest:

April 26

Left for Concord, to see to the transplanting of the apple-trees at "Hillside" and to spend the Sunday with Emerson. Found E. at work on Miss Fuller's Memoir, which he has undertaken to compile and have ready for the press by September. W. H. Channing is preparing his memoir also of Margaret, and the two are to be bound in the same covers. So we shall have the best that can be gathered now of that great woman.

Evening: We have had the Conversation on Webster, Union, Disunion, the Vigilante Committee, and the slave-hunters' work here in Boston.

April 27

All the morning was given to conversation in E's study. After dinner we walked to Walden, and in the evening came Thoreau and Elizabeth Hoar and stayed till 10 o'clock. There was endlessly varied and miscellaneous discourse, which no man may well report.

June 8

These days and nights in Concord with Emerson in study, field, beside Walden Water and woods, are differenced by nameless traits from all days and night in my calendar of experience. There is nothing like them, nothing comparable. Perhaps I best describe them by saying that they make conversation and ideas possible, and the pleasures of friendship without stain like sallies into some fabled cloud-land, remote and golden, they seem, rather than actual scenes on *terra firma*—where minds divested of mortal forms sit sedate and aloft, discoursing free "on fate, free-will, and knowledge absolute."

Add that they have something planetary and astral, and, if I may say so moderately, show the place of our little planet in the solar system, as if the parties had got planted in the sun somehow and were looking through the Lord Rosse and Herschel telescopes at mundane concerns and people.

On returning it takes a day and a night's sleep to restore me to my place and poise for the customary rounds of study. Yet I like these visits to the sun and their great perspectives very well.

June 9

Walked to "Hillside." There is prospect of fruit—apples, peaches, cherries, etc., and a heavy crop of grass.

Dined with Thoreau. We had a walk afterward by the Hosmer Cottage, and back by the rail-track. T. tells me that he read his paper on "Walking" lately at Worcester. He should read this, and the "Walden" also, everywhere in our towns and cities, for the soundness and rectitude of the sentiments. They would have a wholesome influence. I sometimes say of T. that he is the purest of our moralists, and the best republican in the Republic—viz., the republican at home. A little over-confident and somewhat stiffly individual, perhaps,—dropping society clean out of his theory, while practically standing friendly in his own strict sense of friendship—there is about him a nobleness and integrity of bearing that make possible and actual the virtues of Rome and Sparta.

November 10

Plato held that the philosopher might withdraw from the state when it was formed on an imperfect model, and the like freedom was clearly intimated, if not definitely joined, in Christ's teaching also. Moreover, 'tis the dictate

of the instincts and the duty imposed by the moral sentiment, that legislator and president of the royal law is
everyman's soul. The commandment is to "come out of
whatsoever is illegal and base, alike in institutions and ourselves." Nor are we to wait for multitudes to accompany us.
'Tis our individual and personal outcoming from all evils
and impurities of every shade and name. Man is prior to,
and the superior of, states. Caesar's tribute money must
not be levied on God's treasury. An honest man is a brave
man, and heroes can afford to live on nuts, as freemen,
sunning themselves in the clefts of rocks, sooner than sell,
for the state's potage of slavery and wrong, their inborn
liberties. Manliness is all that maintains and makes states
respectable. Man-keeping is the imperial economy. 'Tis a
great age when the state is nothing and Man is all.

December 7

Concord. All day with Emerson and Ideas, the rain
pouring outside also.

But now, as before, nothing remains reportable for
these leaves—yet not lost, but, like some ray from the old
stars, still blending, I doubt not, with the evening and
morning twilights of my experiences, "flattering the mountain tops with sovreign eye."

Say whatever may be said in praise and dispraise of
him, this is the mastermind of our country and time.
Emerson is as necessary to our hemisphere as the day-star
and the evening and morning maiden who feeds her urn at
its beams.

Something about the times, perhaps a feeling that they belonged to an embattled moral minority, was causing the Concord
friends to have a new appreciation of each other. In his own journal, Emerson wrote in 1852 as public events threatened to increase the divisive damage caused by the Compromise, "I am my
own man more than most men, yet the loss of a few persons would

be most impoverishing;—a few persons who give flesh and blood to what were, else, mere thoughts, and which now I am not at liberty to slight, or in my manner treat as fictions. It were too much to say that the Platonic world I might have learned to treat as cloud-land, had I not known Alcott, who is a native of that country, yet I will say that he makes it as solid as Massachusetts to me; and Thoreau gives me, in flesh and blood and pertinacious Saxon belief, my own ethics. He is far more real, and daily practically obeying them, than I."

Still showing little concern about national affairs, Hawthorne and his family left the scenery and socializing of their mountain retreat in the winter of 1851–1852 to occupy the West Newton home of their in-laws, the Horace Manns, while they were in Washington where Mann was serving in Congress. Although their stay at the Manns' was only temporary, it was time enough for Hawthorne to add more fire to Fields's publishing "Steam Engine" by completing *The Blithedale Romance*, a novel in which he once again settled old scores—this time with respect to his disillusioning Brook Farm experience. He made outrageous fun of the hypocrisy and pretensions of the community's do-gooders, who were inspired in part by "Mr. Emerson's essays" and led by a thinly disguised Margaret Fuller to whom he gave the supposedly exotic name of Zenobia. Close to comedy in the beginning, the story reaches a tragic climax in the drowning of Zenobia, a reprise of his account of the drowning he had witnessed in Concord. If there was ever a doubt of how much Hawthorne's realism differed from the idealism of his Concord colleagues, it was dispelled by this book. His was a view as dark as theirs was sunny, but what he did share with them was the aversion to cant that Dickens had spotted in transcendentalism.

Both his blunt honesty and consistently dark view are evident in passages from two Hawthorne novels written years apart—early and nearly forgotten *Fanshawe*, and *Blithedale*. In the former he has his Mr. Fanshawe watching women hover over a dying friend and reflecting that "the disposition which Heaven for the best of purposes has implanted in the female breast—to watch by the sick and comfort the afflicted—frequently becomes depraved into an odious love of pain, and death and sorrow." Then he interrupts the tale for an author's parenthetical statement: "(It is sometimes, though less frequently the case, that this disposition to make 'a joy of grief' extends to individuals of the other sex. But in us it is even less excusable and more disgusting, because it is our nature to shun the sick and afflicted; and, unless restrained by principles other than we bring into the world with us, men might follow the example of many animals in destroying the infirm of their own species. Indeed, instances of this nature might be adduced among savage nations.)" In *Blithedale*, he has his main character, a stand-in for himself, opine, "Most men—and, certainly, I could not always claim to be one of the exceptions—have a natural indifference, if not an absolutely hostile feeling, towards those whom disease, or weakness, or calamity of any kind, cause to falter and faint amid the rude jostle of our selfish existence."

Among the do-gooders whose causes he considered hopeless were prohibitionists. His thoughts on this matter were contained in a paragraph of his original *Blithedale* manuscript that he edited out before publication. He may have thought that it would add to the disapproving gossip about his own habits and those of friends like Franklin Pierce. As written, he asserted that "human nature, in my opinion, has a mighty instinct that approves of wine, at least, if not of stronger liquor. The temperance men may preach till doom's day; and still this cold and barren world will look warmer, kindlier, mellower, through the medium of a toper's glass; nor can they, with all their efforts, really spill his draught on the floor, until some hitherto unthought of discovery shall supply him with a truer element of joy. The general atmosphere of life must first be rendered so inspiriting that he will not need his delirious solace. The custom of tippling has its defensible side, as well as any other question. But these good people snatch at the old, time-honored demijohn, and offer nothing—either sensual or moral—nothing whatever to supply its place; human life, as it goes with a multitude of men, will not endure so great a vacuum as would be left by the withdrawal of that big-bellied convexity. The space, which it now occupies, must somehow or other be filled up. As for the rich, it would little matter if a blight fell upon their vineyards, but the poor man—whose only glimpse of a better state is through the muddy medium of his liquor—what is to be done for him? The reformers should make their efforts positive, instead of negative, they must do away with evil by substituting good."

With the novel finished and the return of the Manns imminent, the Hawthornes began looking around for a home of their own. Nathaniel's books had brought in a little more than three thousand dollars in royalties, and frugal living in the Berkshires had left them with nearly two thousand dollars in savings. When they discovered that the Alcotts wanted to sell Hillside for fifteen hundred dollars, they did not hesitate; they even found five hundred dollars more to buy eight acres across the road from Emerson. Although the house was rather small for a family of five and drably decorated, it was the first place they had ever owned, and they prized it accordingly. Sophia was ecstatic about returning to the haunts of their honeymoon. One reason for her mood was a warm welcome from the Emersons. In her usual glowing letters to her family in late spring and early summer of 1852, she detailed charming instances of this welcome:

> The other morning, at the Middlesex Hotel [where they stayed for the first few days after their arrival until their house was readied], Una remarked that she was going to see Mr. Emerson. I supposed she was jesting; but I missed her soon after, and in about an hour she returned, and said she had been to see him. She had rung at the door, and a servant came, and she inquired for Mr. Emerson! He came out and greeted her very kindly, and said, "I suppose you have come to see Mrs. Emerson." "No," replied Una, "I have come to see *you*." So he politely put aside his studies, and accompanied his young lady visitor over the gardens

and into the Gothic summer-house [Alcott's strange edifice]. I called there on my way here, and Mr. Emerson told me that he would like Una to go in and out, just as if it were her own home. I said that he was Una's friend ever since she had heard "The Humble Bee" and "The Rhodora" [Emerson poems].

Mrs. Emerson invited the Hawthorne family to their annual July picnic for the town's children. Sophia felt obliged to stay home with baby Rose, but "the children had a charming time, and brought back word that each had behaved perfectly. The next day I went to tell Mrs. Emerson why Rose and I did not appear. I found Mr. Emerson, sitting on the side doorstep, with Edith on his knee and Edward riding about the lawn on his pony. Mr. Emerson said that 'the show of children was very pretty. But Julian! *He* makes his mark everywhere; there is no child so fine as Julian!' Was not that pleasant to hear from him? I told him how singular it was that Julian should find in Concord the desire of his imagination for two years—a pony (Mr. Emerson had already superintended the little boy's mounting, and falling off from, Edward's pony); and he smiled like Sirius. 'Well, that's good. Send him this afternoon.' He then called Edward, and bade him go home with me, mount Julian, and bring him back; and this was accordingly done."

Hawthorne's delight in his new home was not in socializing but in the opportunity to be alone. He reported "delectable hours stretched out at my lazy length, with a book in my hand, or unwritten book in my thoughts" on the hillside, and he paced the crown of the hill so often that he wore a path through the brush. He called the hill a place where "I can make my escape when the Philistines knock at the front door." Sooner than he could have imagined it, Hawthorne would be in need of that escape; he found himself engaged in a project that would alienate most of his fellow townsmen, including those leading lights, Thoreau and Emerson. At their convention in June, the Democrats nominated

Franklin Pierce to run for president against his old commander, General Scott, the Whig candidate. As soon as he heard the news, Hawthorne wrote to Pierce that "I hardly know whether to congratulate you, for it would be absurd to suppose that the great office to which you are destined will ever afford you one happy or comfortable moment—and yet it is an end worthy of all ambition, as the highest success that the whole world affords to a statesman." Although he doubtless knew what he was getting himself into, he also wrote, "It had occurred to me that you might have some thought of getting me to write the necessary biography. Whatever service I can do you, I need not say, would be at your command, but I do not believe that I should succeed in this matter so well as many other men."

Pierce evidently thought that Hawthorne was indulging in false modesty and asked him to take on the job. To produce a book in time to affect the election would mean working hard through the summer, which was not Hawthorne's favorite writing season. Worse, he would have to find a way to deal with his friend's pro-slavery stance that angered even his own family. Sophia's sister Elizabeth blasted Pierce for being a militarist as well as being soft on the slavery question; her sister Mary's husband, Horace Mann, used cutting humor to convey their feelings: "If he makes Pierce out to be a great man or a brave man, it will be the greatest work of fiction he ever wrote." Hawthorne responded with a bit of humor of his own: "Though the story is true, yet it took a romancer to do it." Even those who were not appalled by Hawthorne's willingness to support Pierce's political positions faulted him for seeking a remunerative federal appointment as a reward for his work. To them, Sophia wrote that her husband anticipated having "the lowest motives" ascribed to him but that "he never cares a *sou* what people say. He knew he never should ask for an office; and not one word on the subject has ever passed between General Pierce and Mr. Hawthorne."

In the biography that the "romancer" concocted, Pierce is depicted as a statesman and soldier who has devoted most of his working life to public service. To get around the fact that Pierce could claim no notable achievements as a member of the House and Senate, Hawthorne wrote that "instead of thrusting yourself forward in all good or bad occasions, it always required a case of necessity, to bring you out; and having done the needful with as little noise as possible, you withdrew into the background." To counter rumors that Pierce had been a coward in battle, Hawthorne devoted a large section of the book to extracts from Pierce's war journal and other favorable accounts of his actions. Typical and rather crafty in view of Pierce's opponent in the upcoming election was the following rather purple passage of their meeting when Pierce arrived to reinforce the American troops attacking the Mexican positions at Churubusco and San Antonio:

> General Santa Anna entertained the design of withdrawing his forces towards the city. In order to intercept this movement, Pierce's brigade, with other troops, was ordered to pursue a route by which the enemy could be attacked from the rear. Colonel Noah E. Smith (a patriotic American, long resident in Mexico, whose local and topographical knowledge prove eminently serviceable) had offered to point out the road, and was sent to summon General Pierce to the presence of the commander-in-chief. When he met Pierce, near Coyacan, at the head of his brigade, the heavy fire of batteries commenced. "He was exceedingly thin," writes Colonel Smith, "worn down by the fatigue and pain from the day and night before, and then evidently suffering severely. Still, there was a glow in his eye, as the cannon boomed, that showed within him a spirit ready for the conflict." He rode up to General Scott, who was at this time sitting on horseback beneath a tree, near the church of Coyacan, issuing orders to different individuals on his staff. Our account of this interview is chiefly taken from the narrative of Colonel Smith, corroborated by other testimony.

The commander-in-chief had already heard of the accident that befell Pierce the day before; and as the latter approached, General Scott could not but notice the marks of pain and physical exhaustion, against which only the sturdiest constancy of will could have enabled him to bear up. "Pierce, my dear fellow," said he,—and the epithet of familiar kindness and friendship, upon the battlefield, was the highest of military commendation from such a man,— "you are badly injured; you are not fit to be in your saddle." "Yes, general, I am," replied Pierce, "in a case like this." "You cannot touch your foot to the stirrup," said Scott. "One of them I can," answered Pierce. The general looked again at Pierce's almost disabled figure, and seemed on the point of taking his irrevocable resolution. "You are rash, General Pierce," said he; "we shall lose you, and we cannot spare you. It is my duty to order you back to St. Augustine." "For God's sake, general," exclaimed Pierce, "don't say that! This is the last great battle, and I must lead my brigade!" The commander-in-chief made no further remonstrance, but gave the order for Pierce to advance with his brigade.

The way lay through thick standing corn, and over marshy ground intersected with ditches, which were filled, or partially so, with water. Over some of the narrower of these Pierce leaped his horse. When the brigade advanced about a mile, however, it found itself impeded by a ditch ten or twelve feet wide and six or eight feet deep. It being impossible to leap it, General Pierce was lifted from his saddle, and, in some incomprehensible way, hurt as he was, contrived to wade or scramble across this obstacle, leaving his horse on the hither side. The troops were now under fire. In the excitement of battle, he forgot his injury, and hurried forward, leading the brigade, a distance of two or three hundred yards. But the exhaustion of his frame, and particularly the anguish of his knee,—made more intolerable by such free use of it,—was greater than any strength of nerve, or any degree of mental energy, could struggle against. He fell, faint and almost insensible, within full range of the enemy's fire. It was proposed to bear him off the field; but, as some of his soldiers approached to lift him, he became aware of their purpose, and was partially revived by his determination to resist it. "No," said he, with all the strength he had left, "don't carry me off! Let me lie here!" And there he lay under tremendous fire from Churubusco, until the enemy, in total rout, was driven from the field.

Having given his subject heroic stature, Hawthorne used it to justify Pierce's stand with regard to slavery. "Such a man," he wrote, "with such hereditary recollections [his father fought in the Revolutionary War], and such personal experience, must not narrow himself to adopt the cause of one section of his native country against another. He will stand up, as he has always stood, among the patriots of the whole land. And if the work of antislavery agitation, which, it is undeniable, leaves most men who earnestly engage in it with only half a country in their affections—if this work must be done, let others do it.

"These northern men, therefore, who deem the great cause of human welfare all represented and involved in this present hostility against southern institutions, and who conceive that the world stands still except so far as that goes forward—these, it may be allowed, can scarcely give their sympathy or their confidence to the subject of this memoir. But there is still another view, and probably as wise a one. It looks upon slavery as one of those evils which divine Providence does not leave to be remedied by human contrivances, but which, in its own good time, by some means impossible to be anticipated, but of the simplest and easiest operation, when all its uses shall have been fulfilled, it causes to vanish like a dream. There is no instance, in all history, of the human will and intellect having perfected any great moral reform by methods which it adapted to that end; but the progress of the world, at every step, leaves some evil or wrong on the path behind it, which the wisest of mankind, of their own set purpose could never have found the way to justify. Whatever contributes to the great cause of good, contributes to all its subdivisions and varieties; and, on this score, the lover of his race, the enthusiast, the philanthropist of whatever theory, might lend his aid to put a man, like the one before us, into the leadership of world affairs."

How much Hawthorne's biography contributed to Pierce's election could not be measured. Pierce captured an impressive electoral vote, winning all but four states, but he lost Massachusetts to Scott, to the delight of those "northern men" to whom Hawthorne had given the back of his hand. Any joy that the victory might have brought to Hawthorne and Pierce was tempered by personal tragedies. Hawthorne's sister Louisa, coming to visit her brother in Concord for the first time, leaped overboard when fire broke out on the steamer *Henry Clay* en route from Saratoga to New York and drowned. Traveling by train from Boston to his New Hampshire home with his wife and eleven-year-old son a month after the election, the president-elect was involved in an accident that claimed the life of the boy. Shock and sorrow turned Jane Pierce into what all who knew her agreed was a very difficult wife.

In addition to criticism from those who deplored his promotion of Pierce's policies, the book inundated Hawthorne with appeals from friends and strangers to use his apparent influence with the new president to provide them with jobs. In the case of those he found worthy, he was quite willing to do so, and at one point had to advise a supplicant that "there is so much of my paper now in the President's hands that (as the note-shavers say) I am afraid it will be going at a discount." He was quite cynical about the process, as in the advice he gave one young man: "When applying for office, if you are conscious of any deficiencies (moral, intellectual, or educational, whatever else) keep them to yourself, and let those find them out whose business it may be. For example, supposing the office of Translator to the State Department to be tendered to you, accept it boldly, without hinting that your acquaintance with foreign languages may not be the most familiar. If this unimportant fact be discovered afterwards, you can be transferred to some more suitable post. The business is, to establish yourself, somehow and anywhere."

In pleading the cause of others, Hawthorne came to the conclusion that, despite earlier disclaimers, he ought to plead his own. Although his books were doing well enough that Ticknor and Fields wanted to keep the "Steam Engine" going, they were not bringing in the kind of money he needed to repay his debts and secure his family's future. He was earning nothing like Harriet Beecher Stowe, whose *Uncle Tom's Cabin*, a work inspired by the Fugitive Slave Law and beloved by abolitionists, was providing her with unspendable wealth and international fame. Emerson did not attribute her success only to politics, as he noted in his journal: "It is the distinction of *Uncle Tom's Cabin* that it is read equally in the parlour and the kitchen and the nursery of every house. What the lady read in the drawing-room in a few hours is retailed to her in the kitchen by the cook and chambermaid, week by week; they master one scene and character after another." Hawthorne didn't see it quite that way and revealed a case of literary jealousy when he said of women writers that "I wish they were forbidden to write on pain of having their faces scarified with oyster-shell."

Since money was his motive in seeking a government job, Hawthorne tested his friend's gratitude by asking for and getting the most lucrative foreign post—the consulate at Liverpool, Britain's port of entry for commerce with America. When he got the post, Elizabeth Peabody, one of the first to criticize her brother-in-law for prostituting his talents in support of a pro-slavery candidate, struck a very different note in a letter to her father: "Are you not pleased to think that *one* of your children is *rich*?" She had heard that the job would provide some forty thousand dollars annually and estimated that the Hawthornes could spend fifty thousand dollars during the four years he was sure of keeping the post and bank at least a hundred thousand. Accompanied by William Ticknor, who saw to the tiresome details like buying tickets and booking accommodations, Hawthorne took his first trip to

Washington in the late spring of 1853 to get his marching orders from the president. He managed to add the Manchester consulate and another possible three thousand a year in income to his assignment. He indulged freely in the liquor and cigars with which office-seekers wanting his help supplied him—"in the enjoyment of the good things which the Creator has provided with so lavish a hand for the enjoyment of his creatures," as one of them reported. He did try to promote jobs for his friends O'Sullivan and Melville. Possibly because of his additional contacts as a Washington journalist, O'Sullivan was given a post in Portugal, but nothing came of Melville's suit. Hawthorne wrote Bridge that the Washington trip was "a time of much enjoyment, especially of a liquid sort," but added that "Frank was as free and kind, in our personal interviews, as ever he was in our college-days; but his public attentions to me were few and by no means distinguished—only inviting me once to tea, and once to go to a methodist meeting with him while other people were invited to dinner and made much of."

Back in Concord, there would be no more carousing. Hawthorne had to pitch in and help ready the family for a sailing in July. About the time that the Hawthornes boarded the Cunard steamship *Niagara* in Boston harbor—an occasion marked by a cannonade salute in honor of Hawthorne's diplomatic standing and his literary reputation—a young southerner enrolled in Harvard Divinity School showed up in Concord hoping to meet authors he admired. Hawthorne was not one of them. Because of his interest in religion, Moncure Conway first sought out Emerson, whose works were really responsible for his coming to Harvard. Emerson introduced Conway to Thoreau. When Conway expressed great pleasure in meeting the author of *A Week on the Concord and Merrimac Rivers*, which he had enjoyed reading, Thoreau looked startled. "Way down in Virginia you found it," he said. "Must be the only one. It was published way back in '49, and most of the books are still with my publisher."

8

A Transcendental Martyr

ON A DAY IN MAY OF 1854, Massachusetts tasted "the new sweets of Union" almost exactly as Waldo Emerson had predicted in his journal notes on the Compromise of 1850. Although the officers may not have been southern gentlemen, a federal force—an artillery battalion and four platoons of marines—was mustered to escort Anthony Burns, a fugitive slave, from the Boston court-house through an angry mob trying to free him to a wharf where he was put aboard a ship bound for the South. Only a day before this event, Congress had passed another bill calculated to provoke thoughts of civil disobedience from Emerson and his Concord colleagues, Alcott and Thoreau, as had the Fugitive Slave Law. Called the Kansas-Nebraska Act, it had been proposed by Senator Stephen A. Douglas, an Illinois Democrat, who was eager to promote settlement in the West because of his personal land speculations there as well as a belief in America's "Manifest Destiny." To guarantee support from southern lawmakers, Douglas came up with the concept of "popular sovereignty"—that is, that the legality of slavery in these new territories should be decided by a vote of the settlers. As passed with this provision, the Kansas-Nebraska Act effectively did away with the limitations on the extension of slavery in the Compromises of 1820 and 1850. As soon as the bill landed on his desk, President Pierce signed it, just as Douglas had

177

been confident that he would. The president had demonstrated a comforting lack of moral concern about the spread of slavery when he had appointed as secretary of war Jefferson Davis, a Mexican War hero and senator from Mississippi who had resigned from that office to protest the Compromise of 1850.

To Henry Thoreau the ugly incident in Boston was of more immediate concern than the potentially more serious effects of the Kansas-Nebraska Act. When William Lloyd Garrison, the state's leading abolitionist, organized a mass meeting in Framingham to celebrate July Fourth by protesting the seizure of Anthony Burns, Thoreau attended with a speech in his pocket that he had composed from notes in his own journal entitled "Slavery in Massachusetts." The Harvard divinity student Moncure Conway also attended the meeting. Having been in the Thoreau family home while they were in the process of forwarding a fugitive to Canada, Conway was not as surprised to see Thoreau in Framingham as he was to see him rise to speak.

"Thoreau had come all the way from Concord for this meeting," Conway later related. "It was a rare thing for him to attend any meeting outside of Concord, and though he sometimes lectured in the Lyceum there, he had probably never spoken on a platform. He was now clamoured for and made a brief and quaint speech. He began with the simple words, 'You have my sympathy; it is all I have to give you.' It was impossible to associate egotism with Thoreau; we all felt that the time and trouble he had taken at that crisis to proclaim his sympathy with the 'Disunionists' was indeed important. He was there a representative of Concord, of science and letters, which could not quietly pursue their tasks while slavery was trampling down the rights of mankind. Alluding to the Boston commissioner who had surrendered Anthony Burns, Edward G. Loring, Thoreau said, 'The fugitive's case was already decided by God,—not Edward G. God, but simple God.' This was said with such serene unconsciousness of anything shocking in it that we were but mildly startled."

Even as Thoreau was speaking in Framingham, James Fields was writing to a British publisher suggested by Emerson to obtain an English copyright and publication there of *Walden; or, Life in the Woods* by Henry David Thoreau. Ticknor and Fields, he informed the Britisher, planned to have the book out in America that summer. Considering the poor sales of Thoreau's first book, they would be demonstrating considerable faith in this one by an initial run of two thousand copies. The author's technique was the same—a straightforward account of a personal experience, interlarded with thoughtful and thought-provoking digressions—but it was hoped that the idea of a retreat from life's complexities would have more universal appeal than a river trip. Thoreau's meditation on his experience did not advocate detachment from the concerns of ordinary people, as might be expected; it provided a different perspective on them.

On slavery, for instance:

I sometimes wonder that we can be so frivolous, I may almost say, as to attend to the gross but somewhat foreign form of servitude called Negro Slavery, there are so many keen and subtle masters that enslave both North and South. It is hard to have a Southern overseer; it is worse to have a Northern one; but worst of all when you are the slave-driver of yourself. Talk of a divinity in man! Look at the teamster on the highway, wending to market by day or night; does any divinity stir in him? His highest duty to fodder and water his horses! What is his destiny to him compared with the shipping interests? Does not he drive for Squire Make-a-stir? How godlike, how immortal, is he? See how he cowers and sneaks, how vaguely all day he fears, not being immortal nor divine, but the slave and prisoner of his own opinion of himself, a fame won by his own deeds. Public opinion is a weak tyrant compared with our own private opinion. What man thinks of himself, that is which determines, or rather indicates, his fate. Self-emancipation even in the West Indian provinces of the fancy and imagination—what Wilberforce is there to bring this about: Think, also, of the ladies of the land weaving toilet cushions against the last day, not to betray too green an interest in their fates! As if you could kill time without injuring eternity.

The mass of men lead lives of quiet desperation. What is called resignation is confirmed desperation. From the desperate city you go into the desperate country, and have to console yourself with the bravery of minks and musk-rats. A stereotyped but unconscious despair is concealed even under what are called the games and amusements of mankind. There is no play in them, for this comes after work. But it is a characteristic of wisdom not to do desper-ate things.

Then there is a discourse on a favorite Thoreau theme—entrap-ment by things:

What man but a philosopher would not be ashamed to see his furniture packed in a cart and going up country exposed to the light of heaven and the eyes of men, a beggarly account of empty boxes? That is Spaulding's furniture. I could never tell from inspecting such a load whether it belonged to a so-called rich man or a poor one; the owner always seemed poverty-stricken. Indeed, the more you have of such things, the poorer you are. Each load looks as if it contained the contents of a dozen shanties; and if one shanty is poor, this is a dozen times poorer. Pray, for what do we *move ever* but to get rid of our furniture, our *exuviae*; at last to go from this world to another newly furnished, and leave this to be burned? It is the same as if all these traps were buckled to a man's belt, and he could not move over the rough country where our lives are cast without dragging them—dragging his trap. He was a lucky fox that left his tail in the trap. The muskrat will gnaw his third leg off to be free. No wonder man has lost his elasticity. How often he is at a dead set? "Sir, if I may be so bold, what do you mean by a dead set?" If you are a seer, whenever you meet a man you will see all that he owns, ay, and much that he pretends to disown, behind him, even to his kitchen furniture and all the trumpery which he saves and will not burn, and he will appear to be harnessed to it and making what headway he can. I think the man is at dead set who has got through a knot hole or gateway where his sledge load of furniture cannot follow him. I cannot but feel compassion when I hear some trig, compact-looking man, seemingly free, all girded and ready, speak of his "furniture," as whether it is insured or not. "But what shall I do with my furniture?" My gay butterfly is entangled in a spider's web then. Even those who deem for a long while not to have any, if you inquire more narrowly you will find some stored in somebody's barn. I look upon England today as an old gentleman who is travelling with a great deal of baggage, trumpery which has accumulated from long house-keeping, which he has not the courage to burn; great trunk, little trunk, bandbox, and bundle. Throw away the first three at least. It would surpass the powers of a well man nowadays to take up his bed and walk, and I should certainly advise a sick one to lay down his bed and run. When I have met an immigrant tottering under a bundle which contained his all—looking like an enormous wen which had grown out of the nape of his neck—I have pitied him, not because that was his all, but because he had all *that* to carry. If I have got to drag my trap, I will take care that it be a light one and do not nip me in a vital part. But perchance it would be wisest never to put one's paw in it.

Thoreau did not believe that man was doomed to be either enslaved or entrapped. "I went to the woods because I wished to live deliberately, to confront only the essential facts of life, and see if I could not learn what it had to teach, and not, when I came to die, discover that I had not lived," he wrote. During the experiment, he decided that living meant partaking of "the everlasting vigor and fertility of the world," and this could be discovered anew with every dawn:

> The morning, which is the most memorable season of the day, is the awakening hour. Then there is least somnolence in us; and for an hour, at least, some part of us is awake which slumbers all the rest of the day and night. Little is to be expected of that day, if it can be called a day, to which we are not awakened by our Genius, but by the mechanical nudgings of some servitor, are not awakened by our own newly acquired force and aspirations from within, accompanied by the undulations of celestial music, instead of factory bells, and a fragrance filling the air—to a higher life than we fell asleep from; and thus the darkness bear its fruit, and prove itself to be good, no less than the light. That man who does not believe that each day contains an earlier, more sacred and auroral hour than he has yet profaned, has despaired of life, and is pursuing a descending and darkening way. After a partial cessation of his sensuous life, the soul of man, or its organs rather, are reinvigorated each day, and his Genius tries again what noble life it can make. All memorable events, I should say, transpire in the morning time and in a morning atmosphere. The Vedas say, "All intelligences awake with the morning." Poetry and art, and the fairest and most memorable of the actions of men, date from such an hour. All poets and heroes, like Memnon, are the children of Aurora, and emit their music at sunrise. To him whose elastic and vigorous thought keeps pace with the sun, the day is a perpetual morning. It matters not what the clocks say or the attitudes and labors of men. Morning is when I am awake and there is dawn in me. Moral reform is the effort to throw off sleep. Why is it that men give so poor an account of their day if they have not been slumbering? They are not such poor calculators. If they had not been overcome with

drowsiness they would have performed something. The millions are awake enough for physical labor; but only one in a million is awake enough for effective intellectual exertion, only one in a hundred millions to a poetic or divine life. To be awake is to be alive. I have never yet met a man who was quite awake. How could I have looked him in the face?

We must learn to reawaken and keep ourselves awake, not by mechanical aids, but by an infinite expectation of the dawn, which does not forsake us in our soundest sleep. I know of no more encouraging fact than the unquestionable ability of man to elevate his life by a conscious endeavor. It is something to be able to paint a particular picture, or to carve a statue, and so to make a few objects beautiful; but it is far more glorious to carve and paint the very atmosphere and medium through which we look, which morally we can do. To affect the quality of the day, that is the highest of arts. Every man is tasked to make his life, even in its details, worthy of the contemplation of his most elevated and critical hour.

Among the millions leading desperate lives, Thoreau might have counted his friend Alcott. Because of his very nature, Alcott was not quiet about it. On a walk recorded by Thoreau, Alcott talked of his inability to earn a livelihood. He lacked the practical skills for surveying and building that kept Thoreau in bread, and he said that "he could not compete with the Irish in cradling grain. His early education had not fitted him for a clerkship." But how he could talk! In talking he could "affect the quality of the day." Thoreau was undoubtedly one of the people who urged him to follow in Emerson's footsteps and try his "Conversations" in the West. In view of what the women around him were doing to keep the family afloat, Alcott was willing to try anything. A page from daughter Louisa May's journal for 1853—"a hard year"—makes clear his motivation: "In January I started a little school—about a dozen in our parlor. In May, when my school closed, I went to L., as second girl. I needed the change, could do the wash, and was glad to earn my $2 a week. Home in October with $34 for my wages. After two days' rest, began school again with ten children. Anna went to Syracuse to teach, Father went West to try his luck,—so poor, so hopeful, so serene. God be with him! Mother had several boarders, and May got on well at school. Betty was still the home bird."

Alcott was away for months, and from his letters Louisa May concluded that he was "doing as well as a philosopher can in a money-loving world." It was a bit of wishful thinking in light of her report on his return in 1854: "A dramatic scene when he arrived in the night. We were waked by hearing the bell. Mother flew down crying, 'My husband!' We rushed after, and five white figures embraced the half-frozen wanderer who came in hungry, tired, cold, and disappointed, but smiling bravely and as serene as ever. We fed and warmed and brooded over him, longing to ask if he had made any money; but no one did until May said, after he had told all the pleasant things, 'Well, did people pay you?' Then, with a queer look, he opened his pocket book and showed one dollar, saying with a smile that made our eyes fill, 'Only that! My overcoat was stolen, and I had to buy a shawl. Many promises were not kept, and travelling is costly; but I have opened the way, and another year shall do better.'

"I shall never forget how beautifully Mother answered him, though the dear, hopeful soul had built so much on his success; but with a beaming face she kissed him, saying, 'I call that doing *very well*. Since you are safely home, dear, we don't ask anything more.'

"Anna and I choked down our tears, and took a little lesson in real love which we never forgot, nor the look that the tired man and the tender woman gave one another. It was half tragic and half comic, for Father was very dirty and sleepy, and Mother in a big nightcap and funny old jacket."

For Emerson, going west to lecture in the 1850s was a very different story. He had made of himself a national figure who drew full houses and good fees. It was not only what he said but the way he said it that impressed his hearers. Testimony from those who witnessed his performances suggests that he had made of lecturing an art form. The most eloquent description of Emerson on the platform was written by Alexander Ireland, who arranged one of his tours in Great Britain, and it was virtually echoed by Rutherford B. Hayes, a young attorney who heard him in Ohio and would eventually become president of the United States. Hayes found Emerson to be "modest but self possessed, of a good-humored, honest strain, which gives one a favorable impression of his heart and character." But Ireland offers a more indelible image of Emerson in action:

> The first impression one had in listening to [Emerson] in public was that his manner was so singularly quiet and un-impassioned that you began to fear the beauty and force of his thoughts were about to be marred by what might almost be described as monotony of expression. But very soon was this apprehension dispelled. The mingled dignity, sweetness, and strength of his features, the earnestness of his manner and voice, and the evident depth and sincerity of his convictions gradually extorted your deepest attention, and made you feel that you were within the grip of no ordinary man, but of one "sprung of earth's first blood." With "titles manifold"; and as he went on with serene self-possession and an air of conscious power, and set in words of faultless aptitude, you could no longer withstand his "so potent spell," but were forthwith compelled to surrender yourself to the fascination of his eloquence. He used little or no action, save occasionally a slight vibration of the body, as though rocking beneath the hand of some unseen power. The precious words dripped from his mouth in quick succession, and noiselessly sank into the hearts of his hearers, there to abide forever, and, like the famed carbuncle in an Eastern cave, shed a mild radiance on all things therein. Perhaps no orator ever succeeded with so little exertion

in entrancing his audience, stealing away each faculty, and leading the listeners captive at his will. He abjured all force and excitement—dispensing his regal sentences in all mildness, goodness, and truth, but stealthily and surely he grew upon you, from the smallest proportions, as it were; steadily increasing until he became a Titan, a commanding power—

> To whom as to the mountains and the stars,
> The soul seems passive and submissive.

The moment he finished, he took up his MS and quietly glided away,—disappearing before his audience could give vent to their applause.

Even though Emerson was better rewarded in cash and popularity, he did have to endure the same expense and rigors of travel that sent Alcott home in such a sorry state. Discomfort was compounded by the fact that the lecture season was always in winter. Two letters from Waldo to Lidian describe the experience.

From Pittsburgh: "I arrived here last night after a very tedious and disagreeable journey from Philadelphia, by railway and canal, with little food and less sleep; two nights being spent in the railcars and the third on the floor of a canal-boat, where the cushion allowed me for a bed was crossed at the knees by another tier of sleepers as long limbed as I, so that in the air was a wreath of legs; and the night, which was bad enough, would have been worse but that we were so thoroughly tired we could have slept standing. The committee wished me to lecture in the evening, if possible, and I, who wanted to go to bed, answered that I had preliminary statements to make in my first lecture, which required a little time and faculty to make ready, which now could not be had; but if they would let me read an old lecture I would omit the bed and set out for the hall. So it was settled that I should read poor old 'England' once more, which was done; for the committee wished nothing better, and, like all committees, think me an erratic gentleman, only safe with a safe subject."

Springfield, Illinois: "Here I am in the deep mud of the prairies, misled, I fear, into this bog, not by a will-o'-the-wisp, such as shine in bogs, but by a young New Hampshire editor, who over-estimated the strength of both of us, and fancied I should glitter in the prairie and draw the prairie birds and waders. It rains and thaws incessantly, and if we stop off the short street we go up to the shoulders, perhaps, in mud. My chamber is a cabin; my fellow-boarders are legislators. Two or three governors or ex-governors live in the house. But in the prairie we are all new men just come, and must not stand for trifles. 'Tis of no use, then, for me to mag-nify mine. But I cannot command daylight and solitude for study or for more than a scrawl, nor, I fear will my time here be paid for at any such rate promised me."

While Waldo Emerson was slogging through the mud to lecture for uncertain gain, Nathaniel Hawthorne, late of Concord, was find-ing himself called upon in Britain as a newly famous author and a leading representative of the United States to give speeches for the honor of the thing. It was an aspect of his position as consul in Liverpool that he had not anticipated and that, given his shy-ness, might well have kept him from taking the job. Since there was no dodging the obligation he called upon an old friend for help. "I charge myself pretty high with champagne and port before I get on my legs," he wrote, "and whether the business is to make a speech or to be hanged, I came up to it like a man—and I had as lief it should be one as the other." After once leaning on this support, he concluded that "it is easy to speak, when a man is cornered and *corned*." As for the content of his liquefied speeches, he admitted with his disdain for cant that "I flatter myself, however, that, by much practice, I contained considerable skill in this kind of inter-course, the art of which lies in passing off common-places for new and valuable truths, and talking trash and emptiness in such a way that a pretty acute auditor might mistake it for something solid."

As any person who had dined with him would aver, Hawthorne was as fond of food as of drink. Although he often had to sing for his supper in England, it was usually worth it in the circles that they frequented. Sophia recorded a meal they enjoyed at Liscard Vale, the estate of Mr. and Mrs. Charles Holland near Liverpool: "Mr. Hawthorne as chief guest—there were twelve—took Mrs. Holland, and sat at her right hand. The table was very handsome; two enormous silver dish covers, with the gleam of Damascus blades, putting out all the rest of the light. After the soup, these covers were removed, revealing a boiled turbot under one, and fried fish under the other. The fish was replaced by two other enormous dishes with shining covers; and then the whole table was immediately covered with silver dishes; and the center was a tall silver stand holding a silver bowl of celery. It would be useless to try to tell you all the various dishes. A boiled turkey was before Mrs. Holland; and a roasted goose before Mr. Holland; and in the intermediate spaces, cutlets, fricasses, ragouts, tongue, chicken-pies, and many things whose names I did not know, and on a side-table a boiled round of beef as large as the dome of St. Peter's. The pastry of the chicken-pie was of very elaborate sculpture. It was laid in a silver plate, an oak vine being precisely cut all round, and flowers and fruits moulded on top. It really was a shame to spoil it. All these were then swept off in a very noiseless manner. Grouse and pheasants are always served with the sweets in England, and they appeared at either end of the table. There were napkins under the finger bowls, upon each of which a castle or palace was traced in indelible ink, and its name written beneath. The wines were port, sherry, madeira, claret, hock and champagne. I refused the five first, but the champagne was poured into my glass without any question."

One of the first things Hawthorne did with the money coming his way was to repay the loan that had allowed him to work on *The Scarlet Letter*, writing to Hilliard, "Herewith send you a draft on Ticknor for the sum (with interest included) which was so kindly given me by unknown friends, through you, about four years ago. I have always hoped and intended to do this, from the first moment when I made up my mind to accept the money. It would not have been right to speak of this purpose before it was in my power to accomplish it; but it has never been out of my mind for a single day, nor hardly, I think, for a single working hour. I am most happy that this loan (as I may fairly call it, at this moment) can now be repaid without risk on my part of leaving my wife and children utterly destitute. I should have done it sooner; but I felt that it would be selfish to purchase the great satisfaction for myself, at any fresh risk to them. We are not rich, nor are we ever likely to be; but the miserable pinch is over."

Obviously Elizabeth Peabody's exuberant reaction to Hawthorne's appointment was based on erroneous information. Nevertheless, Hawthorne was making more money than any of them had ever seen, but he was earning it the hard way. He had no time or energy to do his own writing, and he had to put up with conditions that he found nearly intolerable. "Liverpool is a most detestable place as a residence that ever my lot was cast in— smoky, noisy, dirty, pestilential; and the consulate is situated in the most detestable part of the city," he wrote to a friend. "The streets swarm with beggars by day and by night. You never saw the like; and I pray that you may never see it in America. It is worth while coming across the sea in order to feel one's heart warm towards his country; and I feel it all the more because it is plain to be seen that a great many of the Englishmen whom I meet here dislike us, whatever they may pretend to the contrary. Myself and my family have suffered very much from the elements. There has not been what we should call a fair day since our arrival, nor a single day when a fire would not be agreeable." If Thoreau had been the friend to receive this letter, he might not have commented, as he did, on Hawthorne's position: "Better for me, says my genius, to go cranberrying this afternoon for the *Vaccinium Oxycocus* in Gowing's Swamp, to get but a pocketful and learn its peculiar flavor, aye, and the flavor of Gowing's Swamp and of *Life in New England*, than to go consul in Liverpool and get I don't know how many dollars for it, with no such flavor."

There was no more escaping the politics of America in Liverpool than in Concord. The Englishmen whose dislike Hawthorne sensed were those of anti-slavery persuasion who had hailed Hawthorne's rival novelist, Harriet Beecher Stowe, as if she were an American queen on her recent visit. They were quite aware that Hawthorne and the American minister in London, James Buchanan, were of President Pierce's Democratic Party that seemed to be seeking ways to extend rather than to curb slavery. When Buchanan took up his post just after Stowe's departure, he gleefully cabled the State Department that "I have learned from a titled lady that the Queen absolutely refused to see Mrs. Stowe either at the Palace or the Duchess of Sutherland's, and that she had refused to attend the concert given at the latter place by the Black Swan, lest she might meet Mrs. Stowe there. My informant says, she remarked very sensibly that American slavery was a question with which Great Britain had nothing to do."

Although the settlers of Nebraska were mostly from the Northeast and quickly elected an anti-slavery legislature, the situation was very different in Kansas. Thousands of armed pro-slavery men called "border ruffians" came into the territory from Missouri and by force and fraud created a pro-slavery legislature. To counter this move a Kansas Aid Society to subsidize settlers was formed first in Massachusetts and then all through New England. As the two groups began shooting at each other, the conflict escalated until the territory was called "bleeding Kansas." Trying to head off catastrophe, Emerson gave a major address at a meeting of the Anti-Slavery Society of New York in 1855. He could see clearly that the growing conflict in Kansas was a kind of dress rehearsal for war on a national scale, and he made a startling proposal:

> Why in the name of common sense and the peace of mankind is not this made the subject of instant negotiation and settlement? Why not end this dangerous dispute on some ground of fair compensation on one side, and of satisfaction on the other to the conscience of the Free States? It is really the great task fit for this country to accomplish, to buy that property of the planters, as the British nation bought the West Indian slave. I say buy,—never conceding the right of the planter to own, but that we may acknowl-

edge the calamity of his position, and bear a countryman's share in relieving him; and because it is the only practicable course, and is innocent. Here is a right social or public function which one man cannot do, which all men must do. 'Tis said it will cost two thousand millions of dollars. Was there ever any contribution that was so enthusiastically paid as this will be? We will have a chimney-tax. We will give up our coaches, and wine, and watches. The churches will melt their plate. The father of his country shall wait, well pleased, a little longer for his monument; Franklin for his; the Pilgrim Fathers for theirs; and the patient Columbus for his. The mechanics will give; the needle-women will give; the children will have cent-societies. Every man in the land will give a week's work to dig away this accursed mountain of sorrow once and forever out of the world.

Emerson's audience sat on their hands. However well reasoned, his appeal came too late for most people in the anti-slavery camp. In the year 1856, when a new national leadership would be selected and the nature of Kansas statehood settled, violence in the territory escalated. A pro-slavery force sacked the town of Lawrence, destroying and looting property and killing a man in the process. In retaliation, John Brown, a Connecticut-born farmer, who had moved with his family of seven sons to Kansas to swell the anti-slavery forces, led a raid at Pottawatomie Creek in which five pro-slavery settlers died. Months later a superior pro-slavery force defeated Brown's men and pillaged Osawatomie. One of Brown's fighting sons was killed and another crazed in the skirmishes. Violence begot violence. The courage of the men they sent west, typified by the Brown family, was much appreciated by the Emigrant Aid groups. At one of their meetings in New Haven, Connecticut, in 1856, the nation's most famous preacher, Henry Ward Beecher, pastor of the Plymouth Church in Brooklyn, New York, and brother of Harriet Beecher Stowe, said that "Sharpe's rifles are a greater moral agency than the Bible" and collected enough money on the spot to ship twenty-five of the weapons to their settlers in Kansas. Back in Brooklyn, Beecher persuaded his congregation to fund another twenty-five rifles, which became known as "Beecher's Bibles."

A party born in Wisconsin in 1854 to protest the Kansas-Nebraska Act and calling itself Republican had grown so rapidly in two years that it fielded a candidate, John C. Frémont, a former California senator and dashing soldier-explorer, to oppose James Buchanan, whom the Democrats nominated to replace Pierce in the national elections. Frémont came close in the popular vote, but, by capturing fourteen slave states and five free states as against the Republicans' eleven free states, Buchanan won the electoral vote. Hawthorne, who had not gotten along well with Buchanan in England, knew that his days at the lucrative Liverpool consulate were numbered and made plans to take the family on a long European trip.

Planless as always, Bronson Alcott had landed a temporary teaching position at a new school called Eagleswood near Perth Amboy, New Jersey, being run by Theodore Weld, an ardent abolitionist and educator of long standing. At Alcott's urging, Thoreau was invited down to survey the school grounds and give a lecture shortly after the 1856 election. Since Horace Greeley had published a number of pieces by Thoreau in his *Tribune*, he invited the pair up to spend a Saturday on his Westchester farm, and they decided to enrich the weekend by going to Brooklyn to meet Walt Whitman, whose new book of poetry, *Leaves of Grass*, was shaking up the literary establishment, though much praised by Emerson.

"We find Greeley at the Harlem Station and ride with him to his farm, where we pass the day," Alcott noted in his journal. "He takes us to see his acres, his ditches, the barn he is building of rubble-stones and cement, and tells of his crops, his proposed improvements, etc. But I doubt the wisdom of his farming and predict nothing of it." The next day being Sunday, they breakfasted at their New York hotel and crossed "afterwards to Brooklyn and the Plymouth Church to hear Ward Beecher. Thoreau called it Pagan, and was restive under it; but I pronounced it very good, very well suited to priest and people, the best I had heard lately, and hopeful for the coming congregations."

They could not find Whitman on Sunday but finally cornered him on Monday in his lodgings, where Alcott found himself an amused witness to the dance of two egocentric poets:

> He receives us kindly, yet awkwardly, and takes us up two narrow flights of stairs to sit or stand as we might in his attic study—also bed chamber for himself and his feeble brother, the pressure of whose bodies was still apparent in the unmade bed standing in one corner, and the vessel scarcely hidden underneath, a few books were piled disorderly over the mantel piece and some characteristic pictures—a Hercules, a Bacchus, and a satyr—were pasted, unframed, upon the rude walls. He is very curious of criticism of himself, or his book, inviting it from all quarters, nor suffering the conversation to stray very wide away from Walt's godhead without recalling it to that high mark. I had hoped to put him in communication direct with Thoreau, and tried my hand a little after we came down stairs and sat in the parlour below; but each seemed planted fast in reserves, surveying the other curiously,—like two beasts, each wondering what the other would do, whether to snap or run, and it came to no more than cold compliments between them. Whether Thoreau was meditating the possibility of Walt's stealing away "out-of-doors" for some sinister ends, poetic or pecuniary, I could not well divine, nor was very curious to know; or whether Walt suspected or not that he had here, for once, and for the first time, found his match and more at smelling out "all Nature," a sagacity potent, penetrating and peerless as his own, if indeed not more piercing and profound and peerless, finer

and formidable, I cannot say. At all events, our stay was not long.

Thoreau would not have long to meditate on matters poetic, because early in 1857 a young Harvard graduate, Franklin Sanborn, who had been persuaded by Emerson to start a school in Concord, brought a famous visitor to town. He was John Brown on a tour of the East to raise funds for his fight in Kansas. Concord was a stop worth his time. The year before its citizens had raised some thirteen hundred dollars for Kansas relief, as Emerson noted in his journal. Sanborn brought Brown to the Thoreaus' for lunch; he would also meet Emerson before his speech at the Town Hall. A wiry man of medium height with a weather-tanned face, he looked more the farmer he once had been than the fierce fighter he had become. His tone and attitude were calm and friendly in conversation but as fierce as the look in his eye when he told the Town Hall audience about the killing of one son and the torture of another by pro-slavery ruffians until he lost his mind. Nevertheless, he argued, freeing the slaves was a cause that the Lord had ordered him to join, a cause worth dying for. Both Thoreau and Emerson were moved enough to contribute, and Emerson brought Brown home from the meeting to spend the night at the Bush. The next day, Emerson reported to his journal only that Brown had given "a good account of himself," but his daughter Ellen would later write of the animal stories with which Brown entertained her and the other children. "When I was present he was talking on peaceful subjects, his conversion, and stories of things he had seen and known, very pretty stories—not about slavery," she reported.

That their fight in Kansas and elsewhere would be a hard one became even more apparent to the anti-slavery people when, just two days after the new president was sworn in, the Supreme Court, dominated by southern justices, published a five-to-four ruling against Dred Scott, a Missouri slave who sought his freedom on the grounds that his master had once taken him to live for a time in Illinois north of latitude 36°30′, where slavery was forbidden by the Missouri Compromise. By their ruling, which was the first time that the Court had declared an act of Congress unconstitutional since 1803, slavery was made legal in every state and territory. This act by the land's highest court caused Emerson to give deeper thought to John Brown's denouncing "the folly of the peace party in Kansas, who believed, that their strength lay in the greatness of their wrongs, and so discountenanced resistance." If there was no way to prevail through government on a clear issue of morality, wasn't it necessary to use force? John Brown thought so. His claim to the moral high ground and his willingness to sacrifice his life to hold it made it almost impossible for Emerson and Thoreau not to wish him well.

Not long after Brown went on his way, Thoreau had a part in another Concord event that took his mind off national events for a while. The Alcotts asked him to survey a property next to the Wayside that they were thinking of buying. Still considering Bronson one of his best friends, he went at the job with a will and not surprisingly came up with what Alcott called a "fair plot," containing twelve acres and sixty-six rods. An enthusiastic Bronson, who had come to Concord to look over the property, wrote to his wife that they could have the land for $345 and the house on it in great need of repair for $600. The decision would be hers, because she controlled the money she had managed to lay by from the sale of Wayside to the Hawthornes and saved from the erratic income of family members. Abba did not hesitate. Their daughter Beth's health had been declining slowly for about a year, ever since a severe bout of scarlet fever had led to "consumption." Abba wanted to care for Beth in a place where she had been happy, and nobody could predict how long the girl's life would last. As to this unknown, they had a stroke of luck. The Hawthornes were still in Europe, and they were able to make arrangements to occupy part of Wayside immediately while work went on at their own home, which they christened the Orchard House.

By a curious coincidence, the Hawthornes were also dealing with a daughter's potentially failing illness. They had settled down in Italy—wintering in Rome, summering in Florence—for an indefinite period. Una came down with what they called "Roman fever," and for thirty days and nights Sophia sat by her nearly comatose daughter's bedside, sleeping only a few daylight hours in her chair when a friend was on hand to keep watch. There came a time when the mother gave up, as described by son Julian in his family biography: "All at once her feeling changed. It was one of those apparently miraculous transformations that sometimes come over faithful loving hearts. 'Why should I doubt the goodness of God?' she asked herself. 'Let him take her, if He sees best. I can give her to Him. I will not fight against Him anymore.' Her spirits were lighter than at any time since the illness began; she had made the sacrifice, and found herself not sadder but happier. She went back to the bedside, and put her hand on Una's forehead; it was cool and moist. Her pulse was slow and regular, and she was sleeping naturally. The crisis had passed favorably."

Una's illness had brought to the Hawthornes' Roman lodgings a kind of warmth that had nothing to do with the Italian climate. To their door came well-wishers and friends, both new and old. One of these was poet Elizabeth Barrett Browning. The Hawthornes had become friendly with Elizabeth and her even more poetic husband, Robert, during their sojourn in Florence. Sophia was particularly touched by this visit, since a delicate Mrs. Browning "almost never goes upstairs." But the Hawthornes' doctor was not pleased by the soup that the poet left behind. He had all food for the patient prepared to his own prescription. When he sniffed the Browning offering, he said, "Tell Mrs. Browning to write her poesies, and not meddle with my broths for my patient." Another appreciated visitor was an ex-president of the United States. Franklin Pierce was traveling abroad to recover from a disappointing presidency. As soon as he arrived in Rome, he sought out his old college mate. By then, Una had survived the crisis but was still very ill. "I recollect the first evening that Pierce came to our house, sat in the little parlor, in the dusk, listening to the story of Una's illness," Julian Hawthorne wrote. "'Poor child! Poor child!' he said occasionally in a low voice. His sympathy was like something palpable,—strong, warm, and comforting. He said very little, but it was impossible not to feel how much he cared. He knew of his own experience what it was like to lose children. He stayed in Rome several weeks, and he and Hawthorne talked over all their former years and adventures, since they were boys in college together." Of Pierce's visits, as often as three times a day, Sophia wrote home, "I think I owe him, almost my husband's life. He was divinely tender, sweet, sympathizing and helpful."

Back in Concord, the story had a very different ending in the early months of 1858, and it was recorded feelingly in Louisa May Alcott's journal:

> *January, 1858,*—Lizzie is much worse. Dr. G. says there is no hope. A hard thing to hear; but if she is only to suffer, I pray she may go soon. She was glad to know she was to "get well," as she called it, and we tried to bear it bravely for her sake. We gave up plays; Father came home; and Anna took the housekeeping, so that Mother and I could devote ourselves to her. Sad, quiet days in her room, and strange nights keeping up the fire and watching the dear little shadow try to wile away the long sleepless hours without troubling me. She sews, reads, sings softly and lies looking at the fire,—so sweet and patient and so worn, my heart is broken to see the change. I wrote some lines one night on "Our Angel in the House."

> *February,*—A mild month; Betty very comfortable, and we hope a little.

> Lizzie makes little things and drops them out of windows to the school-children, smiling to see their surprise. In the night she tells me to be Mrs. Gamp, when I give her her lunch, and tries to be gay that I may keep up. Dear little saint! I shall be better all my life for these sad hours with you.

March 14th,—My dear Beth died at three this morning, after two years of patient pain. Last week she put her work away, saying the needle was "too heavy." And having given us her few possessions, made ready for the parting in her own simple, quiet way. For two days she suffered much, begging for ether, though its effect was gone. Tuesday she lay in Father's arms and called us around her, smiling contentedly as she said, "All here." I think she bid us good-by then, as she held our hands and kissed us tenderly. Saturday night she slept, and at midnight became unconscious, quietly breathing her life away till three; then, with one last look of the beautiful eyes, she was gone.

A curious thing happened, and I will tell it here, for Dr. G. said it was a fact. A few moments after the last breath came, as Mother and I sat silently watching the shadow fall on the dear, little face, I saw a light mist rise from the body, and float up and vanish in the air. Mother's eyes followed mine, and when I said, "What did you see?" she described the same light mist. Dr. G. said it was the life departing visibly.

For the last time we dressed her in her usual cap and gown, and laid her on her bed,—at rest at last. What she had suffered was seen in the face; for at twenty-three she looked like a woman of forty, so worn was she, and all her pretty hair gone.

On Monday Dr. Huntington read the Chapel service, and we sang her favorite hymn. Mr. Emerson, Henry Thoreau, Sanborn and John Pratt, carried her out of the old home to the new one at Sleepy Hollow chosen by herself. So the first break comes, and I know what death means,— a liberator for her, a teacher for us.

Family and friends speculated that Beth Alcott was too innocent and good for the world she left behind, and the ominous signs of coming catastrophe were confirming. It was no thanks to the Buchanan administration that Kansas would be joining the

Union as an anti-slave state. When two separate conventions sent pro- and anti-slavery constitutions to Congress, the president urged passage of the former. More concerned with proving his policy of "popular sovereignty" than gaining southern support by advancing slavery, Senator Douglas brokered a bill requiring a territory-wide vote in Kansas that resulted in victory for the anti-slavery constitution. Up for reelection in Illinois, Douglas was nevertheless challenged to debate by an upstart lawyer named Abraham Lincoln running for the new Republican Party. Douglas argued that the voters of any state regardless of geographical location had the right to decide the slavery issue and that states of different persuasion could continue to tolerate each other as they had in the past. Lincoln claimed that "a house divided against itself cannot stand," and that "the government cannot endure, permanently half *slave* and half *free*," but that "it will become *all* one thing, or *all* the other." But what put heart into the thinkers of Concord was Lincoln's assertion that slavery was a moral issue. He said that the political difference was "between the men who think slavery a wrong and those who do not think it wrong. The Republican party think it wrong—we think it is a moral, a social and a political wrong." Although Lincoln lost to Douglas, there was real promise that the moral issue would be *the* issue in the national elections in 1860.

Meanwhile, the existence and nature of the moral issue were brought close to home for the people of Concord by another visit from John Brown in the spring of 1859. With Kansas behind him, he was moving onto a national stage, raising funds and making plans to inspire a slave insurrection throughout the South—peaceful if possible, violent if necessary. He was inspirational rather than specific about his plans in the Concord speech, attended by Alcott, Emerson, and Thoreau. After the meeting Alcott had a brief talk with Brown, shook his hand, and went home to write a mysteriously prophetic line in his journal: "This is the man to do the Deed." Alcott was as surprised as his friends that fall when the news came through of Brown's bloody and unsuccessful raid on the federal arsenal at Harpers Ferry, Virginia, where he hoped to get weapons for the intended insurrection. It was not the deed that they had anticipated, and yet, unlike most public figures of every state and party, they did not repudiate him.

Thoreau was the most vocal and the most passionate defender of a man whom he thought to be a martyr when the first reports said that Brown had been killed by a U.S. Marine force led by Colonel Robert E. Lee. For any who cared to hear, Thoreau said, "When a government puts forth its strength on the side of injustice, as ours (especially today) to maintain slavery and kill the liberators of the slave, what a merely brute, or worse than brute, force it is seen to be!" When in fact it turned out that Brown was alive, though severely wounded, and was summarily tried and sentenced to death, Thoreau announced that he would deliver in Town Hall on October 30 "A Plea for Captain Brown." He had to ring the bell himself to summon the people since nobody else offered to do so. By using the military title that Brown's followers bestowed on him, Thoreau could liken Brown to a soldier under orders—in this case his own perception of what God wanted him to do. Brown was, said Thoreau, "a transcendentalist above all, a man of ideas and principles."

Thoreau's plea was "received here by our Concord folks with great favor," according to Alcott, but it fell upon deaf ears in Richmond and Washington. On the day that the execution was carried out, December 2, 1859, there was a quiet service for John Brown in Concord at which Alcott, Emerson, Sanborn, and Thoreau all gave readings. Emerson nearly lost his emotional cool when he called Brown a "new saint" who would "make the gallows glorious like the cross." It had been five troubling years since Thoreau first stood up before a crowd at Framingham to proclaim his sympathy for "Disunionists" in the cause of ending slavery, and the movement had come to this. Little wonder why Alcott would find himself telling his journal that, despite getting the selectmen's permission "to have the bell of the first parish tolled at the time Captain Brown is being hung, the bells are not rung. I think not more than one or two of Brown's friends wished them to be."

9

A Time for Dying

HEARTS WERE LIFTED IN CONCORD, MASSACHUSETTS, early in that critical election year of 1860 when they learned of Abraham Lincoln's visit to New York in search of the Republican Party's nomination. Despite a bitter February night, some fifteen hundred distinguished New Yorkers went to hear him speak at Cooper Union. He brought them to their feet with his closing call: "Let us have faith that right makes might, and in that faith, let us, to the end, dare to do our duty as we understand it." And he made his sentiments clear on the Sunday following by crossing over to Brooklyn to attend the church that had sent the "Beecher's Bibles" to Kansas. With the prospect that a man of that persuasion might be elected and put moral backbone into the nation's leadership, the thinkers of Concord turned thankfully to more personal and pleasant affairs.

It was a true spring in the lives of the inhabitants of Orchard House. At long last and at age sixty, Bronson Alcott had a job that was perfectly suited to his ambitions and tastes. He was superintendent of Concord Schools. On his rounds about the time of Lincoln's speech, he stopped at the village post office and picked up a copy of the March *Atlantic Monthly*, which featured a story by daughter Louisa May entitled "Love and Self-Love" that should, as he wrote in his journal, "encourage and lead her to some appreciation of the fair destiny that awaits her if she will be true to her gifts as she has begun." But the climax of their joy came in May when, on the Alcotts' thirtieth wedding anniversary, their oldest daughter, Anna, was married to John Pratt. It was, in Alcott's words, "a day of fair omens, sunny after showers of days past. Apple blossoms luxuriant, and a company of true and real persons present to grace the occasion." That company included Thoreau and the Emersons. Although Louisa May's journal account reflected the same kind of joy, she could not refrain from indulging in a bit of sisterly jealousy: "Mr. Emerson kissed her, and I thought the honor would make even matrimony endurable, for he is the god of my idolatry."

For Thoreau and Emerson, the wedding provided a pleasant break in their concentration on self-appointed tasks. Thoreau at this time was described by his observant friend and neighbor, Ellery Channing, as being "busy as a shoemaker." He had taken over running the family pencil business following the death of his father that winter and continued being involved in surveying, building, planting projects, wherever and whenever he found himself needed. But his heart was in an ongoing effort to observe, measure, and record the development process in nature as seen in leaves, crystals, trees. "I confess that I love to be convinced of the inexhaustible vitality of Nature. I would rather that my body should be buried in a soil thus wide awake than in a mere inert and dead earth," he wrote of this preoccupation.

Emerson's occupation was, as always in Alcott's view, "emancipating the mind of his own time from the errors and dreams of past ages." At this particular point in his time, he was readying for the press a new book of essays entitled *Conduct of Life*. In this work, Emerson was endeavoring to look above and beyond the current state of the nation that had been engaging so much of his thought and time. Out of his own experience and extensive reading, he wanted to give his readers food for thought about managing their own lives. Just as Emerson's lectures were thinking out loud, his essays were thinking in print. He considered thinking the hardest kind of work, and work was one of the many subjects he treated in *Conduct of Life*:

I look on that man as happy, who, when there is a question of success, looks into his work for reply, not into the market, not into opinion, not into patronage. In every variety of human employment, in the mechanical and in the fine arts, in navigation, in farming, in legislating, there are among them numbers who do their work perfunctorily, as we say, or just to pass the time, and as badly as they dare,—there are the working men, on whom the burden of the business falls,—those who love work, and love to see it rightly done, who finish their task for its own sake; and the state and the world is happy, that has the most of such finishers. The world will always do justice at last to such finishers; it cannot otherwise. He who has acquired the ability, may wait securely the occasion of making it felt and appreciated, and know that it will not loiter. Men talk as if victory were something fortunate. Work is victory. Wherever work is done, victory is obtained.

Some of his thinking was heretical, as on religion:

The religion which is to guide and fulfil the present and coming ages, whatever else it be, must be intellectual. The scientific mind must have a faith which is science. "There are two things," said Mahomet, "which I abhor, the learned in his infidelities, and the fool in his devotions." Our times are impatient of both, and specially of the last. Let us have nothing now which is not its own evidence. There is surely enough for the heart and imagination in the religion itself. Let us not be pestered with assertions and half truths, with emotions and snuffle. There will be a new church founded on moral science, at first cold and naked, a babe in the manger again, the algebra and mathematics of ethical law, the church of men to come, without shawms, or psaltry, or sackbut; but it will have heaven and earth for its beams and rafters; science for symbol and illustration; it will fast enough gather beauty, music, picture, poetry.

Or on immortality:

Of immortality, the soul, when well employed, is incurious. It is so well, that it is sure it will be well. It asks no questions of the Supreme Power. The son of Antiochus asked his father, when he would join battle? "Dost thou fear," replied the King, "that thou only in all the army wilt not hear the trumpet?" 'Tis a higher thing to confide, that, if it is best we should live, we shall live,—'tis higher to have this conviction than to have the lease of indefinite centuries and millenniums and aeons. Higher than the question of our duration is the question of our deserving. Immortality will come to such as are fit for it, and he who would be a great soul in future, must be a great soul now.

Aware that most men are more concerned with success in this life than with life ever after, Emerson had this to say:

Concentration is the secret of strength in politics, in war, in trade, in short in all management of human affairs. One of the high anecdotes of the world is the reply of Newton to the inquiry, "how he had been able to achieve his discoveries?"—"By always intending my mind." Or if you will have a text from politics, take this from Plutarch: "There was, in the whole city, but one street in which Pericles was ever seen, the street which led to the market-place and the council house. He declined all invitations to banquets, and all gay assemblies and company. During the whole period of his administration, he never dined at the table of a friend." Or if we seek an example from trade,—"I hope," said a good man to Rothschild, "your children are not too fond of money and business; I am sure you would not wish that."—"I am sure I should wish that; I wish them to give mind, soul, heart, and body to business,—that is the way to be happy. It requires a great deal of boldness and a great deal of caution, to make a great fortune, and when you have got it, it requires ten times as much wit to keep it. If I were to listen to all the projects proposed to me, I should ruin myself very soon. Stick to one business, young man.

By June 1860, Concord could boast of another author with another new book on the market with another kind of heresy. The Hawthornes returned to occupy Wayside. Before coming home Hawthorne had gone from Rome to England, where he had stayed long enough to finish a new novel, *The Marble Faun*, and arrange for its publication there and in America. He had concocted a strange and mysterious story set in Italy and reflecting all that he had observed of life and art during his stay. One character is an expatriate artist named Hilda with an "inheritance of New England puritanism" very like his own. She had always been fascinated with the magnificent art to be seen in Rome's holy places, but only personal problems led her to a mind-opening encounter with the religion inspiring the art:

> Restless with her trouble, Hilda now entered upon another pilgrimage among the altars and shrines. She climbed the hundred steps of the Ara Coeli; she trod the broad, silent nave of Saint John Lateran; she stood in the Pantheon, under the round opening in the Dome, through which the blue, sunny sky still gazes down, as it used to gaze when there were Roman deities in the antique niches. She went into every church that rose before her, but not now to wonder at its magnificence, which she hardly noticed, more than if it had been the pine-built interior of a New England meeting-house.
>
> She went (and it was a dangerous errand) to observe how closely and comfortingly the Popish faith applied itself to all human occasions. It was impossible to doubt that multitudes of people found their spiritual advantage in it, who would find none at all in our own formless mode of

worship, which, besides, so far as the sympathy of prayerful souls is concerned, can be enjoyed only at stated and too infrequent periods. But, here, whenever the hunger for divine nutriment came upon the soul, it could on the instant be appeased. At one or another altar, the incense was forever ascending; the mass always being performed, and carrying upward with it the devotion of such as had not words for their own prayer. And yet, if the worshipper had his individual petition to offer, his own heart-secret to whisper below his breath, there were divine auditors ever ready to receive it from his lips; and what encouraged him still more, these auditors had not always been divine, but kept, within their heavenly memories, the tender humility of human experience. Now, a Saint in Heaven, but, once a man on earth!

Hilda saw peasants, citizens, soldiers, nobles, women with bared heads, ladies in their silks, entering the churches, individually, kneeling for moments, or for hours, and directing their inaudible devotions to the shrine of some Saint of their own choice. In his hallowed person, they felt themselves possessed of an own friend in Heaven. They were too humble to approach the Deity directly. Conscious of their unworthiness, they asked the mediation of their sympathizing patron, who, on the score of this ancient martyrdom, and after many ages of celestial life, might venture to talk with the Divine Presence almost as friend to friend. Though dumb before its Judge, even Despair could speak, and pour out the misery of its soul like water, to an advocate so wise to comprehend the case, and eloquent to plead it, and powerful to win pardon, whatever were the guilt. Hilda witnessed what she deemed to be an example of this species of confidence between a young man and his Saint. He stood before the shrine, writhing, wringing his hands, contorting his whole frame, in an agony of remorseful recollection, but finally knelt down to weep and pray. If this youth had been a Protestant, he would have kept all that torture pent up in his heart, and let it burn there till it scared him into indifference.

The Hawthorne returning to Concord was not the Adonis of his honeymoon days. By his own admission, he was graying and "wrinkled with time and trouble." But his next-door neighbor, Alcott, did not notice the change, according to his journal notes for June 28, the day of their arrival: "Evening: We call at Hawthorne's, my wife and I, and see them all. He looking well, and full of thoughts of 'Hillside' [Alcott never accepted Hawthorne's new name for the place] and the repairs he wishes to make on the buildings and improvements generally in the grounds. Asks my suggestions and counsels. I shall delight to assist him and build for him in my rustic way, restoring his arbours if he wishes." On the next evening, Alcott reported, "Eat strawberries and cream at Emerson's with Hawthorne, Thoreau, Sanborn, Hunt and the artist, Keyes, and Cheney—a party made to welcome Hawthorne home to 'Hillside' and Concord."

Despite the warm welcome, Hawthorne quickly reverted to his search for solitude. He did not seek Alcott's help on additions to the house but hired a couple of local carpenters to build a tower with a study on top to which he could retreat, according to his son Julian, who also reported that his father "took few or no long walks after his return to America: Walden Pond (about two miles distant) was the limit of his excursions; and he generally confined himself to his own grounds, except on Sundays, when we all strolled together about the neighboring fields and wood paths. His physical energy was on the wane, and he lost flesh rapidly." Alcott would later complain of never seeing his near neighbor except as a ghostly figure pacing his hilltop alone. When he once confronted Hawthorne and asked why they could not see more of each other, Hawthorne was tactless enough to say that he could not abide Mrs. Alcott. Alcott overlooked even that in his continuing efforts to be friendly. Fortunately, Hawthorne's antisocial

Handsome Hawthorne returned to Concord after his long stay in Europe "wrinkled with time and trouble," as he put it. He was ambivalent about the issues involved in the oncoming civil war, and he was never afterward able to write anything notable, although he struggled to do so.

attitudes did not affect the rest of the family. Julian recalled that he and his sisters enjoyed school dances and picnics and "hospitable entertainment" at the Alcotts' and Emersons' and that "there never was and never will be such a genial Concord—for young people at least."

Alcott could overlook Hawthorne's peevishness because he had more important matters on his mind. The nation's political struggle was intruding on his transcendental meditations. Lincoln had been nominated by the Republican convention in May, and in June the Democratic Party split, with a northern faction nominating Senator Douglas and a southern faction nominating John C. Breckinridge of Kentucky. Although that split almost guaranteed Lincoln's election, there was too much at stake for any serious citizen to count on it. Alcott had a daily reminder of the need for some solution to the slavery question. With Beth's death and Anna's marriage, they had room to spare in Orchard House and

Nathaniel and Sophia Hawthorne pose in front of Wayside with the additions they added after their return to Concord. Hawthorne used the tower more as an escape to pander to his shyness than a place to work. Despite his increasing health problems and reclusive attitude, his family found Concord warm and welcoming.

had given John Brown's daughters refuge as boarders. The result of Alcott's concern was spelled out succinctly in his journal entry for November 6, 1860: "At Town House, and cast my vote for Lincoln and the Republican candidates generally—the first vote I ever cast for a President and State officers."

Emerson's journal entry about the same event declared that the election of Lincoln was "sublime, the pronunciation of the masses of America against Slavery." Thoreau stayed true to form, as noted by Alcott on November 11: "Thoreau is here and discusses the suffrage. Thinks a freeman cannot vote for the President, candidates, etc." Despite these differences in approach to what they regarded as bad government, Alcott and Thoreau were seeing a lot of each other—too much, as some would later claim. In late November, Alcott attended a gathering of the Massachusetts Teachers Association in Boston and caught a cold from "the draughts at the teacher's Meetings" that he passed on to Thoreau when he stopped by to report on the affair. By going out in early December in the rain to count rings on young hickory trees on Fair Haven Hill, Thoreau exacerbated his cold and came down with what he called variously bronchitis or flu so severe that he was mostly housebound for the rest of the winter.

Alcott recovered and plunged into school affairs, as a pleased daughter Louisa May recorded with her usual flair in her journal for February 1861:

> Father had his usual school festival, and Emerson asked me to write a song, which I did. On the 16th the schools all met in the hall (four hundred),—a pretty posy bed, with a border of proud parents and friends. Some of the fogies objected to the names Phillips and John Brown. But Emerson said: "Give it up? No, no; I will read it." Which he did, to my great contentment; for when the great man of the town says, "Do it," the thing is done. So the choir warbled, and the Alcotts were uplifted in their vain minds.
>
> Father was in glory, like a happy shepherd with a large flock of supportive lambs; for all did something. Each school had its badge,—one pink ribbons, one green shoulder-knots, and one wreaths of pop-corn on the curly pates. One school to whom Father read Pilgrim's Progress told the story, one child after another popping up to say his or her part; and at the end a little tot walked forward, saying with a pretty air of wonder,—"And behold it was all a dream."
>
> When all was over, and Father about to dismiss them, F.H., a tall, handsome lad came to him, and looking up confidently to the benign old face, asked "our dear friend Mr. Alcott to accept of Pilgrim's Progress and George Herbert's Poems from the children of Concord, as a token of their love and respect."
>
> Father was much touched and surprised, and blushed and stammered like a boy, hugging the fine books while the children cheered till the roof rung.

His report was much admired, and a thousand copies printed to supply the demand; for it was a new thing to have a report, neither dry nor dull; and teachers were glad of the hints given, making education a part of religion, not a mere bread-making grind for teacher and irksome cram for children.

At the time of this pleasant and peaceful celebration in Concord, the structure of the nation was falling apart. Southern states had begun seceding in January, and two days after Alcott blushingly accepted his presents, the once senator from Mississippi and secretary of war, Jefferson Davis, was sworn in as provisional president of the Confederate States of America, almost a month before Lincoln would take his oath of office in Washington. On April 12, Confederate guns opened fire on Fort Sumter in the mouth of the harbor at Charleston, South Carolina, and days later Concord responded to President Lincoln's call for seventy-five thousand volunteers by sending a troop of forty-five off toward Washington. "A busy time getting them ready, and a sad day seeing them off," wrote Louisa May Alcott in her journal, "for a little town like this we all seem one family in times like these. At the station the scene was very dramatic, as the brave boys went away perhaps never to come back again. I've often longed to see a war, and now I have my wish. I long to be a man; but as I can't fight, I will content myself with working for those who can."

In their public statements and actions, the inhabitants of Orchard House and the Bush left no doubt as to their all-out support of the war. At the Wayside, Julian, too young to enlist, began drilling with his schoolmates in the hope that the war would last long enough to allow him to follow in the footsteps of the "heroes" he had seen off at the station. His father's attitude was more ambivalent. Writing to his friend Horatio Bridge, paymaster of the navy, he said, "The war, strange to say, has had a beneficial effect upon my spirits, which were flagging woefully before it broke out. But it was delightful to share in the heroic sentiment of the time, and to feel that I had a country—a consciousness which seemed to make me young again. One thing, as regards this matter, I regret, and one thing I am glad of, the regrettable thing is that I am too old to shoulder a musket myself, and the joyful thing is that Julian is too young. Though I approve the war as much as any man, I don't quite understand what we are fighting for, or what definite result can be expected. If we pummel the South over so hard, they will love us none the better for it; and even if we subjugate them, our next step should be to cut them adrift. Whatever happens next, I must say that I rejoice that the old Union is smashed. We never were one people, and never really had a country since the Constitution was formed."

As for Thoreau, he seemed to be disenchanted with the whole political process. Alcott described his friend as "impatient with the politicians, the state of the country, the State itself, and with statesmen generally, accuses the Republican party of duplicity." Thoreau himself wrote a friend that "though Lincoln has been president for nearly a month, I continue to feel as if I lived in an interregnum, & we had no government at all." Thoreau's outlook was undoubtedly affected by his health, which had not improved, as hoped, with the coming of spring. He was very clearly dealing with "consumption," and his doctor prescribed a change of climate. He chose to go west, hoping to see the "real frontier," with seventeen-year-old Horace Mann Jr., then a Harvard student, as his companion. He got as far as Mackinac Island, Michigan, making notes and collecting specimens to enlarge his knowledge of natural phenomena on the way, but a friend of Emerson's who met Thoreau in Chicago wrote back that "he would hesitate for an instant now and then, waiting for the right word, or would pause with a pathetic patience to master the trouble in his chest." Thoreau was back in Concord in early summer in worse health than when he left.

The rest of 1861 was a very trying time for almost everyone in the North. Impatient warriors could not understand how their larger army could suffer so many defeats and refuse to take the fight to the enemy. Impatient abolitionists could not understand how

Lincoln did nothing about freeing the slaves. Emerson was particularly distressed by this bit of foot-dragging since his southern-born friend Conway had convinced him that an immediate emancipation declaration would shorten the war. Conway's argument was that when slaves began taking advantage of the declaration and leaving the plantations, Confederate soldiers would desert to go home and take care of their properties. Emerson included this thought in an address he called "American Civilization," and he was invited by Massachusetts senator Charles Sumner and others to deliver it at the Smithsonian Institution in Washington in January 1862 in the hope that the message would reach the right ears in Congress and the White House. As ever, Emerson did not dwell on a single thought in his address but took a sweeping and optimistic look at the conflict in the context of America's destiny.

He told his Washington audience:

The destiny of America is mutual service; labor is the corner-stone of our nationality,—the labor of each for all. In the measure in which a man becomes civilized he is conscious of this, and finds his well-being in the work to which his faculties call him. He coins himself into his labor; turns his day, his strength, his thought, his affection, into some product which remains as the visible sign of his power; to protect that, to secure his past self to his future self, is the object of all government. But there is on this subject a confusion of mind of the Southern people, which lends them to pronounce labor disgraceful, and the well-being of a man to consist in sitting idle and eating the fruit of other men's labor. We have endeavored to hold together these two states of civilization under one law, but in vain; one or the other must give way. America now means opportunity, the widest career to human activities. Shall we allow her existence to be menaced through the literal following of precedents? Why cannot the higher civilization be allowed to extend over the whole country? The

Union party has never been strong enough to kill slavery, but the wish that never had legs long enough to cross the Potomac can do so now. Emancipation is the demand of civilization, the inevitable conclusion reached by the logic of events. The war will have its own way; one army will stand for slavery pure and one for freedom pure, and victory will fall at last where it ought to fall. The march of ideas will be found irresistible, and this mountainous nonsense insulting the daylight will be swept away, though ages may pass in the attempt. But ideas must work through the brains and arms of good and brave men, or they are no better than dreams. There can be no safety until this step is taken.

With Sumner as guide, Emerson was introduced around Washington and most warmly received by Secretary of State William Seward, an abolitionist so fervent that he had lost the Republican nomination to a more moderate man. After an Episcopal church service on Sunday, Seward took Emerson to the White House, where they first had a talk with the Lincoln boys and got a glimpse of the president's domestic life before he appeared. "You have not been to church today," Seward chided him. "No," Lincoln admitted and then confessed that he had spent the time reading Senator Sumner's speech on the *Trent* affair. An American warship had boarded the British ship *Trent*, bound for England, in the Bahamas and taken two southern agents, Mason and Slidell, off it. Lincoln reported that he had been congratulated by both England and Spain for releasing the men to Great Britain, thus easing international tensions. Then he turned to Emerson and said, "Oh, Mr. Emerson, I once heard you say in a lecture, that a Kentuckian seems to say by his air and manners, 'Here am I; if you don't like me, the worse for you.'" It was said with a chuckle and much appreciated by Emerson, who was quite aware that Mrs. Lincoln came from one of the first families of Kentucky and had blood relatives fighting on the Confederate side.

"The President impressed me more favorably than I had hoped," Emerson wrote in his journal. "A frank, sincere, well-meaning man, with a lawyer's habit of mind, good clear statement of his fact; correct enough, not vulgar, as described, but with a sort of boyish cheerfulness, or that kind of sincerity and jolly good meaning that our class meetings on Commencement Days show, in telling our old stories over. When he has made his remark, he looks up at you with great satisfaction, and shows all his white teeth, and laughs." Emerson headed home with intimations—but no promise—of emancipation to come, and he remained a defender of Lincoln, saying, "If Mr. Lincoln appear slow and timid in proclaiming emancipation, and, like a bashful suitor, shows the way to deny him, it is to be remembered that he is not free as a poet to state what he thinks ideal or desirable, but must take a considered step, which he can keep. Otherwise his proclamation would be a weak bravado, without value or respect."

A month after Emerson's return, Hawthorne took a trip to Washington in an effort to lift his spirits and benefit his health. He had been virtually unable to write since the start of the war, and there was a promise from James Fields of using an article in the *Atlantic Monthly* about his observations. On Sunday, March 16, he addressed an informal report to daughter Una: "I have never a moment's time to write, for I move about all day, and am engaged all the evening; and if ever there is a vacant space, I want to employ it in writing my journal, which keeps terribly behindhand. But I suppose mamma and the rest of you remember there is such a person, and wish to know what I am about. I went up yesterday to Harper's Ferry (a distance of eighty miles from Washington) by invitation of the directors of a railroad; so that I made the whole journey without expense, and partook of two cold collations besides. To be sure, I paid my expenses with a speech; but it was a very short one. I shall not describe what I saw, because very likely I shall print it in the 'Atlantic Monthly'; but I made acquaintance with some rebel prisoners and liked them very much. It rained horribly all day, and the mud was such as nobody in New England can conceive of. I had shaken hands with Uncle Abe, and have seen various notabilities, and am infested with people who want to exhibit me as a lion. I have seen a camp, and am going in a few days to Manassas, if the mud of the Sacred Soil will permit. Tell mamma that the outcry opened against General McClellan, since the enemy's retreat from Manassas, is really terrible, and almost universal; because it is found that we might have taken their fortifications with perfect ease six months ago, they being defended chiefly by wooden guns. Unless he achieves something wonderful within a week, he will be removed from command, and perhaps shot,—at least I hope so; I never did more than half believe in him." His article, as written and published that summer, would reflect his disgust with the way the war was going and his sympathy for rebels and would not go down well at all with the patriots of the North, by whom he was surrounded in Concord.

About the only person in Concord for whom Hawthorne really cared, Henry Thoreau, was gradually dying all that spring. He kept his wits about him, working when energy permitted on putting his affairs in order and receiving friends and neighbors. Sam Staples, the man who had once jailed him, stopped by and reported to Emerson that he had never seen anyone "dying with so much pleasure and peace." Snatches of his conversation revealed long-held secrets, such as when he told his sister that he had "always loved" Ellen Sewall. He also showed flashes of humor. When he was asked if he had made his peace with God, he quipped, "I didn't know we had ever quarreled." He could be philosophical. One old friend said tactlessly, "You seem so near the brink of the dark river that I almost wonder how the opposite shore may appear to you." A weary Thoreau said, "One world at a time."

Henry David Thoreau slipped away from his first world peacefully on the morning of May 6, 1862. He was only forty-four. Alcott bustled around making arrangements for a funeral in the church from which Thoreau had resigned at Emerson's insistence and interment in the New Burying Ground, from which his body would later be removed to Sleepy Hollow Cemetery. At the church,

Emerson delivered the eulogy, in which he said that "his soul was made for the noblest society; he had in a short life exhausted the capabilities of this world; wherever there is knowledge, wherever there is virtue, wherever there is beauty, he will find a home." Thoreau had impressive obituaries in the New York and Boston papers. The *Boston Transcript* reported "a large company of his townspeople, with some votive pilgrims from parts beyond" at the funeral, and added, "And though the church bell—after affecting old custom—tolled the forty-four years he had numbered, we could not deem that *he* was dead whose ideas and sentiments were so vividly alive in our souls."

Those who knew him best would regret that Thoreau had not lived a few months more to become aware of the brightening prospects in his old world. The Union forces began winning battles that spring, mostly in the west under General Ulysses S. Grant, and when the army in the east scored a victory at Antietam Lincoln lived up to Emerson's faith in him by issuing a proclamation that slaves would be free in the rebellious states as of January 1, 1863. One of the few people not cheered by these events was Hawthorne, whose deteriorating health was reflected in his spirits. He was having trouble writing and was starting and putting aside efforts at a new novel. He did, however, manage to put together articles that he had written on England into a volume called *Our Old Home*. A sentence from the preface reflected his mood: "The Present, the Immediate, the Actual, has proved too potent for me. It takes away not only my scanty faculty, but even my desire for imaginative composition, and leaves me sadly content to scatter a thousand peaceful fantasies upon the hurricane that is sweeping us all along with it, possibly into a limbo where our nation and its polity may be as literally the fragments of a shattered dream as my unwritten romance."

Hawthorne's wife, Sophia, was either in denial or trying to rise above her husband's gloom. In a letter dated December 11, 1862, to Una, who was visiting relatives to recover from a recurrence of her "Roman fever," Sophia wrote, "Great events seem thickening here. Louisa Alcott has had her summons to the Washington

Hospitals; and Abby came to ask me about some indelible ink she had, and I offered to do anything I could for Louisa. She said if I could mark her clothes it would assist very much. So I went over, in the divine afternoon, and marked till dusk, and finished all she had. Mrs. Alcott says she shall feel helpless without Louisa, and Mr. Alcott says he sends his only son. Louisa is determined to make the soldiers jolly, and takes all of Dickens that she has, and games. At supper-time Julian came in with the portentous news that the battle has at last begun, and Fredericksburg is on fire from our guns. So Louisa goes into the very mouth of the war. Now, to-day, is the Bible Fair. I carried to Mrs. Alcott early this morning some maizena blanc-mange which Ann made for papa, and turned out of the sheaf-mould very nicely. . . . Papa has not a good appetite, and eats no dinners except a little potato. But he is trying to write, and locks himself into the library and pulls down the blinds."

During 1863, it became apparent that emancipation was not demoralizing the Confederate armies as Emerson had hoped, although a regiment of free blacks—the 54th Massachusetts—was organized in Boston, and a regiment of escaping slaves—the First North Carolina Colored Volunteers—was brought together under the command of Colonel James Beecher, Ward Beecher's brother and a minister turned warrior. Both regiments were in combat before the year was out. Lincoln was almost frantically changing generals in command of the Army of the Potomac, which seemed in stalemate with General Robert E. Lee's Army of Northern Virginia until Lee broke through into northern territory at Gettysburg, Pennsylvania. When the then current northern commander, General Meade, drove him back but failed to follow, Lincoln was in near despair, which may account for the brevity of what was thought to be his disappointing address at the dedication of a cemetery at the battlefield. Only in the west where Grant and naval forces led by Rear Admiral David G. Farragut were opening up the Mississippi River was the news arriving in Concord favorable.

As to be expected, war was beginning to make life difficult on the home front. In a letter to brother William, Emerson wrote that war "has found me in quite as poor a plight as the rest of the

Americans. Not a penny from my books which usually yield five or six hundred a year . . . no dividends from the banks . . . almost all income from lectures has quite ceased. Meantime we are trying to be as unconsuming as candles under an extinguisher. . . . But far better that this grinding should go on, bad and worse, than we be driven by any impatience into a hasty peace, or any peace restoring the old rottenness." To remedy this situation, Emerson pushed harder on his lecturing in 1863, an effort that was given a boost by Lincoln's appointing him to the Board of Visitors at the military academy at West Point. Bronson Alcott had to make a trip to Washington to bring his "only son" at the front home when Louisa May fell ill due to strain and infection from her work as a nurse. Beginning to be the only real moneymaker in the family, she was able to turn her experience into income by getting out a book called *Hospital Sketches*, about which her proud father wrote that it was "likely to be popular, the subject and style of treatment alike commending it to the reader, and to the Army especially. I see nothing in the way of a good appreciation of Louisa's merits as a woman and a writer. Nothing could be more surprising to her or agreeable to us."

Things were not going as well at the Wayside next door, where Hawthorne was becoming ever more isolated and miserable. In early 1864, Sophia wrote to a friend that Nathaniel had "really been very ill all winter, and not well, by any means, for a much longer time; not ill in bed, but miserable on a lounge or sofa, and quite unable to write a word, even a letter, and lately unable to read." Having been, in her words, "immaculately well all his life," Hawthorne refused to see a doctor. But in March he did agree to try a trip south with William Ticknor in the hope that it might pick him up as their Washington trip had done two years before. From the Astor House in New York, Ticknor sent back an encouraging report that Hawthorne was "looking better, and says he feels very well. He seems afraid he shall eat too much, as he says his appetite is good." But in Philadelphia, the first sunshine of the trip led them to leave their rooms in the Continental Hotel on April 7 for a ride through Fairmount Park. It was still chilly and Ticknor had given his coat to his ailing friend, with the result that he caught cold. A doctor was called in and prescribed pills and powders that Hawthorne tried to administer faithfully, but Ticknor died three days later. It was a devastating experience to a man in such bad shape that he thought death had "made a mistake and claimed the wrong man." When he finally got back to Concord, he could not hire a carriage at the station and literally staggered to Wayside, where he frightened Sophia by being "so haggard, so white; so deeply scored with pain and fatigue was the face, so much more ill than I ever saw him before."

Something had to be done for him. Remembering how tender Frank Pierce had been with Una in Rome, Sophia wrote to him about Nathaniel's condition. Pierce immediately proposed meeting Hawthorne in Boston and taking him on a trip through New Hampshire in the pleasant weather of early May. Sophia accompanied her husband to Boston, having written secretly to James and Annie Fields, who were hosting them, to arrange "in some ingenious way" for Dr. Oliver Wendell Holmes to see Nathaniel. As an old literary friend, it was natural for Dr. Holmes to call on Hawthorne and suggest a walk, during which he observed that Hawthorne "seemed to have shrunken in all his dimensions, and faltered along with an uncertain, feeble step, as if every movement were an effort." He got Hawthorne to admit that he was having a lot of abdominal discomfort but could make no more accurate diagnosis than to tell Annie Fields that "the shark's tooth is upon him."

Sophia had used good judgment in calling upon Pierce and trusting what she called their "boy associations." The two men had one of those fortunate friendships that start in youth and survive despite differences in matters like politics that develop with age. At some cost to himself, Hawthorne had very recently demonstrated his loyalty to that friendship by dedicating *Our Old Home* to Pierce, who was widely viewed throughout the North as being disloyal to the cause. Whether they even discussed politics is doubtful, and one of the values in this friendship was that they could be silent together. They had just such a silent carriage ride one afternoon, during which, as Pierce told it, Hawthorne's eye "was quick to catch every object striking or beautiful." When he did break silence, Hawthorne, recalling Thackeray's death, said, "What a boon it would be, if when life draws to a close one could pass away without a struggle." Hawthorne was granted that boon on May 19, 1864, at the Pemigewasset House in Plymouth, New Hampshire. As had become his practice, Pierce left the door between their rooms open when they went to bed early the night before so that he could check on his friend. At midnight, Pierce found Hawthorne sleeping "in a perfectly natural position, like a child with his right hand under his cheek"; at three in the morning, he found him in the same position but lifeless. "He had passed from natural sleep to that from which there is no earthly waking—without the slightest struggle—evidently without moving a muscle," Pierce wrote. Hawthorne was sixty years old.

Another funeral for a man who seldom, if ever, darkened its door was held in the Concord church. Pierce sat with the family, and pallbearers included, besides Alcott and Emerson, such literary lights as Dr. Holmes, James Fields, James Russell Lowell, and college classmate Henry Wadsworth Longfellow, who described the day as "all sunshine and blossoms and the song of birds. You cannot imagine anything at once more sad and beautiful." The minister who had married the Hawthornes, James Freeman Clarke, led the service. As recorded by Emerson, Clarke said that Hawthorne "had done more justice than any other to the shades of life, shown a sympathy with the crime in our nature, &, like Jesus, was the friend of sinners." Hawthorne was buried in Sleepy Hollow Cemetery on a hilltop and under the pines, a place very like the hill behind his Wayside where he had so often sought solitude.

In their written remarks on their departed friend and neighbor, both Alcott and Emerson expressed bafflement at the man's reserve. Emerson thought that the minister should have stressed "a tragic element in the event—a painful solitude which, I suppose, could no longer be endured, & he died of it. I have found his death a surprise & disappointment. I thought him a greater man than any of his works betray, that there was still a great deal of work in him, & that he might one day show a pure power.

It would have been a happiness, doubtless to both of us, to have come into habits of unreserved discourse." Alcott wrote that "there was something of strangeness even in his cherished intimacies, as if he set himself afar from all and from himself with the rest; he most diffident of men; as coy as a maiden, he could only be won by some cunning artifice, his reserve was so habitual, his isolation so entire, the solitude so vast. How distant people were from him, the world they lived in, how he came to know so much about them, by what stratagem he got into his own house or left it, was a marvel. Fancy fixed, he was not to be jostled from himself for a moment, his mood was so persistent. There he was in twilight, there he stayed."

Less than a year later, Concord would be in mourning again—this time for a distant friend. In his journal of April 15, 1865, Alcott wrote, "Appalling news of Pres. Lincoln's assassination in the Washington theater last night, by Booth the actor. Sec. Seward also stabbed and his sons, nor likely to survive. The country is in woe, all men sorrowing at this calamity. The Chief Magistrate falls a martyr to his adherence to justice and republicanism. The sacrifice is doubtless to knit us in closer and more religious bonds to God and the right, and redound to the preservation of our national honor and glory. None but the hand of a traitor to liberty and the foe of mankind could have struck this blow at the life of both. See Emerson, who feels smitten with shame at the event." Four days later he would add, "At the National Funeral. The Town all at the Church."

As the town's leading citizen and a featured speaker at this service, Emerson said of Abraham Lincoln, "He is the true history of the American people in his time. Step by step, he walked before them, slow with their slowness, quickening his march by theirs, the true representative of this continent; an entirely public man, father of his country, the pulse of twenty millions throbbing in his heart, the thought of their minds articulated by his tongue." Victory had come before this death; this man had not let the people of Concord, or anywhere else in the nation, down.

10

A Long Good-bye

AFTER THE DEATH OF NATHANIEL HAWTHORNE, Bronson Alcott noted in his journal, "Fair figures one by one are fading from sight. Thoreau, once the central figure in our landscape, has disappeared from it; and Hawthorne no longer traverses his hill-top near my house. Only Emerson and Channing remain of our village circle. I meet the first familiarly, though seldomer than I could wish, but catch no more of the last named than a glance as he passes by my door once in a long while, or crosses my track in the streets." It would not be long before Alcott would discover to his dismay that the figure he had relied upon so long for intellectual stimulation and financial support was also fading. The long and smiling decline of Ralph Waldo Emerson began shortly after the end of the Civil War, as if his major mission of spreading freedom from old fears and concepts had been accomplished.

Before the beginning of the long ending, however, Emerson enjoyed a kind of climax of rewarding personal and professional events. For some years the Emerson family had been adopted by a wealthy businessman, John Forbes, who entertained them every summer at his place in Naushon on the shore. The happy result was that in the fall of 1865, Emerson's younger daughter, Edith, was married to the scion of the Forbes family, Colonel William Forbes. In 1866 Emerson was given an honorary doctor of laws degree by Harvard, the university that had shunned him for so long, and in 1867 he was invited once more to deliver the Phi Beta Kappa oration at Harvard and made an overseer of Harvard College. In that year, too, he delivered eighty lectures, the most in any year of his career. But it was the last year of Emerson's working life, according to his son Edward, who had graduated from Harvard and become a physician.

In those postwar years, increasing involvement with their matured children and grandchildren would begin to take the place of their own work and ambitions for both Alcott and Emerson, and there is a notable lack of reference to public affairs in what became known as the Gilded Age in their letters and journals. Alcott lost his job as school superintendent in 1865, but the slack was more than taken up by Louisa May, whose book on her hospital experiences had been a good seller, as her father had foreseen, and who would top that with the publication of *Little Women* in 1868. Older daughter Anna was providing grandchildren to brighten their days with visits to the Orchard House, and youngest daughter May, pursuing her artistic interests in Europe, found love and marriage. Alcott himself was reaping psychological, if not financial, rewards by conducting his "conversations" in the West where transplanted New Englanders hungered for a taste of the old culture.

Edward Emerson may have dated his father's decline from 1867, because in that year Emerson read to his son his poem "Terminus," with moving lines like these:

> It is time to be old,
> To take in sail:—
> The god of bounds,
> Who sets to seas a shore,
> Came to me in his fatal rounds
> And said, "No more!" . . .
> As the bird trims her to the gale,
> I trim myself to the storm of time,
> I man the rudder, reef the sail,
> Obey the voice at eve obeyed at prime:

"Lowly faithful, banish fear,
Right onward drive unharmed;
The port, well worth the cruise, is near,
And every wave is charmed."

The waves coming Emerson's way after he wrote the poem were indeed charmed. In 1871, the closer ties with the Forbes family brought about a trip by private Pullman car all the way to California with a party made up by John Forbes. In addition to enjoying the spectacular scenery and interesting people he met, such as the naturalist John Muir, Emerson by all reports relished the food—pie, if possible, for any meal—wine, and cigars provided by his host. With his optimistic nature, Emerson always welcomed new sights, experiences, inventions, and thoughts. Change was likely to be for the better in his evolutionary view. He wrote a confirming journal entry in the year of that trip: "In my lifetime have been wrought five miracles; 1, the Steamboat; 2, the Railroad; 3, the Electric Telegraph; 4, the application of the Spectograph to astronomy; 5, the Photograph;—five miracles which have altered the relations of nations to each other. Add cheap postage; and the mowing-machine and the horse-rake. A corresponding power has been given to manufactures by the machine for pegging shoes, and the power-loom, and the power-press of printers. And in dentistry and in surgery, Dr. Jackson's discovery of Anaesthesia. [This was Lidian's brother, who claimed to have discovered ether, as did a host of others, but Emerson was loyal to the family.] It only needs to add the power which, up to this hour, eludes all human ingenuity, namely, a rudder to the balloon, to give us dominion of the air, as well as of the sea and land. But the account is not complete until we add the discovery of Oersted, of the identity of Electricity and Magnetism, and the generalization of that conversion by its application to light, heat and gravitation. The geologist has found the correspondence of the age of stratified remains to the ascending scale of structure in animal life. Add now, the daily predictions of the weather for the next twenty-four hours for North America, by the Observatory in Washington."

Not long after that pleasant trip, a totally charmless wave hit the Emersons. As recounted by Edward, "About half past five in the morning of July 24 [1872, my father] was waked by the crackling of fire, and saw a light in the closet, which was next the chimney. He sprang up, and, not being able to reach the part that was in flames, ran down partly dressed to the front gate and called out for help. He was heard at a considerable distance, and answered instantly. The neighbors came running in from all sides, and, finding it too late to save the house, applied themselves to removing the books and manuscripts and then the furniture, which was done with so much promptitude and skill and by such a concourse of persons eager to help that, of the movables, but little of value was destroyed or even injured; hardly anything except some papers in the garret where the fire began. One of his kind townsmen was in the chambers and barely escaped when the roof fell in. By half past eight the fire was out; the four walls yet standing, but the roof gone and the upper parts much injured. It had been raining in the night and everything was soaked; a circumstance which saved the trees Emerson had planted close to the house, but also the cause of many colds and rheumatisms. Emerson himself had a feverish attack from walking about in the rain, partially clad, in his solicitude about the letters and papers from the garret, which were carried about far and wide by the wind."

Edward, who was interning in a London hospital at the time, reconstructed his account later from family memories, but Concord's next most famous writer, Louisa May Alcott, set down a vivid and immediate eyewitness report in a letter to a friend:

> We had a topsy turvy day at the fire. I saved some valuable papers for my Ralph, & most of their furniture, books and pictures were safe. The upper story is all gone & the lawn strewed with wrecks of beds, books & clothes.
>
> They all take it very coolly & in a truly Emersonian way. Ellen says, she only regrets not selling the old papers & rags up garret. Mrs. E. floats about trying to find her clothes, & Mr. E. beams affably upon the world & remarks

with head cocked up like a sparrow—"I now see my library under a new aspect."

He looked pathetically funny this morning wandering about in his night gown, pants, old coat & no hose. His dear bald head lightly covered with his best hat, & an old pair of rubbers wobbling on his Platonic feet.

Our entry is full of half burnt papers & books, & the neighbors are collecting the clothes of the family nicely mixed up with pots & pans, works of art & cinders. Sad but funny. The house was insured & will be built right up at once. "Our turn next," Ma darkly predicts.

Cousin Elizabeth Ripley invited the Emersons to stay at the Old Manse, and Judge Hoar arranged for Emerson to have a room in the courthouse for an office. Insurance or no, within days friends raised some fifteen thousand dollars to help with restoration of the Bush and to send Emerson abroad with daughter Ellen as companion and guide to recuperate from the shock. Although he was having increasing difficulty in finding the right word to say what he wanted to say and experiencing lapses of memory, Emerson was refreshed by the trip, which took them from England through Europe to Egypt and lasted nearly a year. In England they got to see Edward— looking "gaunt" to his sister—and Una Hawthorne, who had accompanied her mother to London after her father's death and was staying on to do settlement work even though her mother had died in 1871. Emerson's old friend Carlyle, very hale and hearty at seventy-seven, greeted Waldo with a bear hug, and they exchanged two hours' worth of memories. Among other notables they met were Gladstone, John Ruskin, and Charles Dodgson, who, as Lewis Carroll, wrote *Alice in Wonderland*. But by the spring of 1873 it was time to return to Concord and a welcome surprise, described by Alcott in his journal entry for May 27:

The village bells announce Emerson's coming by the 12 train. Then comes a telegram, that he will arrive here at 3:30 p.m.

The procession in carriages and on foot await him at the Station. Mr. Hudson receives and conducts him to the barouche. Sanborn conducts Ellen, and Mrs. Forbes and family take their seats in a second carriage.

Mr. and Mrs. Sanborn, Louisa and myself, take our places in the procession of carriages following the Concord band, Judge Hoar, Mr. Reynolds and Mrs. Hoar beside us, and other carriages abreast behind. Then Emerson and Ellen, Will. Forbes, in their open barouche, the school children and footmen in the rear,—All march down Main Street and Lexington to the triumphal arch over the street by his gate. He passes between rows of children singing "Home Sweet Home" and other melodies. After alighting and meeting his family within, he reappears at his gate and thanks the neighbors for "this trick of sympathy to catch an old gentleman returned from his wanderings, being unmistakably the old blood surviving to compliment him." The whole company then give him three hearty cheers and retire, leaving him to the privacy of his home. Thus the whole village honor their returned townsman, and it is good to see the enthusiasm illuminating their faces as they look and shout lustily at his gate.

'Tis a charming spectacle. Whatever doubts any may have had respecting its agreeableness to him, were instantly dissipated by the hearty response and cheer with which he returned this expression of his townsmen's regards. It was a surprise to him, "What meant this gathering? Was it a public day?" Ellen could not contain her joy at the compliment thus shown her father. Standing in her carriage, she smiled thanks all around to the friends waving their handkerchiefs, all happy to catch a glance from her eye. Both seemed in fine health, browned by travel, and in the familiar spot again. The prettiest sight was the gate, the children singing as the open barouche passed under the arch, ornamented with laurels running up the columns, and the word "Welcome" surmounting it. I did not hear his speech distinctly, but trust someone gifted with a faithful memory will preserve it.

It is a novelty in the history of this our historic revolutionary village, this honoring of scholars publicly. It stirs the latent patriotism which has slumbered unfelt perhaps in the old citizens, descendants of the patriots of 19th April, and now rekindled at the fame of their townsman.

Although Emerson had given up lecturing, he continued to make an appearance on ceremonial occasions by reading from some previous speech or essay. An invitation that he could not turn down came from the committee staging a celebration of the hundredth anniversary of "the shot heard round the world" on April 19, 1875. For an occasion like this, he felt obliged to struggle with creating something new. For the last speech he would ever write he managed to come up with a very novel thought about how and why the Revolutionary War came about:

In the year 1775 we had many enemies and many friends in England, but our one benefactor was King George the Third. The time had arrived for the political severance of America, that it might play its part in the history of this globe, and the inscrutable divine Providence gave an insane king to England. In the resistance of the Colonies, he alone was immovable on the question of force. England was so dear to us that the Colonies could only be absolutely disunited by violence from England, and only one man could compel the resort to violence. Parliament wavered, but the king had the insanity of one idea; he was immovable, he insisted on the impossible, so the army was sent, America was instantly united, and the Nation born.

This anniversary year was a good one for Bronson Alcott. He returned that spring from a six-month tour of the West, during which he had held "conversations" in twenty-eight towns, to find that he had been elected an honorary member of Phi Beta Kappa at Harvard. This prompted a memory: "I have a very pleasant and flattering reminiscence of my first introduction to Harvard College. It was on Phi Beta Kappa Day, and soon after my becoming acquainted with Emerson in 1835. The usual procession of members of the Fraternity was being formed to pass into the Church where the annual exercises were held. Standing near Emerson and dubious as to whether I should follow after the procession and find a seat, he suddenly seized my arm, saying, 'We will not mince matters. You are a member by right of genius,' and he took me willingly along with the rest to a seat near the Orator, receiving my thanks for this unexpected generosity."

Although continuing forty years later, the relationship with Emerson was no longer as supportive, as evidenced by Alcott's journal entry for May 1, 1875:

Home is home; yet I should enjoy a wider and more intimate association than opens for me here in my immediate neighborhood and throughout New England. Life seems a little tame after the closer fellowships of the last months in the West. With Longfellow and Johnson at Cambridge the other day we had snatches of conversation only too short, and which rendered my last evening with Emerson, by contrast, somewhat disappointing. The old themes and the new dragged more heavily. Was I still the visionary enthusiast, whom he must check by his moderated sense and less hopeful mood? Or was he in the subjunctive? Enthusiasts carry their ideals into age, themselves youthful still. Is my Tithonous being touched by age? To suspect this were almost an impiety. Yet my friend complains of growing old, says that his memory is gone, and that his Diary has few entrances in these late days. Does he exaggerate, as the rhetorician must? I have known not a single scholarly acquaintance whose memory of words was ready and retentive like his. His mortification must be extreme if the facts be as he states. I observe, however, in his conversation, how aptly he suggests by circumlocution his loss, his opulent vocabulary serving the while.

Let us concede the fact that we are ancients unmistakably. If one plead to infirmity of memory, the other may to that of hearing, though both may still attempt fellowship with satisfaction. I should add the qualifying circumstance that Emerson falls latterly into his more subdued tones in conversation and renders our intercourse the less satisfactory to myself.

Alcott was in denial about his friend's problem, but the members of his family were not. Son Edward wrote that

the decay of some of the vital machinery began to make itself felt in ways that can not be denied. He began to find extraordinary difficulty in recalling names, or the right word in conversation. By degrees the obstruction increased, until he was forced at times to paraphrase his meaning, and to indicate common things—a fork or an umbrella— by pantomimic representation, or by a figure of speech; often unintentionally, as one day, when he had taken refuge from the noontide glare under the shade of a tree, he said, in a casual way to a companion, who was sitting in the sun, "Isn't there too much heaven on you there?" Meeting him one day in the street in Boston, seemingly at a loss for something, I asked him where he was going. "To dine (he said) with an old and very dear friend. I know where she lives, but I hope she won't ask me her name," and then went on to describe her as "the mother of the wife of the young man—tall man—who speaks so well," and so on until I guessed whom he meant. For himself, he took a humorous view of his case. Once, when he wanted an umbrella, he said, "I can't tell its name, but I can tell its history. Strangers take it away." But the disability led him at last to avoid occasions of conversation with persons with whom he was not intimate, thinking it unfair to them. He spoke of himself as a man who had lost his wits, and was thereby absolved for anything he might do or omit, only he must learn to confine himself to his study, "where I can still read with intelligence."

People who did not see Emerson regularly were likely to rely on their memory of his cool competence and press him into service. This would account for why he was called upon to give aid and comfort to the Alcott family when May, far away in Europe, was sick with fever and dying after giving birth in December 1879 to a daughter she had named Louisa. Knowing that her sturdy mother had died in 1877 and that Louisa May was ailing from overwork on her books, May instructed her husband to contact Mr. Emerson if she did not recover. As ever the best reporter of family doings, Louisa May recorded Emerson's involvement in her journal:

> "*Wednesday, 31st.*—A dark day for us. A telegram from Ernest to Mr Emerson tells us "May is dead." Anna has gone to B.; Father to the post-office, anxious for letters the last being overdue. I was alone when Mr. E. came. Ernest sent to him knowing I was feeble, and hoping Mr. E. would soften the blow. I found him looking at May's portrait, pale and tearful, with the paper in his hand. "My child, I wish I could prepare you; but alas, alas!" There his voice failed and he gave me the telegram.
>
> I was not surprised, and read the hard words as if I knew it all before. "I *am* prepared," I said, and thanked him. He was much moved and very tender. I shall remember gratefully the look, the grasp, the tears he gave me; and I am sure that hard moment was made bearable by the presence of this our best and tenderest friend. He went to find Father but missed him, and I had to tell both him and Anna when they came. A very bitter sorrow for all.

The dear baby may comfort E., but what can comfort us? It is the distance that is so hard, and the thought of so much happiness ended so soon. "Two years of perfect happiness," May called these married years, and said, "If I die when baby comes, don't mourn, for I have had as much happiness in this short time as many in twenty years." She wished me to have her baby and her pictures. A very precious legacy! Rich payment for the little I could do for her. I see now why I lived,—to care for May's child and not leave Anna all alone.

A little over a year later Emerson got his reward for his neighborly act when the Alcotts dropped by, as Bronson wrote it:

May 25—This is Emerson's birthday anniversary, being seventy-eight years of age. Louisa accompanies me with little L., and a bunch of rhodoras, his favorite flower in her hand, verses hidden within the leaves, and presents to her poet. He takes her in his arms and carries her about, presenting her with smiling face to Ellen and Dr. and Mrs. Furness, guests of his from Philadelphia. It was a pleasant surprise, apparently, and pleasant to us as well. I had a few words with him; but he does not incline voluntarily to conversation with any one, I am told. He listened to my adventures approvingly. His chief inquiry, and repeated was, had I found any new men in those parts. I could only reply, none, in his estimation of newness. Having enjoyed for so many of his prolific years his company and participated in the ideas common to us, I may not dwell sadly on the reticence that has overflowed his genius during these later years of his.

Meditating on what was happening to his friend, Alcott tried his hand at putting his feelings into verse in February 1882:

Oft I recall those hours so fair and free
When all the long forenoon we two did toss

From lip to lip, in lively colloquy,
Plato, Plotinus, or some schoolman's gloss,
Disporting in rapt thought and ecstasy,
Then, by the tilting rail, Millbrook we cross,
And sally through the field to Walden wave,
Plunging within the cove, or swimming o'er,
Through woodpaths winding, he, with gesture quick
Rhymes deftly in mid-air with circling stick,
Skims the smooth pebble from the leafy shore,
Or deeper ripples raises as we lave—
Nor will his pillow press, though late at night,
Till converse with the stars his eyes invite.

Whatever was happening to his mind, Emerson tried to keep his body in shape by following his usual routine of walking. On that date of such importance in Concord, April 19, of that year of 1882, he went out for an evening walk without his overcoat and was caught in a chill spring rain. He came down with a cold that rapidly turned into what his doctor son, now practicing in Concord, diagnosed as pneumonia. By April 26 he was bedridden when Alcott came to see him and afterward wrote:

> I walk this cloudless morning to Emerson's, and am admitted to his sick chamber. On being announced by Ellen, he turns his kind glance, smiling as none other, upon me, and taking my hand, he said, "You are quite well?"
>
> "Yes," I replied; "and am not used to find you in bed."
>
> Smiling, he seemed confused, and uttered words too indistinctly to be discerned. Leaving his bedside and about going, he signified his wish to speak further with me, and, returning to his bed's head, he took my hand affectionately and said in strong but broken accents: "You have strong hold on life, and maintain it firmly," when his voice faltered and fell into indistinctness.
>
> I came away questioning if this might not be my last interview with my long and faithful friend. Though the

sun shone brightly above, the light that had illuminated our friendship so long seemed overcast, and I was soon to be left alone. My little maid smiled upon me as I reentered my home, and stole away by her prattle and pretty ways the saddening eclipse. Concord will be shorn of its human splendor when he withdraws behind the cloud.

That cloud came down the next day. When Edward found his father in pain on Thursday, April 27, he followed the advice of a specialist he had called in and gave the patient some of his uncle Jackson's ether. "In the quiet sleep thus produced, he gradually faded away," Edward wrote. That evening the bell of the church with which the Emersons had so long been associated tolled seventy-nine times. At the funeral in the church, Alcott read a sonnet he had written for the occasion, and Judge Hoar spoke for the people crowding the pews: "Throughout this great land and from beyond the sea will come innumerable voices of sorrow for this great public loss. But we, his neighbors and townsmen, feel that he was *ours*. He was descended from the founders of the town. He chose our village as the place where his lifelong work was to be done. It was to our fields and orchards that his presence gave such value; it was our streets in which the children looked up to him with love, and the elders with reverence and pride." Emerson was buried in Sleepy Hollow Cemetery, again in the company of Thoreau and Hawthorne.

Judge Hoar was right about the national interest in this death. Newspapers in all the major cities took note of it, and the *New York Times* gave it three columns on the front page and two more inside. The message in this unsigned tribute was that Emerson's "influence has in all likelihood been greater upon the American, and in less degree the English, mind than any other writer in the Nation. Emerson appears to have acted his own definition of a philosophy—he reported to his own mind the constitution of the universe."

The always ailing Lidian Emerson lived on another ten years, with Ellen to care for her. Alcott did find the "new men" that

Emerson had asked about. As he had predicted when he returned from his first trip to the West with only a dollar in his pocket, he had made contacts there that finally paid off handsomely when one of the men he met came east to help him found a Concord School of Philosophy that met with Orchard House as its head-quarters every summer until his death in 1888. Alcott's last com-panion and supporter, daughter Louisa May, debilitated by the illness she contracted while nursing in the Civil War and by in-cessant overwork, died two days after her father.

Although the people who hallowed it were all called away, the village of Concord was—and remains—a shrine to the life of thought.

Bibliography

Material for this narrative of a very special friendship was drawn from the following sources. Since the subjects were superior and prolific writers, this writer has chosen to tell much of the story in their own words to let the reader see their lives, their work, their relationships, and the world as they saw them. In view of their enduring fame, it is not surprising to note that a great deal of their thinking remains relevant to our lives today. The only intrusions on their words are set apart in brackets; material in parentheses is in the original.

Alcott, A. Bronson. *Concord Days*. Philadelphia: Albert Saifer, 1872.

Allen, Gay Wilson. *Waldo Emerson*. New York: Viking, 1981.

Baker, Carlos. *Emerson Among the Eccentrics*. New York: Penguin, 1991.

Bode, Carl, ed. *The Portable Thoreau*. New York: Penguin, 1947.

Borst, Raymond R. *The Thoreau Log: A Documentary Life of Henry David Thoreau, 1817–1862*. New York: G. K. Hall & Co., 1992.

Cabot, James Elliott. *A Memoir of Ralph Waldo Emerson*. 2 vols. New York: AMS Press, 1969.

Cheney, Ednah D., ed. *Louisa May Alcott: Her Life, Letters, and Journals*. Cambridge, MA: University Press, John Wilson and Son, 1889.

Chipperfield, Faith. *In Quest of Love: The Life and Death of Margaret Fuller*. New York: Coward-McCann, 1957.

Conway, Moncure D. *Emerson at Home and Abroad*. New York: Haskell House, 1968.

———. *Life of Nathaniel Hawthorne*. New York: Haskell House, 1968.

Derleth, August. *Concord Rebel: A Life of Henry D. Thoreau*. Philadelphia and New York: Chilton Company, 1912.

Durant, Will. *The Story of Philosophy*. New York: Simon and Schuster, 1933.

Emerson, Edward Waldo. *Emerson in Concord*. London: Sampson, Low, Marsten, Searle & Livingston, 1889.

Emerson, Ellen Tucker. *The Life of Lidian Jackson Emerson*. Edited by Delores Bird Carpenter. Boston: Twayne Publishers, 1980.

Emerson, Ralph Waldo. *Essays and Lectures*. New York: Library of America, 1983.

Gussow, Mel. "Rosy Days of Fatherhood, Far from 'The Scarlet Letter.'" *New York Times*, August 11, 2003.

Hawthorne, Julian. *Nathaniel Hawthorne and His Wife*. 2 vols. North Haven, CT: Archon Books, 1968.

Hawthorne, Nathaniel. *Collected Novels: Fanshawe, The Scarlet Letter, The House of the Seven Gables, The Blithedale Romance, The Marble Faun*. New York: Library of America, 1983.

———. *Life of Franklin Pierce*. Boston: Ticknor, Reed and Fields, 1852.

———. *Mosses from an Old Manse. The Centenary Edition of the Works of Nathaniel Hawthorne*. Columbus: Ohio State University Press, 1974.

Holmes, Oliver Wendell. *Ralph Waldo Emerson*. Boston: Houghton, Mifflin and Company, 1885.

Hough, Henry Beetle. *Thoreau of Walden: The Man and His Eventful Life*. New York: Simon and Schuster, 1956.

Lathrop, Rose (Hawthorne). *Memories of Hawthorne*. New York: Ames Press, 1897.

Lincoln, Calvin D., ed. *The Bicentennial Almanac*. Nashville/New York: Thomas Nelson, 1975.

Mellow, James R. *Nathaniel Hawthorne in His Time*. Boston: Mifflin Company, 1980.

Miller, Edward Haviland. *Salem Is My Dwelling Place: A Life of Nathaniel Hawthorne*. Iowa City: University of Iowa Press, 1991.

Miller, Perry, ed. *Margaret Fuller, American Romantic: A Selection from Her Writings and Correspondence*. Gloucester, MA: Peter Smith, 1969.

Morison, Samuel Eliot. *The Oxford History of the American People*. New York: Oxford University Press, 1965.

Morrow, Honoré Willsie. *The Father of Little Women*. Boston: Little, Brown and Company, 1927.

Myerson, Joel, ed. *Emerson in His Own Time*. Iowa City: University of Iowa Press, 2003.

Perry, Bliss, ed. *The Heart of Emerson's Journals*. Boston and New York: Houghton Mifflin, 1926.

Richardson, Robert D., Jr. *Emerson: The Mind on Fire*. Berkeley, Los Angeles, London: University of California Press, 1995.

———. *Henry Thoreau: A Life of the Mind*. Berkeley, Los Angeles, London: University of California Press, 1986.

Shepard, Odell. *Pedlar's Progress: The Life of Bronson Alcott*. New York: Greenwood Press, 1968.

Shepard, Odell, ed. *The Journals of Bronson Alcott*. Boston: Little, Brown and Company, 1938.

Van Doren, Mark, ed. *American Poets 1630–1930*. Boston: Little, Brown and Company, 1933.

Wagenknecht, Edward. *Hawthorne: Man and Writer*. New York: Oxford University Press, 1961.

Index

Page numbers in *italics* refer to illustrations.